THE OTHER SIDE OF CHARM

Your Memoir

H. G. Beverly

FIRST EDITION, JANUARY 2014

Copyright 2014 by H. G. Beverly

ACKNOWLEDGEMENTS

Love and gratitude for my children first and most of all. They have been though more hardship than anyone deserves, and they still manage to lean into their strengths and talents. They are amazing people.

I will never stop trying to elevate their lives.

Next to my parents, who have suffered and endured the pain of alienation right alongside me. I know at times they've felt like they were losing their grandchildren completely, and I know that's been a horrifying experience. My parents are warm, loving people who cherish family more than anything, and without their steadfast support, I would have nothing. Not this computer I type on, not a home, not hope. They are my safety net, and I am forever grateful. I still hope we can look forward to a day when this experience of alienation will not define our lives.

Thank you for standing by me.

TABLE OF CONTENTS

PROLOGUE

I'm going to start you off by talking about psychopaths. Why not? I can't think of a better way to start off a story about how a charming, apparently caring man can maintain a sparkling smile as he devastates you. Maybe you'll recognize some of these tendencies in people you know. Maybe you'll be surprised.

So let's talk about it.

Psychopath. Sociopath. Antisocial Personality Disorder. The labels are muddled and confusing because the field is equally so. The terms "psychopath" and "sociopath" are used interchangeably in the literature and by professionals. The exception to this is while establishing a formal diagnosis, because then it's most proper (at least in 2013) to use the label "Antisocial Personality Disorder." But to keep it basic, all of these words refer to a specific diagnosis that research has indicated can be applied to 1 out of every 25 people in our general population.*

1 out of 25.

That's a pretty prolific diagnosis.

But it's also a confusing diagnosis. What's it called? Why all these different labels? What does it look like? What does it mean? How does a sociopath behave and how can I tell?

Most people can't.

Most people get confused. And not just by the *niceness* of many sociopaths, but by the messy complexity of properly

9

applying the established diagnostic code. For example, it's easy to confuse and misread the behaviors of a person with an Attachment Disorder with the characteristic sociopathic tendencies. But you have to be careful. Because while a sociopath may be incapable of forming attachments, the criteria for diagnosis are broader. They're different disorders. The issue is that it's apparently difficult for clinicians to see, experience, and identify the differences accurately. A clinician may look at the sometimes cruel or violent behavior of a traumatized and neglected individual who is suffering from Attachment Disorder and think "psychopath" and pursue the diagnosis of Antisocial Personality Disorder. The same clinician may feel the warmth behind the smile of a hand-shaking client who talks incessantly about family values and how his daughter may need a bit of help because she's been hearing voices lately and is saying things that just don't make sense. This clinician will not likely think "psychopath" and will not immediately suspect that the daughter is starting to speak the truth about family incest and that her sociopathic father is simply ensuring that no one will believe her. She may be hospitalized. Institutionalized. Her father may run your local Rotary Club and coach your son's team. He may show up for everything. He may be the most likable person you ever met. He may be a sociopath.

If he is, he will never feel remorse. That's the key. He may fully believe that his daughter brought it on herself, and he won't care, anyway, as long as he wins.

He has no conscience.

He will hug her and may even cry over her declining mental health when the camera's pointed at him.

You will never see him for who he is. What's scary is that

most clinicians won't, either.

I'm not an expert, I'm not a researcher, and I'm not leading the field. I'm an average clinician with limited experience—as are most mental health professionals that any of us will encounter in our lives. I simply have enough knowledge and personal experience to understand that any human being who is involved in the prevention, diagnosis, or treatment of any form of abuse in any vulnerable population needs more training in the assessment of sociopaths, psychopaths, or individuals with Antisocial Personality Disorder. The fact that we don't have a clear and consistent way to talk about these individuals is a small indication of a huge, confusing mess.

A mess.

Who can see us through it? Research shows that untrained college students are as accurate in detecting deception as CIA and FBI agents.** That none of us—no one, anywhere, at any level of training—can detect a liar as well as we think we can. You know what that means?

It means we're all vulnerable.

Even the professionals. But we'd all like to know who's out to get us. So let's talk just a bit more about identifying these individuals and labeling them through diagnoses. The fields of psychiatry, counseling, psychology, social work, psychotherapy, and so on generally utilize a manual for establishing diagnoses that is called the Diagnostic and Statistical Manual, or DSM. I was trained in the fourth edition, the DSM-IV. In 2013, clinical professionals are in the process of being trained to use the fifth edition, the DSM-V. Essentially, this manual standardizes mental illness and provides clinicians with a common language and code for diagnosis along with a uniform system for obtaining payments from health insurance companies. Choosing a diagnosis is not an option—if a clinician wants to be paid through health insurance or if a client needs or wants to continue in therapy in a way that is supported and reimbursed by an insurance company, then a diagnostic code is mandatory. You get a label.

That being said, the creation and use of the DSM is controversial. Who wrote the book? Who defines mental illness for our society? Who is diagnosing who and for what benefit? Who is it that benefits? Those questions are not the overarching topic of this book. My point is simply to educate—to make unfamiliar readers aware of issues that do exist in the field. It's always important to question whether a certain group of professionals or body of work are benefiting humanity—and ask how they might do better.

I'm a licensed mental health professional. Today, I can pick up the DSM-IV and eventually the DSM-V, and I can legally use it under supervision to assign diagnoses to my clients. Not only can I do this, but I am impelled to do this by the system that manages our health care and well-being. Using the DSM-IV, I can diagnose a psychopathic or a sociopathic individual as having "Antisocial Personality Disorder."

My issue with this power that I have is that I have absolutely zero training—nothing—*nada*—to guide me in this specific type of assessment.

But that doesn't necessarily stop other untrained clinicians from jumping right in. In fact, we're encouraged and even pressured (under supervision) to do so. If you work for a practice or a clinic or an agency, they want paid. The way to get paid is to get their clinicians to assign a label.

Diagnoses are tied to paychecks. But I'm cautious.

I don't want to give the diagnosis of Antisocial Personality Disorder and be wrong. Yes, I'm supervised. And yes, I have to admit that at this point in my life, I probably have a better ability to detect these traits than probably 90% of the professionals in my field. The number may be higher. But I'm not bragging. It's the reverse—I'm simply pointing out that the number of professionals who can accurately diagnose another human being with Antisocial Personality Disorder (a psychopath or sociopath, remember) is so small that most of us will not get it right.

And that's scary.

And if this "disorder" affects 1 in 25 people,* then it seems to me that we all need further training in assessment—*stat.* Especially when you realize that this disorder is incurable and potentially has a physiological basis.*** Especially when you realize that a troubled teen who is acting out his or her own abuse and neglect may be labeled "Antisocial" and have to share that mislabel with "true" psychopaths both internally and on record for the rest of his or her life. Especially when you realize that the presence of an unidentified sociopath in group therapy or family therapy or any other type of therapy will completely change the success rates of that therapeutic process for everyone involved. How can a family heal in therapy when a sociopath is dropping bombs on their progress and no one, not even the clinician, can see what's happening behind the smoke and mirrors of an incredibly charming and manipulative human being? In individual therapy, I would venture to guess that every therapist I know has been fooled into thinking that their undiagnosed sociopathic client was making big progress and really embracing the work.

It's a fool's game.

Even further, the failure to identify sociopathic individuals extends far beyond the mental health field. I've witnessed and experienced enormously devastating systemic failures in the legal, justice, and law enforcement systems to date, and I've also experienced the gaps between these institutions. It's even bigger than confusion and a lack of education. Court-approved (admissible) forensic psychiatric evaluations cost thousands and thousands of dollars each, and their success depends entirely on the training and capabilities of the administering clinician. These assessments are reserved for the rich and can potentially be used as a weapon to hurt and label the victim of a better-funded (potentially sociopathic) individual. It's easy to label people who are suffering. It's sometimes impossible to label a perpetrator. I've watched for years as very clear sociopathic behaviors have been missed entirely by mental health professionals and educators and advocates who are trained to see but remain blind— sometimes by charm, sometimes by choice. And I've watched my children suffer trauma and degradation almost daily for the past ten years as a result of these ineptitudes—in a system that not only fails to protect them, but prevents parents and caregivers like me from doing it as well.

I believe there are millions living out this story in the United States.

That belief makes this story not only mine, but yours.

Your memoir.

The Sociopath Next Door, Martha Stout, PhD
**Predators: Pedophiles, Rapists, and Other Sex Offenders*, Anna Salter, Ph.D
***Without Conscience: The Disturbing World of the Psychopaths Among Us, Robert Hare, Ph.D

{If you knew me, you would be ashamed.}

PART I
How it begins

.01
LOVE FEST

Many of the most hurtful people
never go to prison
or any other facility.
Instead, they construct a
façade of normalcy
and move right into your life,
nearly always getting
exactly
what they want.

You will fall in love. Your love will come to you from the southeast in some kind of subtle-sparkle-smoke fog coming in through the cracks around your door sweeping across the room to you there where you'll be reading on your sofa he'll be reaching his hands down around your waist filling your eyes with his glow so intense that you will not keep yourself from looking over and away. Lids half closed to shield your eyes. Your love will not be able to stay away will come to you in the morning and in the afternoon and in the evening and in the middle of the night your love will wake you from a dream with strong coffee will relax your rigid bones with a glass of wine will make you wonder why you've been working so hard all this time you'll watch him coming toward you and his smoke will serenade your heart *so this is passion.* Your love will take you on a night walk stroll behind you pushed up against you stride for stride and the rhythm will tell him you're a perfect fit *look at us walking. We're a perfect fit.* He will be fascinated. With your plans and dreams *they're so much in line with mine* if only he hadn't been traveling through the south these last years you could've been building a life together ever since college or high school or maybe even junior high your fit is just that marvelous your feet will sweep across the earth like matchsticks lighting a fire. Every step another spark. Will fly to the sky *I can't believe I didn't see this in you before should've known when I first saw you as a child but I've never known love like this in my life let's spend every moment making up for lost time. Let's start with a dance. Yes, right here. Right now.* You'll swing around the living room you'll swing across your lawn you'll spin sideways down the sidewalk you'll follow his lead with your eyes you'll talk freely about the future *so this is love.* Your love will teach you all about *love* you will say *I didn't know it could be like this* your last relationship will have been with someone more regular *no smoke* that last one will have cooked chili too late and his nose will have run and dripped while he stirred and you'll have watched him wipe it with the side of his hand while cutting hot peppers but *no smoke.* You won't have known what it could be what might happen in your heart when the sparks start flying to the sky when the light show creates a fog and you won't have known what love could feel like to be lost what the smoke might do to your heart all engulfed in that glittering, hazy mist no time to come up for air you won't even bother trying. You won't have known what it could be until it finds its way in through the cracks and then you'll know that nothing was like this before *so this is the one* there's no way of saying no when God sends you the smoke you don't question your destiny.

You won't question your destiny.

You'll fall forward into it you'll fall off the face of the earth you'll fall sideways through the sky no one will be able to find you for months. *Where is that girl.* You will land on the earth wearing short shorts and your legs will be perfect in the sandals with slight heels that you'll wear every day and all summer they're the only ones you'll have with you at his tiny rented cottage tucked into the corner of his family's farm. This new man. You'll scarcely go back to your own home you won't show up for things won't show up for anything won't have ever been so reckless before he'll show you a better life he'll show you how to relax *just live for once. Let's go get some dinner.* And he won't go to work you'll never have met anyone so capable of earning a living on just a few phone calls a day *how does he do it* seems he has everything figured out you will watch him in wonder wish you could've figured it out like that all you've ever done is work and all he's ever done is *live it up* enjoy every moment and yet he's somehow still so successful drives a company car *maybe it's the smoke* maybe there's some secret you don't understand but you won't have time to think about it for long he'll be with you in every moment day and night your clothes will smell like his clothes your dog will sleep with his dogs your breath will smell like his breath your thoughts will be distant sentences floating in fragments and pieces drifting silently through the smoky sky. Every once in a while your eyes will catch the clear horizon and you'll remember what it was to breathe a different kind of air in a different kind of place where it would hit your lungs like a break from all this hazy heat and slumber where it would hit your lungs with a cold strike and the bits and pieces of your thoughts would come home from the sky and land in their proper order and your stomach would take on an ease and tell your mind that what it's thinking's absolutely right. Some call that clarity. And you'll need clarity at some point and so you'll head for the solitude of your own space *I really need to study, this biochemistry exam is going to be crazy and I have to get an A. It's just one night and I will miss you so much.* So you'll head back to your own little home for one more night alone before you move on and it fills up with someone else's things but he'll show up, anyway, and ask to sit with you at the table and then sleep on your sofa or even better in your bed. Just needs to feel his heart beat up next to yours he just didn't feel like he was at home without you. And since no man's ever shown up against your wishes before and since the smoke will creep in to announce him you'll be seduced before you even open that door will forget all about that biochemistry and there he'll stand, filling the doorway with all that denim and fresh flannel in the mist. You'll feel so irresistible he can't keep himself away from you. And that's what he'll say as he notices that you're breathing in the same pattern as him while you fall asleep in his arms. Breathe in, breathe out. Breathe in, breathe out. It must be some kind of sign. It must be an absolute miracle.

He will very quickly and courageously start talking to your parents. *Traditional*, he'll say, and *family*. Words like *children* and *farming* and even *for life*. He'll show up for everything hold the door every time. Change tires for the elderly. Take you to small country restaurants to meet wrinkled men in bib overalls for fruity drinks *you'll never drink so much in your life*. Build a brick sidewalk with his dad without really knowing how you'll be right there next to him in his parched flower beds framed in by old telephone poles, hoping the petunias will survive. You'll know nothing about soil at the time. Later, when the petunias are dying off and the sidewalk bricks start cracking off the sides into the grass, you'll stick close to the middle so your ankles won't roll on your way to the car.

(You'll be the second woman to stay in that house in six months.)

But you won't really know that at the time all you'll know is that his old girlfriend followed him up from the south *kind of like a stalker* they'll say and you'll ask *where is she now*, they'll say *please don't get into all that she really hurt Wyatt took a bunch of his stuff please don't bring up all those painful memories we're just so glad you're practically in the family now you're just nothing like her and we're so happy we think you're so wonderful*. So you'll wrinkle your eyebrows for a moment and let it go what you will focus on

24

instead is that the stars fall from the sky when you lay on the blanket together in the side yard at midnight. You'll know that it's time to leave your job when it just won't work to commute so far from his little cottage anymore. And he'll stay there with you, most days, making drinks in the blender that he'll like to call *naughty but healthy*. It will all blow your brains out you've been such a boring little girl since you went to college getting all straight A's and working so hard to get into vet school. *So this is what it's like to have fun. I almost forgot.* It will be so much fun that he'll hit the roof of his car with a *hoop hoop* every time a good song comes on, dancing himself right out of his seat. The jokes will roll. The sun will rise. Your parents won't even wonder where you are, anymore, he'll talk to them almost more than you do. *It's a match made in heaven.* That's what the preacher will say when you sit down to talk about marriage. Your test scores will be perfectly matched. No other couple has known each other so long, had so many similar interests, had such perfectly matching families—not to mention identical life dreams. Your stomach will tingle. You'll smile every time you see him. You'll feel like you won something amazing. Some kind of magical life prize. Where the 4H crush of your Midwestern childhood comes back after conquering the world to pick you up in his bulging arms and carry you over the finish line.

You'll drop out of veterinary school that fall. Your parents will object at first, but after he spends some time with them talking about *parenting* and *traditional families* and *student loans*, they'll see it his way. Just like you do after he talks to you about it every day for months. After a while, everything he says starts to make sense. *Why go to school if you want to raise your own kids? Why have kids if you don't raise them yourself? Don't you want kids? You want their first steps to be with a sitter? So why take on the loans? Why not just utilize your assets and live the life you really want to live? If you could stay home then why would you have someone else raise your kids? You agree that sitters aren't an ideal way to grow up, right, and so why would you do that to your kids just for some kind of hobby job? Your mom stayed home for you, didn't she? Did you like that? Think that was better? Then why spend years training for a position that will work you round the clock for half the pay I'm making as a starting salesman, anyway? Especially when I never have to go to work?* He'll work maybe 15 hours a week most people are jealous of him. A few calls here and there. One late night on the computer. And that's it.

You'll be amazed by his relaxed quality of life. *He must know something I don't know.* And without work, days will find you walking hand in hand down the abandoned railroad tracks. To the creek. To the abandoned house with all the peeling layers of newspaper on the walls. Through the cornfields on both sides no one can see you there's never anyone else around. You'll mess around. Make hay together with your dad. With his dad. His family will all be so impressed by a girl who can hold her own on the hay wagon not many girls do. You'll smile at your own wiry strength didn't spend your whole life working your ass off for nothing and it always feels so good to shock the men. Road crews. Farm crews. Construction crews. You'll have done it all by then you'll have shocked every one of them it always makes your dad smile, too. You'll even have built your own house with your grandpa and you'll love that house love pulling right into the garage at the end of a long day you'll love washing your car in the driveway you'll love landscaping all around you'll love watching the sunset over the pond. But that was before the smoke rolled in now you're no fool ignorant of God you'll pack up all your things won't think twice about renting out that first perfect home you ever made for yourself you'll be leaving it for a *person* and you know not to second guess the best people the best relationships in life. These are your chances don't take them for granted. Pack two pairs of shorts in a basket and maybe a toothbrush to go. And you'll go. At 24. Because that's the year you'll fall in love. And it's the same year that you'll be married.

Seven months later.

Seven was always your lucky number so you'll marry under a white tent at the edge of the lake where you grew up. Dreamy white horse and carriage *my parents are such loving miracle workers* they will pay for and pull off the whole thing with little notice. Raw silk dress you'll find it with your mom after trying on maybe a thousand of them even though you both hate to shop. You'll smile at each other when you know. And have it altered very quickly *you know we really don't have time. To think. There's no time to deliberate now. We have a wedding to plan.* So before you blink you'll find yourself in that silk dress under an arbor on the water, surrounded by pumpkins and fall flowers, listening to a string quartet. Ladybugs in your veil. You'll be smiling over every detail your designer aunts will make everything perfect. The last thing you'll be hoping for is that your miracle man will cry when he sees you. Surely the smoke will roll in and all around him bringing the water to his eyes to the eyes of a man who has never cried no he's never cried but you just know he will this time surely this will be his big moment surely he will cry with this miracle of coming together surely he will cry at the way your stars aligned.

He won't cry.

But it's nothing to take personally he didn't even cry when his grandpa died he just isn't the type.

And so that's ok. You'll cry a bit, and that will be enough. The whole thing will be more than enough and the amazing thing about a wedding is that you'll only remember a few moments of it, later. One moment will be when you pull up to the white tent in your carriage and find the lighting inside glowing as if a spirit came to dance over the flowers when you see it you'll feel something come together in your heart. Another moment will come on the dance floor when your whole crazy extended family will gather hands and spin in a

27

circle, spin in a double circle, there will be too many of you and you'll all be laughing, *we are family*. Your beautiful tiny flower girl will take both your hands and lean backward, smiling up at you and to the sky. Her perfect angel face will stay with you forever. Her face and your dancing, spinning Uncle Will in the background.

Later that night, he will take you. Through the McDonald's drive-through he knows this was his part to plan but he ran out of time didn't have a moment to put together that romantic picnic. You'll wrinkle your nose and think that a drive-through is some kind of strange and terrible way to end a wedding but you won't want to be a snob and so you'll make sure you understand. *I understand.* You'll wonder what else is in store. For the evening. And you'll smile you're sure there'll be more *way more* but then you'll stand hanging your head over the sink pulling out 1,224 hairpins and tossing them in he'll lay on the bed will fall asleep as you talk about the day from underneath your now overdone hair. *I think I'm going to have to shower I look like Tina Turner.* You'll turn for a smile he won't respond you'll stand still and upright for a moment and watch him sleep look around the stale room and think *why did we come here why would he pick some cheap state park lodge two hours away should I have planned this part, too?* Then you'll bathe and rinse and consider trying not to wake him when you climb in but he will stir almost resentfully to climb on top of you it's so late now but after all his friend came in from Florida *I can't exactly leave the wedding early when people travel so far to see me.* You'll understand. *I understand.* But when the darkness takes over and you lay under him looking up you'll feel the ocean of the night in your ears and the moon will sound of emptiness. Only you will hear it will notice that things aren't what you expected at all you won't know what you would've expected at the time but only later will you remember searching for his eyes he won't have looked at you won't have run his hand down your side won't have smiled a knowing smile won't have told you that you're beautiful or that he loves you and most of all there won't be any smoke. *Where is his fire why is he in a rush I don't want this and he must be exhausted?* His face will be as flat as yesterday's bread your body will empathize *he's tired* even as it aches for a loving touch you will want to make a joke about it *wow, we slept through that one* but will know already not to joke with this man about anything personal and certainly never about his sex *he's so sensitive* and the bottom line will be that you should've suggested waiting for another night. It's your own fault. But even then your left over anticipation will ask you where is that mesmerizing buzz you imagined when you dreamed that the roof might blow off a ski lodge somewhere on your real first night of marriage all the snow would melt down the mountains with your heat. Aglow. But you'll have to wait for ski season you'll take a real honeymoon in a couple months. To the snow. *Wyatt doesn't really want a tropical honeymoon so we're going to go west later in the fall.* And so for now, on your fake wedding night, you'll throw the scratchy bed cover with the plastic threads right off of that bed. Then you'll snuggle in next to his sleeping bulk and try to get warm under the sheets.

02.
MARRIAGE

We swim in a sea
of our relationships,
and our capacity for closeness
can greatly enhance our well-being.
Unless there's a predator involved,
in which case
our ability to be close
will be used
to eat us alive.

You will be married. You will not take that promised honeymoon won't blow the top off a ski lodge in fact you will never take a vacation together again. From that point on, all travel will be separate he'll start traveling with work and you'll only go places if someone else asks you and offers to help you pay for it. So you won't travel much for years.

You will be surprised.

You will also be pregnant right away your sister will guess almost immediately she'll offer you a glass of wine at your grandpa's favorite Italian restaurant with one eyebrow cocked and ready for your response. *I'm just not in the mood.* But you love wine, she'll say, *when have you ever said no.* And she'll say this with a wink and her wink won't float across the room like a butterfly, no, this one will be the kind that jumps straight down your throat and stirs it up in there so much that your face will catch fire from the heat. And then she'll know.

You will be married you will be pregnant you will make lifelong friends with change.

Your aunts will be happy for your marriage. And secretly bewildered. Where did their studious young feminist go? They thought you left this whole pleasing-the-male phase behind in high school. You won't have brought up politics or art in months or given your whole speech about the way the plastic world tells women it owns their bodies and their babies. And no writing and no journaling *have you been to the new exhibit at the art museum have you seen a show lately?* They'll know this Wyatt's into everything at least that's what you'll keep saying *we've been doing more of a simple life in nature kind of thing but he's into everything he fully supports all my interests* but honestly, they'll have some concerns especially about you leaving vet school. Vet school! They'll wonder if they should talk to you they will start to talk to you briefly but then they'll see your face and not want to intrude will file their concerns away for later in the back of their brains and find themselves showing up for everything. *We brought some flowers for you. How are things going?* They'll take you out to dinner and treat you to a pedicure they'll smile when you move into the farmhouse they grew up in everyone will be happy about that, you will buy it back from the bank when another family loses it in divorce *what a great deal what beautiful timing we're so glad to have it back in the family.* Your parents will lend Wyatt thirty grand to help him contribute to the purchase you will keep the loan quiet to protect Wyatt's pride you will quickly pull a credit line on that house you already own *I have so much equity in that house since I built it myself and so it just makes sense plus that little house and its barns are paying all our mortgages with the rent I'm bringing in and they can cover the payment on the credit line, too, and so life is good. But let's be careful with how we talk about it so Wyatt doesn't feel weird* you will set up a credit line you will pay your

32

parents back yourself the spring after you wed. You will be delighted with your opportunities you will be twenty-four years old you will move right into your grandma and grandpa's old house with joy you will have big plans.

You will stay there a full week before your wedding, alone with your little girl memories you will spend your first few hours wandering around through the piles of trash and abandoned furniture left behind for you to take care of you will pick up a half empty glass of rotten milk and carry it carefully out the door. Peek into the stairwell attic and remember the ancient dolls your grandma used to store in there. Where did they go? Trace your fingers over the velvet wallpaper *I remember when I thought this place was a palace.* Walk down the back stairs. Walk up the front stairs. Two sets of stairs! *Our kids will make a fort in the balcony where grandma used to keep her sewing machine.* You'll imagine them sliding down the steps on diapered bottoms, one boom at a time. You'll remember your mom and grandma folding clothes at the table in the kitchen you'll remember your mom and grandma folding clothes in the living room on the floor in front of the TV. You'll remember your mom and grandma feeding the farm hands at noon on a hot summer day you'll remember the kitchen table bulging with all the food and sweaty bodies. You'll remember one of them was a homeless man named Shorty who set up house in the barn long before your grandpa built him a little apartment in the corner you'll think of the way Shorty's breath smelled like candy syrup and silage how his hand would shake shake shake until every pea fell off his spoon before it ever hit his lips. You'll remember standing next to his chair as a little girl so you could stare more closely at his shaking hands at his watery eyes his stubbly cheeks with all their folds and creases you'll remember that he was somehow the world's expert in getting along with animals and the weather you will remember him sharing the most fascinating facts. You'll remember where your grandpa used to sit to read the paper you'll wander the house again and carry out the trash and fill it instead with your memories you'll think of everything that week *it's just amazing how the stars align when you find the perfect person.* And Wyatt will call you every hour or so to check in, *he's so attentive.* You're so in love can't stand the time away from each other you've never been apart a single day. Until that first week in your grandparents' house, anyway, and it'll be such a let down when he tells you he has to work all week you'll want to say *you never had to do that before* but with the wedding just days away there's just no time for conflict and a whole lot to do so he'll remind you *maybe your dad can help you lift a few things. Get you started.* Ok, you know, you'll understand. And after a full seven months of uninterrupted play with late dinners after late naps, it will actually feel purifying to scrub the floors and windows, anyway. Turn up the radio and dip your hands into the bucket of water make it as close to scalding as you can. Fill the dumpster one armful at a time. Dirty socks and a rotten futon mattress. You're making it as a team both of you working so hard across the miles and you really missed hard work you will cherish the ache in your arms you will ruin your fingers for the manicurist when it comes to your wedding day *what have you been doing* she'll ask. *Bought grandma and grandpa's house back. Ouch, that stuff is burning my thumb. I'm so excited and I really want to make it grand again. Just paint them a neutral color. I can never keep the paint on, anyway.*

After the wedding, you'll take over the finances, the remodeling, the cooking, and all the cleaning. You'll be the one staying home so why not, and it'll feel like love to have dinner ready when he arrives. Or comes inside. Most days, he won't have to work again after you're all settled and you'll feel so lucky he's somehow mastered the rat race and you can stand together in the side yard at two in the afternoon and talk about where to put in a garden. With a baby inside, you'll zero in on words like *wholesome* and *organic* like you never have before. Homestead. *What better way to raise a child than wrapped in a cloth diaper and standing in fresh soil?* You'll build a dream of a debt free life. Carefully track every bill and every bank statement every month. Work hard to meet every challenge you've always been a girl with a project. When he tells you that *Devon's wife only spends $150 a month on groceries, and they even have two kids* you'll start studying recipes to see which ones have the cheapest ingredients. Beans are a must. You'll study cans of beans to see which ones are five cents less. You'll go for simple, simple, simple, maybe you can even make your own clothes someday. For now, it's curtains. Thirty-five double sets *this house has a lot of tall windows.* You'll paint the nursery. Bunnies peeking out from around the window frame smiling sun looking down on the crib. A tree. Happy birds and squirrels and butterflies. In the kitchen, you'll sing along with you think it's the Carpenters as they serenade your baby, *on the day that you were born the angels got together, and decided to create a dream come true... so they sprinkled moon dust in your hair with golden starlight in your eyes of blue...*

Will you have a baby with eyes of blue? Or maybe hazel green, like yours. Blonde hair or brown? Maybe white hair, like Wyatt and your brother. Maybe the baby will have black curly hair, like your dad. Sticking up everywhere like a giant halo of curls, that would be so cute. Hands on your tummy, you'll sometimes cry with the wonder of wondering what's happening in there. Who you're going to meet. And when. You'll focus on it more and more and once the fights begin because for all its ups and downs it'll be the most positive part of your life.

And the fights will begin.

Every couple has a hard time adjusting in the beginning. We have to learn how to live together. That's a big deal. You'll remind yourself that you married a man of late naps and late dinners never really established a stable home before didn't even have to take care of the company car so you can't expect him to be something different from that he has to have time to grow.

You'll remind yourself that you're staying home now and you've always been the drill-sergeant-taskmaster type and so while you felt you were on vacation for the past seven months you have to know that those ways were actually his normal life and you can't suddenly expect different and plus you left vet school so you have to work through that on your own and that's a big adjustment for you in terms of ego. It's probably about your ego. Because you loved when the doctors would ask your opinion on morning rounds and sometimes you'll have cried about it since. Brushing your hair in the bathroom, you'll one morning remember the thrill of an unexpected diagnostic insight. The respect and kindness of the older students *she's just a beginner but she gets it.* There'll be a lot for you to let go of, and there'll be no one standing around at home telling you that you're amazing for having the laundry completely done every day even when you're pregnant and working to restore a grand house there'll be no one standing around at home telling you that you're amazing at anything. *She's just a beginner and yet she does so much.* In fact, it'll be quite the opposite it'll seem that you haven't gotten the groove right yet he won't like the way you just throw things in the dryer without shaking them with a snap first. He'll want to hear a snap with each and every item that's the way his mom does it. And he'll also come to think that reusing a towel is disgusting. This will be all new, and it'll make you angry. *You practically used the dog towel when we were dating and I don't want wash a towel every single time you take a shower. And when I do the laundry, I do it my way.* But after the 50th or 100th time of him coming in when he hears you loading the dryer to stand behind you with a glass of wine and comment on the snap, sometimes setting his glass down to show you again, you'll find yourself throwing a fit. *Leave me alone or do it yourself!* He will take a step back and look clearly and strangely amused and then he'll begin. *I don't know why you're so uptight about everything. Are you seriously going to cry? Is it that big a deal to snap out the towels? They don't dry right if you don't.* You'll throw the towels down and stomp *why are you doing this again I know*

36

how to dry towels I get the towels dry why can't you just leave me alone! And his blue eyes will blacken on you shoulders stiff and square he will take a moment to turn the wine round in the glass and then stare you down. *You know, you're a lot like your aunts. Have to have things your way, don't you. Lindy can't even keep a man around she's so selfish you know it and you're just like her aren't you you're just a selfish ugly bitch.* You will stagger backward a bit with that one and inside your chest your heart will blow. Crying, *what did you just say why would you say that to me?* Stomping, *it's just the laundry can't you let me have my thing?* Swinging your arms, *I'm pregnant and I'm so tired and I'm sick of painting everything and how can you say I'm selfish?!* You will sob. *How can you say that to me?* He will watch you without expression before taking his wine glass out the door. *Where are you going? How can you just walk away don't you care how I feel?*

He won't turn around.

Instead, he'll walk right out of the house and into the back yard. Down the hill to stand under the empty clothes line. You'll follow him *no one has ever talked to me like that in my life.* What are you doing wrong? The heat inside your ears will pound so hard your brain will squeeze downward and block your throat. Your hands will shake. A selfish bitch? *Am I a selfish ugly bitch?* The thought will bring you almost to your knees you've led such a sheltered life because even when your brother called you a bitch once he said right away that he didn't mean it especially after you slammed the door so hard it wouldn't open again. You were thirteen, then, and he was ten and scared to death so you teamed right up to fix that door before your dad got home and your brother hugged you and you hugged him, too. But now this. Now this was different. What am I doing wrong? No hugs doesn't he love me? *How could you say that to me? How could you say that to me? Everything's changed since we got married.* And that's when he'll be the one to fall to his knees there in the grass under the clothesline. But he'll only stay there for a second before he'll be coming right up and at you. *Did you seriously just say that to me? Seriously just say that to me? You going to say something like that to your HUSBAND? I'm your husband what kind of wife says such a thing to her HUSBAND? You think everything's changed? You think it's so bad? That's because you only think about your selfish self, princess.* His arms will swing wide and then back together and then wide again, the whole time bouncing up and down he will pound out every word. Sometimes they will reach toward you, and you will step out of their reach, backing slowly across the back yard he will be coming with you. *You were raised to be a princess and now you're a spoiled bitch. You want to tell me things have changed? I can't even look at you. I can't even look at you. You think you can just say that? Hurt me like that? Get away from me, you stupid ugly princess.* And with that he will give you a push, your first push. Hands to the shoulders, like I want you out of my way I'm going to put your body over there now. It won't be a hard push, but it'll leave you shaking there on the lawn. *Get out of my way.* He'll only look back once over his shoulder *I can't believe you would say that to me* and then he'll be gone.

Please don't leave, you'll cry up the hill to him. *Please don't leave.*

You'll hear his car as he pulls away. Where does he go? You'll never get to know. But when he comes back and you add up two more days of *fuck yous* and fighting about it, you'll be too worn out to care. *He can leave and come back when he wants to. There's just not enough energy in the world it's not worth it.* And when it comes around to the laundry, you'll start snapping out the loads. At least when he can hear because it's just not worth him coming to stand right there behind you.

When he's not around, you'll lob huge globs of wet clothes right in.

Some things just aren't worth fighting about.

03.
BIRTH

Growth-fostering
relationships mean
we both get to develop
to our fullest, and
increasing the sense
of relatedness
between us is
intrinsically

good.

You will have three children. You will have them in the morning and in the middle of the day and in the middle of the night. You will have them in a hospital, you will have them in a birthing center, you will have them at home. You will have them with screaming and moaning. You will have them in a meditative trance of quiet and peace. You will have them standing up and sitting up and lying down. You will have them both with and without medication. You will have them with red-faced strength. You will have them with focus and gratitude. You will cry to God when they are born. *Thank you, thank you, God. Oh, thank you, thank you, God.* You will lay them on your chest and nurse them right away and all the time. They will gain weight from day one and keep right on gaining. You will thank God again. *Thank you, God.* You will start thanking God every day. You will pack them in a sling, in a front pack, in a back pack. They won't want to be put down. When they're a little older, they'll sample your recipes as they peek over your shoulder from the pack. Watch you chop vegetables and pour three glasses of water. Doze with their cheek smooshed up against the side rail as you run the vacuum. Bounce with your stride around the park. They will do everything.

And they will be everything. So much the center of your every decision that you won't even know to say it out loud. Like water in a lake—you won't think to wonder whether it might all suddenly fly up to the sky. Because some things just are. And so you'll take 4,000 photos a day won't want to let a single sideways glance to go by unnoticed. You'll take them to the indoor pool. You'll take them to the library. You'll let them paint each other in the yard. You'll read about childrearing. *You are Your Child's First Teacher.* You'll read for the long-term. *7 Habits of Highly Effective Families.* You'll read Daniel Goleman and Rudolph Steiner and Maria Montessori. You'll put bowls of glue in front of your toddlers *just so they can experience it.* You'll walk and carry your tiny ones back through the fields for regular visits to Granny Apple Tree. Your little environmentalists will decide to clean up every piece of hundred-year old fencing that happens to be stuck in her branches. They'll feel like superstars and you'll all serenade Granny Apple with a poem before walking home with pants stuck full of thistle. It will be apparent to everyone who sees you who spends even a moment of time with you. *She has such a gentle nature she's so patient with her kids listen to the way she's explaining that to him.*

And that connection, the strongest connection of your life, will also be your weakest spot. There are at least two sides to everything you know, and it will be the perfect target it will be the bomb that explodes later in your heart. *If you want to destroy someone, figure out what they love.* Because not everyone who's watching you will feel touched by what you do or how you do it. Some people are the kind you just can't touch, but that doesn't mean they don't know how to read you. Sometimes it even seems they can read you better than you can read yourself. And so sometimes you'll only understand after, by what they work to destroy, what has always looked to the rest of the world like your greatest strength. Then, and only then, you'll be able to say, *I was once really good at that.*

And it meant more to me than anything, anything at all.

You might not be able to get that last part out.

04.
A GOOD WIFE

A relationship is not a place
or a thing.
You don't have to be
near a person to feel
your ties, and
you might even say
that what we see
when we look at each other
are our relationships
made visible.

Two or three or four years will go by. Your oldest will be learning to read and your next one down will be learning how to chase away the hens if they happen to surround him in the yard. You'll be skinnier than ever before in your life something like a tight sack of bones that's a little dry and brittle around the eyes. Your aunts will give you some eye cream *you need to take care of yourself it's better to start early*. Your mom will show up with new jeans and T-shirts twice a year. *It's amazing what a new shirt will do for you*. Your sister will show up everywhere to help you strip wallpaper or rake rocks. You won't write, you won't draw, and you'll never watch TV. You won't read the newspapers, you won't go to the movies, and you won't know the popular music. You'll be down to one or two distant girlfriends and have to fight almost daily to keep them as your own. Mostly, you'll talk to them when he's not there. Mostly, you'll follow your man.

You'll follow him to horse auctions when he decides he wants to plow. With horses now that you're living all bumped up against your family's land *there's no end to the possibilities.* You wonder about a riding horse you'd really rather have something to ride. But you'll end up with a Clydesdale filly you can see why it's a good idea after the seven hour drive you'll spend listening to Wyatt explain why it's a good idea. *I can train her myself. So can you, after the baby comes.* You'll buy her with that handy credit line you have on your house you'll buy everything with that handy credit line you'll pay for all the fencing and all the remodeling and all the equipment, too. He'll quickly start telling people that your little place is his house *it's great there's so much equity and it pulls $1,800 a month in rent.* You'll also sign for a round pen (gotta train her), a manure spreader (she'll make plenty of it), and a mower (we'll have to make hay). You'll sweep the barn aisle every day you really like to keep it tidy and it's nice to listen to her chew her grain in the quiet.

And that's the extent of it. Once you get her home, he'll never touch her outside of a couple runs across the back yard when your brother stops in to see her. You'll be pregnant and willing take the blame *his mom says I don't let him have any time for these things* so within a year, she'll be sold off and he'll come up with another horse he just has to have, a big old Percheron named Butch who'll be so chill that his bottom lip will droop down about six inches when he's dozing in his stall. It'll make you giggle. You'll instantly fall in love with this 2,000 pound Butch and his five pound lip he'll be so wonderful to brush and so easy to deworm he'll just kind of stand there and say *oh well, I guess it's for the best.* He'll say that about everything and in all the years you'll know him you won't remember a single time he ever jumped. Over time, you'll become fast friends, and even though you'll never ride or hitch him, you'll keep the burrs out of his mane and you'll scratch him all over and he'll follow you cn the other side of the fence when you wander to the garden then droop his head over the top to watch your tiny boys digging in the sand down below. Pretty soon, your in-laws will show up with two more horses and two or three full sets of harness—a surprise gift for your man they love to support a fun hobby and you know, *he works so hard he needs a good hobby and you ought to be more supportive, too.* Despite your initial doubts and frowny eyebrows—after all it's a lot of work for you to feed and water Butch let alone pull the burrs out of his mane and keep the flies off him and sometimes it's hard to get out there in the winter with a baby—but then despite all that you'll fall in love with these mares within a week you're such a sucker for animals and they'll be just as big and perfectly black as Butch. White star on the forehead. Hooves that a-e bigger than your head. Bonnie will be the gentlest, the most like your Butchie. Princess will have a little kick-and-vinega- to her spirit, but over time you'll find that she never actually kicks. She just thinks about it. Practices sometimes out in the field *she wants to keep her game.* And so when your in-laws show up with these one-ton horses, your man will almost dance with joy over all the *stuff.* All those pounds of muscle and good, old-timey bulk. Harness. You'll need harness hooks to hang it all up, you know. You'll need to hit an auction and buy some within a week. He'll go to auctions every Saturday for years he'll love to stand with the Amish men and smack them on the back. And his face will light up over the pie from the ladies under the tent he'll also love to make them smile and blush. And he'll know this one guy he can talk into selling him anything for nothing. A Schwartzentruber—that's the oldest subgroup around they don't make any modern compromises. After every visit to this Schwartzentruber's farm, your man will laugh and laugh over the deal he got from that guy. *Doesn't seem to care about money at all can you believe he practically gave me this thing what a joke.* And he'll take it into his shop where it'll lay on the floor for the next five or seven years. All that harness, in giant piles. Even the hooks. Piles on top of tools his dad gave him and old wooden boxes and saddles and weed-eaters and stuff. Piles up to your eyeballs, literally. And there will be more auctions and more purchases. Wagons. A potato plow. Collars and straps and tools. *You need to be more supportive.* And you'll want to be more supportive you will decide to be more supportive and eventually, it will be your hobby, too, you're all certain. When the babies get a little bigger. When the garden's established. When the house is fixed up and the orchard repaired. There's just not time right now there's so much to do on this farm.

You will decide to be more supportive you will embrace the work *I've loved hard work all my life* you will decide. To move from your small farm to a much bigger one it will back up to your parents' property it will come to you in another perfectly timed opportunity so you will sell your grandparents' home after two years of solid work you will sell your little rented home and all your barns and you will not look back *don't turn down life's perfect chances.* Like a woman on fire you'll land in this new place with more energy and excitement than you've ever known. You'll walk the fields touch the tops of the grasses love the way they bounce off your hands you'll love the sky. Love the fencerows. Love the birds. More pheasants and turkeys and bobolinks than you knew lived in this world. You'll love the little farm pond. The ancient two-track driveway with grass growing down the middle *seems like it's a mile long* the privacy the sweeping landscape the view to the south the rising hillsides dotted with million dollar thoroughbreds who are your only visible neighbors. You will marvel *this is my life's dream come true* you always wanted to live on a farm watch little toddlers sprinkle chicken seed in the grass for puffy-butt hens and you'll have one who insists on sleeping in the garage, the coop being just a bit to crowded for her liking. This farm will be your everything your one and only soul mate it might take you a while to get over the junk piles and the empty space and really attach, but once you do, that farm will be the best partner you have in your life *the sky is bigger up here and I am with this place this land knows me and I know this land.* And in the coming years when desperately need a companion, that farm will hold you in its arms on the gentle slope to the west. It will rock you and talk to you about the stars. It will warm your soul with the sunshine. The fields will sing a whistling melody to your children in the afternoon *there is no better way to live.* No better way to live. Nothing material will ever mean so much to you, you will have no regrets you will feel perfectly safe even when Wyatt acts up and by the time you get to the farm it will be very clear that sometimes Wyatt acts up so you will be just a little more cautious and you'll buy the place in a self-protective kind of way *I'm not entirely stupid I have almost 115 acres that are just mine. Wyatt and I only share the remaining five acres and the house, and that's where we have the mortgage. Two parcels. It's the way you have to buy a farm, anyway. Separate the producing acres from the non-producing acres and set up the mortgage on the non-producing. The house.* You'll explain things carefully to yourself but you won't say out loud that you're scared of what he might do. You'll never talk about that at all. Instead, you'll take some protective measures in silence and continue to focus on the positive *my kids get to grow up here this is some kind of a perfect blessing from God we have 118 acres who could have dreamed it would back up to my parents' farm the whole back side the kids will be able to take a long hike and end up at Grandma's house.* 118 acres. That number will make you cry. And it'll come complete with two giant barns, a long lane with vista views, a broken windmill, a chicken coop stuffed with junk, and a couple mobile homes. Also stuffed with junk. It'll come with an '80s tract house that the last owner built after he burnt down the old grand farm home you will mourn the loss of that home *it had two sweeping staircases going up each side to meet at a balcony in the middle.* The neighbor will remember that she always wanted to get married there when she was a little girl. But it'll be long gone *he burnt it to pocket the insurance money and then threw together the shittiest, cheapest house he could possibly build.* The neighbors will tell you the details and they'll be so glad he's gone *it's well known that he left suddenly in the night* he also left the house completely stuffed with stuff so you'll roll up your sleeves and get to work once again *the basement has such a strange smell must be all that food that sat in there for months it's creepy* and you'll hand scrub the whole thing. You'll donate the piles of clothing along with two pairs of reading glasses left sitting on the kitchen table *where did that guy run off to? Why did he leave?* You'll vacuum the brown indoor/outdoor carpet and thank your parents over and over for at least changing all the flooring upstairs from the purple jungle leaf print carpet. They'll show up to carry junk out for weeks they'll do everything to help by the time you get to the farm because everyone except for Wyatt's parents will know it's the only way you'll ever get help with anything you want to get done. Seems your man has a sudden business trip every time things get tough.

And so when you move in, you'll have horses and cats and dogs and a healthy little boy and another on the way. And with all of these blessings, there'll be no room to complain. Your man will travel more and more, and after you buy the farm he'll spend days and weeks away. At first it'll make you nervous to stay there alone in the middle of all those dark fields but after a few months the loneliness will become your favorite thing. Your friend it'll be like something more than a habit, even, and once things start to happen, it'll be the one thing you can rely on in the night. *Oh, you're right there thank goodness I couldn't find you for a moment.*

Because lots will happen.

And when lots happens, decisions have to be made. And maybe there are limits to the number of decisions we all get to make in life you won't really know it then but you'll understand later that you spent lots of time putting off decisions you needed to make you'll think later that you must've been saving it all up for one big thing. One big

48

moment. You'll understand, only after, that it's easier for you to move forward than to sit still or go back, and so you'll have a habit of ignoring people who are hurting you *there's no time to deal with that now and it's not going to take me down it's not going to hold me back I've got to get moving I've got to keep moving.* Only later will you regret all your deciding to not decide. Only later will you wish you'd made decisions all along the way. Later you'll know regret, when you finally have to decide that something big and it takes you all the way back. To the very first hurt you decided to ignore in your race to move forward with your dreams.

In the meantime, you'll work hard to get the laundry done every day because you like to dress your children in clothes that smell like fresh air. Kiss their cheeks so many times they'll turn red after a bath and it just won't be helped they'll smell like baby powder at the end of a long day of smelling like dirt. They'll eat a lot of dirt. They'll try to eat some bugs. They'll scratch themselves climbing in the hay. They'll scratch each other when they fight, grabbing each other's cheeks and arms *it's just awful but they're only twenty months apart.* That's what you'll tell the teen employee at the grocery store as you work to rebuild the pyramid of oranges they tumbled into. They will spend whole days in their jammies, and when their Papau pulls in the drive in his red truck they'll bounce around in their stocking feet and scream with joy. *Papau's truck! Papau's truck!* And that joyful chant will be the beginning of the end of your man's relationship with your dad and it may even be the very first seed planted for the end of your boys' relationship with your dad, too, but you won't know it at the time because even though your man may never touch a diaper unless someone's watching *oh, look at him. What a great dad. I wish my man ever did that* and even though he may never care to read them a story unless you pull out a camera for a photo op (or give them a bath or rock them to sleep or keep them at home while you run to the store *I actually have some calls I need to make,* he'll say). He may not teach them how to dribble or shoot hoops or how to throw or how to kick (when you oldest starts basketball at five and is the only one on the team who doesn't know what to do, you'll bring him home and tear the indoor/outdoor carpet right up with a knife and teach him how to dribble yourself. Bang, bang, bang, the sound will echo around the house). But even though your husband won't care to do any of these Midwestern masculine fatherly things, he will not even begin to tolerate your boys having these screaming happy fits about their Papau pulling up the lane. If he's there, he'll come into the room and stand behind them as they bounce, staring them down with shark eyes and swirling his wine in his glass. Other times, he'll pull them both backward into a wrestling match and then whisk them upstairs for a tickle fight so intense they'll forget how to even breathe for a moment. Your dad will come into the house on his own. *Where are the guys, are they up? I found a snapping turtle crossing the road and I want to show it to them.* And you'll hear the boys trying to pull away from their father you will go to the bottom of the steps and holler up, *Papau's here!* and Wyatt will accelerate the tickling your dad will stand and wait for five minutes in the kitchen shifting his weight back and forth in his muddy boots *I can come back or you can just bring them over later if that's better but I have an appointment I just wanted to show them this turtle* you will yell *Papau's gotta go!* and start up the stairs to get them you will say *Wyatt, quit it* the boys will be trying to pull away from him with red faces and hysterical laughter as he grabs their arms and tickles them some more you will say *dad's gotta go just let them go see this turtle* they will jump and wriggle away he will grab at them and laugh and tease *you better get back here, boy* and then go all shark-eyed again as they dash back down the steps to find their Papau and climb up on his shoulders for a peek into the bed of his truck Wyatt will watch from the window with those darkened eyes before opening it and putting on a celebrity smile *you better get back in here, boys, I'm going to tickle the snot out of you* and they will laugh in his direction but stick for just a moment with their Papau and his turtle they will delight in their time

50

with him now, but the end has already started for your dad. It's just that no one will know how to see it at the time.

Because you will not know no one will know lots of things. Later, you'll think it's like decent people don't even have the eyes to see. You'll think *it's not that Wyatt wants to hurt anybody* because he talks so much about family *he really loves family life* so you'll think maybe some of his competitiveness or whatever you call it it just because he had a hard time with his own dad leaving for other women while he was growing up you will tell your mom *yes, that must have an impact on the way Wyatt is it must've made him jealous or insecure because I guess his dad left every few years it's just that no one ever knew it but when his aunt got so drunk at Thanksgiving she told me all about it. Out of no where plus I want to tell you something you can never bring up with him and this is so sad but she told me his grandpa committed suicide when his dad went away to community college. I think he wanted him to stay on the farm, but I don't really know the story. Yeah, seriously. She said he tried several times and that one time he threw himself into the hay baler in front of Wyatt's dad to make the point can you even believe that. It doesn't even seem real it's so awful and it's a taboo subject I mean all of this is all of it so don't say a word seriously his family does not talk about these things* you will pause but just for a moment because you'll be agitated by telling the truth you will sip your coffee and look out the window your mom will sit quietly and wait for you to continue *you know, his sister sat down at the table the other day and said she feels sorry for divorced families she can't imagine it because she grew up with such a perfect family life. No shit. There's so much hidden betrayal there and it has to change how you respond to the world he wouldn't know how truly committed parents operate and he must think that yelling and hurt and hiding things I guess are part of a normal marriage. Wouldn't he? If that's all he knew?* Your mom will nod her head to agree. *Plus, the pressure of keeping it all so normal as a kid and no one can know a thing about his dad's cheating. Not even me not anyone. Actually, he did tell me one thing he hardly shares anything but this one night he actually opened up kind of quietly and said that he doesn't remember anything hardly except one time when*

51

he was three or four he visited his dad at an apartment somewhere and they built a little blue truck. When he got home, he smashed it and his mom spanked him hard and told him he was bad. And what a wreck that would be he's never been allowed to feel anything you know so maybe if we can just be patient enough, or if we can be consistent enough—always there for him—then maybe our love will make a break through to the part of him that needs to be touched. He's so sensitive, really, and so maybe all he needs is a little commitment and TLC. He really seems to enjoy other people he always has so much fun with everyone. It seems like he's really happy when everyone's together and he talks about family all the time. So I just need to focus on the good things. And try to be more supportive through all the rest.

That's what you'll tell yourself that's what your whole family will tell themselves. And while you're doing that, he'll continue to distract and disorganize the boys every time their Papau comes around. Or their Mamau or Aunt Rachel or Uncle Wesley or anyone at all and it won't be obvious that he's *disorganizing children* to people who don't even know the phrase no one will notice that he goes from zero interest to high speed chaos the moment another person walks in and wants to hug his child no one will notice the part that he doesn't care unless there's a sense of competition inside his head and that when he feels the competition it will be game on he will bounce off the walls he will take his children with him for the ride *Daddy is the most fun ever aren't we having the most fun ever isn't this the funniest tickle fight we've ever had? You can't even breathe that's so funny you can't even breathe, now quit that crying I'm just playing around. My God. Here, catch this think twice catch it here you go!* He will pull them from the room. Play with them wildly at the back yard party. Throw them up higher than ever before laughing hard enough for every person around to take notice of how the best dad in the world is playing with his babies *they're pretty enough to be in a commercial.* He'll bounce like a jackrabbit when he feels the attention, leap and land on his back in the grass. Stand the boys on his hands and lift each of them up higher than their Papau *ever* does when he stands them up like that. Aren't they as amazing as little blonde circus boys aren't they as spectacular as the sun aren't they mirror images of their father it's some kind of miracle from God that they all look absolutely perfectly alike. Blonde hair. Blue eyes. Big, athletic builds. When they hit junior high, he'll tell them that they're from the Aryan race, which makes them better than anyone else in the world. *If you lived in Germany, everyone would tell you that you're the perfect human being.*

But that's for later. For now, they're round-faced cherubic boys with toads in the front pockets of their overalls. They'll talk to each other. *You have to be gentle, Levi. Toady doesn't like that.* They'll take their toads to their Granny's house. They'll take their toads to the store. You'll create tiny toad habitats in clear plastic boxes with handles so they can transport Toady on the go. You'll build big huge toad habitats for Toady at home on the farm. You'll spend time with your toads every day of the summer and release them in the garden before the fall. You'll build toad huts right there on the spot just in case they choose to use one for winter housing. (They will choose!) You'll feed them insects and earth worms and then watch in horror as Mr. Big Toad picks up a big juicy one with his two tiny hands and crams the whole thing into his chomping mouth, Jabba the Hut style. Gulp, gulp, gulp. The end will be dangling out until he crams it in with his little fist. *That poor worm!* You'll all be glad that toads aren't bigger than you *they would be scarier than a dinosaur.* And then you'll head inside to wash up for a story and a nap. *Frog and Toad.*

Sometimes, you won't leave your farm for weeks you'll buy enough milk and have enough of everything else in the freezer you will walk the ducklings down to the frog pond to see the first swim of their lives and the singing of the meadows will become your favorite silence. The whistling and ever-rustling grasses. Pheasants calling. Turkeys gobbling. Even the song of the quail families that will venture into your orchard for a bite. You'll love the way they bob to peck at things. The way they seem to chatter with each other. *I got your back! I got your back! I found a horsefly! I found a horsefly!* Three golden red does will spend the afternoon bedded down on the north slope of your yard, flicking their ears against the gnats and chewing their cuds as they take on the breeze. You won't go out *they're only twenty feet from the house and it's the middle of the day* but you'll watch from your window and wonder whether you've moved to some kind of Disney-Bambi-Land where the animals aren't afraid and the sky is always blue. You'll call your girlfriend *Maggie, there are deer bedded down in my back yard not thirty feet from my house. Right now! It's crazy. Yes, I'll take a picture.*

And then he'll come home.

When he's there, a different kind of atmosphere will fall over you it will be the silence of a heavy fog at five in the morning in the flatlands it will drown out the song of the fields and the trees it will cloud up your brain. You'll lose focus of your daily schedule it will suddenly be 3:30 and you won't have put the kiddos down for a nap. He'll keep you up at night with mixed drinks so strong *I had no idea you put so much in there* you'll be hung over the next day from just one glass and you won't be able to believe that you ran around the back yard naked in your muck boots *who was that person, anyway? What was that about?* You won't remember anything. You won't remember most things. But you will try almost anything to build a good moment and you will try a lot of self-help-save-your-marriage tactics because you'll know you've been through a lot together in a short time and you'll really want to have a strong relationship so you'll work hard to figure out what men like and what would make him look at you what would bring that sparkle-smoke back down from the sky you will show up to get him at the airport with a secret red garter belt under your jeans. Left the boys with Granny and Papau brought a simple bouquet of flowers just to be unexpected but you'll know it's all wrong as soon as he steps out of the tunnel and looks embarrassed his eyes will flash dark. *What's this? You don't get flowers for a MAN.* He'll be whispering these words will be zeroing in on you. *Carry those and come on.* So you'll come on, trying to keep it chatty in the car. *How was your trip? Did you eat anything good?* He'll describe how he heard two married-to-other-people sales team members having sex through the hotel wall and he'll remind you that he would never do such a thing *those people are unbelievable.* You'll redouble your determination to keep him occupied and pleased, hinting at the garter *and the kids are with my parents.*

And he'll think it sounds like fun. Always up for a good time, he thinks he'll take you. He'll take you every time. There'll always be a hand on the back of your head, telling you what to do. There'll always be a request. *You know what I'd really like is if you'd stand on your tiptoes over there and look back at me over your shoulder like you're all innocent and surprised. That's it.* He'll take you in the car and in the barns and in your bed when you're sick with the flu. He'll take you when you want to and when you really don't. After your first four hundred *no's* when he shows up naked at 3 a.m., you'll learn that it just isn't worth the energy of staying up all night long so he can tell you what a selfish bitch you are how could you treat him like that he works so hard. Once you're worn out, he'll take you pretty much any time he wants. When you're nursing your wee babies, you'll push him away *not right now* cover them up with a blanket so they can't see what he's trying to do. When you're in labor with your first, you'll feel scared and anxious *I need to relax* he won't notice what you're saying will just push you and push you and push you until you'll yell at him and he'll yell back and tell you all the ways you're *unbelievable* and then you'll feel a contraction and not want to spend your labor fighting and he'll say *can't you just go down on me come on* and so you'll finally just give up and get it done. Later, you'll worry about the splinters in your knees. It's your own fault, anyway, you'll think, for wanting to do those pregnant-naked photos before the baby came. Last minute like that. It was too much for him to take it really turned him on it's easier to just get down and love him one last time. Plus, it's better than a fight *I really want this birth experience to be something beautiful.*

He'll take you into a cloud where no one else lives you will stay there for years you will know not to bother trying to describe it to anyone else even after you begin to notice but it will take you years to notice. You'll know not to describe anything to people who can't see the cloud you'll keep it to yourself won't want them to tell you that you're crazy or that only bad wives talk about their men like that and you'll want to be a good wife, won't you. You got yourself into this and you'll figure out a way to make it work. Your friends won't wonder where you are anymore which will be better, really, than the weeks you'd have to spend before or after any visit defending them *they're not really sluts I don't know why you're even worried about that and who would care even if they were we are grown ups what is the big fat deal* he won't even want you to hang out with his own sister he'll go on and on *she drinks too much and she's a cheapskate did you notice that they got us like two towels as a wedding gift? Nice. I got them a full set of silverware and they get us two towels? You don't want to be that way and I don't even want them around Trent's just an ass, I really can't stand being around him sometimes I want to punch him in the face he's such a wannabe country boy.* At the holidays, his sister will love and gush on you she will say *Trent and I had some hard times with Wyatt in the past, but you really brought the family back together.* You'll smile and hug her, but you'll be thankful that there's at least one area where you strongly agree with your man. And that's Trent. You will bond with Wyatt over your complaints you will get along for a moment it will be like eating candy. *Who calls his two-year-old son a pussy if he wants to ride in the stroller after walking half a mile? A crybaby? Max was crying and chasing the stroller with his little arms out. Who does that? I had to call him out on it I'm not going to stand there and watch that, Wyatt. I don't want to fight with your family, but some things have to be said.* So when the holidays roll around, you'll let his mom make you one of her strong drinks and you'll run around with all of them creating happy family moments with a numb happy smile like a good wife does.

A good wife also knows how to be accountable. So when something goes wrong, you'll know how to apologize and take credit for your part. When you burn all your old journals and everything you ever wrote in your life, you'll do it because he was so hurt he couldn't keep himself from reading them even after you duct-taped them into a box he'll pull the box apart and pore over them and lament *how could you write such things? You're not the person I thought you were.* You will hate being a let down and you'll get sick of the explanations so you'll throw them all into a fire one hot afternoon in August. You'll try hard not to hurt him at all and when you're down in the city and don't find a pay phone to call every couple hours, you'll agonize over the fact that you've probably made him really worried and that there's going to be a couple days' hell to pay when you get home. You won't give up on him taking on his part, for sure, it'll just be harder to see over time what that is. Does that make sense? No, probably not. Not if you're not there yet, in the middle of it, living it. Everyone on the outside, later, would say, *why didn't you leave him right from the start?* Your therapist will ask you, *why do you think you let him treat you like that? What part of you let that happen? Did you know that you could just walk away?* And you will say, *no, I didn't think I could just walk away—I got married. Married is married my parents made it through some tough times and they got married when they were seventeen and eighteen. And I thought I was doing something wrong or else it would be better, like when we were dating. Or like it could be sometimes when we were in public. We'd have our moments. When people were watching, he'd act like he adored me. At least most of the time. And I've known him since I was nine, and everything I've ever known about him was that he's a happy-go-lucky, family kind of guy. Maybe a little self-proud or something, but so likable. And so I thought it must be about me or about how hard it can be to move or to add children and I thought I could work through those things and try harder I thought I could make it work. Plus everyone loves him. So I thought it* was about me and most people would probably say it's about me because he sets it up to look that way and that's really hard to overcome. Public opinion. He always made me seem crazy like one time he left me in the car for an hour with two screaming babies while he ran into a store for just one thing, he promised. But then he ran into a friend in there and caught up with the guy and I could see him standing there chatting through the window and I kept calling his phone and the boys were absolutely screaming and I'd watch him click it off and this went on for about an hour and he knew the boys were crying before he even went in so when I finally stormed up and knocked on the window he looked at me with this big smile of disbelief and laughed with the guy about what a psycho I was and how I was always a crabby bitch to poor Wyatt and by the time he got back in the car I was so angry for being left in there and I was so angry that he laughed at me and I was so angry that he made me look bad and I was so angry that the boys were miserable and needed naps and so I yelled at him and the conversation immediately flipped into how I was attacking him and it turned into what a bitter person I was and how insecure and jealous I was to get upset about him trying to catch up with an old friend and it's amazing how relentless and convincing he can be and how worn down I could get after hours of that and so I'd lose sight of being wronged and I'd start focusing on things I thought I could impact like relighting the fire or saying things to him in a way that would spark a connection. I wanted his love back so badly I thought I just had to find the right way to say stuff. And you know what? I was confused. I was confused as hell. I didn't know where the guy went that I dated or why he was still so nice to everyone else—unbelievably helpful— and so unhelpful and degrading and mean to me I thought I must be doing something wrong that made him change like that behind the scenes and hate me. He was always, always right. And he never cared how I felt. I threw up and passed out once when we were moving because I had no help and was lifting too much because he was out of town for the week so when I got mad at him for leaving me there to do everything with the boys he got even more mad at me for being unsupportive and a selfish whiner and for not doing my part. And you know, other people agreed with him and got mad at me, too. I packed and moved us four times on my own, and on the fifth time, I left him to do it except he didn't have the kiddos to care for and professional movers were coming to help. And

I got three phone calls from angry people saying how could you leave him with all of that but no one ever got angry when he left me alone with our children and an entire move to take care of myself. And that's our whole society chipping in. To why I didn't stand up for myself. He has a whole culture working to his advantage. A culture with clear ideas about what a woman should do. And that's pretty much everything. So it's the easiest thing in the world for him to get people to feel sorry for him about what he tells them I'm doing or not doing. Like he told everyone and still talks all the time about how he always cooked every meal and people get really defensive and angry about that, thinking that he had to work all week and still feed everyone mashed potatoes, too. He created a giant army of people who were against me—right from the beginning of our marriage. And I could never figure out why he'd do that. Or I couldn't understand why he'd lie. Because once we were married, he never cooked again. Not even to help when I had babies. Except I have to say that after I had Levi, he did heat up some leftover tuna noodle casserole once from the fridge. I hate tuna noodle casserole, but he loves it. With peas. And so after that, whenever a visitor came to the house to see the baby, he's say right off "I made her some tuna noodle casserole first thing because she needed to eat I wanted her to eat." He'd show them a photo he took of the plate of food. "I made her some dinner. I made her some food. She sat right down and ate it.. What do you think of that? Wasn't that sweet? I made her first meal and I brought it right to her."

And even though that's the only time in your entire marriage that he'll ever make you anything besides grilled foods (if he has an audience) or a glass of *naughty but healthy* anytime, other people will be taken. *Did you see how proud he was over that food? That's pretty cute. It's so cute the way he gets so excited over everything. Why doesn't she seem happy? He's so loving he just adores her you can see and he's so fun he's a lot more fun to be around than she is and she's actually kind of a dud anymore she must bring him down I wonder what's going on with her and I feel bad for that guy.* Every person on the street will get his captivating smile and a touch and every visitor to your house will get his personal tour. *See this door handle? It was facing the wrong way, like this here. See this?* He'll lean in close and put his hands on the backs of your guests for a subtle almost-massage, pulling them up close. *Do you see that? I changed it around this way, the right way, for her. I did this for her. You see?* Then he'll look at your guest for affirmation, maybe he'll be three inches away from her face. And maybe it'll be your grandma, who will stagger a couple steps back, overwhelmed by so much touch but never really able to put her finger on any strange thing. *He's such a good guy. He works really hard for her.* And then she'll sit at your table enjoying coffee with your mom and remind you that he does, indeed, work really hard. And *at least he's not hanging out every night in the bars.*

You'll find out some years later that he is indeed hanging out every night in the bars. It'll be long after you stopped caring where he goes. It'll be long after you stopped asking questions at all. But you'll figure out at some point that he's a local favorite in town that he buys drinks for everyone all night long and that he also has several key seats at bars in the best flannel-man-gone-upscale taverns in your closest city, an hour away. Maybe it's time to get to that now. To the place where you'll find out everything. To the place where you will have to make some *decisions.* It'll start after a move to Colorado and the birth of your daughter. Yes, you will move away from your beloved farm for his work he will want an adventure he will sell you on any adventure he wants you will rent out your home all over again, and your parents will manage the renting, mowing, and maintenance plus all the animals while you're gone. Your sister will also move out west to have her own adventure and help you along. Wyatt will start a new job that keeps him traveling several weeks out of every month and he'll feel better about his work life than ever, laughing to you later that all these people are so easy. Even the persnickety old men he will say *Dale Carnegie knows exactly what he's talking about.* He can get them to buy whatever he's selling and the women are always the easiest of all he'll say they have no real sense of self-respect he can always get them to do whatever he wants. *They shouldn't even be in the field.*

60

You'll give an almost silent *uh-huh, sure* and concentrate on your fresh salsa, your neighbor has the best recipe and it's always best for the kids to avoid some big ugly discussion about women and self-respect.

But it will become impossible to avoid every big ugly discussion because you never were the kind to stay quiet so over time your words will be harder and harder to hold back. There will also be some words that will have been gone too long from your life and you will ache to hear them again you will strain to shut yourself up as much as you strain to hear words you need to hear. Words like *wonderful*. Or *kind*. Or *beautiful*. Or *I care*. Whole phrases will have disappeared. Like *how you doing? You doing ok? Need anything? Thank you. I'm so grateful. You're my best friend*. You will strain to hear you will keep straining you will have waited six years to hear that your pretty or *you want a glass of water? I'm having one*. You'll have waited your whole marriage to know whether he feels good about you it will feel like you've been waiting your whole life. You will look in the mirror and cry and ask him outright for the feedback you need but the best he'll be able to do is *you know you're good looking*. So you'll be lonely. You'll feel empty. And run down. And so when you give birth to your daughter one mountain-sunrise morning at 6 a.m. and then stop off to shop for a cake before 10 a.m. on your ride home, Wyatt will say *why don't you run in and get it you're the one who knows what cake to buy* and you will run out of any energy you were using to keep your mouth shut you will go home to your Colorado house and fall into your mom's care like a bruised peach that needs special placement in your lunch bag. You'll barely get off the couch for a couple days *it's been so long*. You will watch your mom do everything you will watch your man stand behind her with his glass of wine, using his paternity leave to make suggestions. *You know, what would be really good in that is corn*. You will watch your man stand around and laugh at a show while your mom works to get by him with a crying toddler under one arm and a laundry basket under the other.

You will listen to his excuses *I said I'd get that*. You will hear your mom start to snap back here and there. *That was three days ago now*. You will hear the echo of his voice through the house when he asks you what's for dinner or whether the boys are up and ready. And then on a certain Tuesday he will let the dogs back into the house three times in thirty minutes, he will let them right into the bedroom to lick your face while you're trying to nap with the baby and you'll finally after the third time go bursting out and ranting into the kitchen like an explosion you'll imagine later that the top of your head actually blew off *now I SAID get the God-damned dogs OUT of here I already asked you THREE times why the FUCKING hell are you letting them in this bedroom I just had a BABY and I'm TRYING to SLEEP!* He'll be shocked by your ridiculous behavior and you'll know as he laughs and smiles at you and calls you a *piece of work* you will know that you are going to leave Colorado. You'll wait a day to bring it up, but it will come you will start with your mom over coffee. *Mom, I'm going to go home with you I'm so sick of this and I just had a baby.* She'll raise an eyebrow at you and rub her hand up and down your arm. She'll say *you know* (long pause) *I know how he is. I could punch him sometimes* and she will rub her fist in her hand, thinking about it *but I think you really need to stay here and keep making your family.* You'll absorb her answer in silence, too tired just then for words. But moments later, you'll take a long glance around the room at what staying here looks like, and the words will come right out you'll find yourself saying something out loud to Wyatt from across the room *it sure is nice to have some help here. Mom's doing such a great job I really wish you could help do some of this stuff for a while when she's gone.* His back will be to you as you say this, and you'll see it stiffen from across the room.

If you want help from me, he'll say, *you're going to have to do my job.*

I WORK.

He won't turn around. And that's when you'll decide to leave. Colorado. With three kids under the age of four, you'll fly home to Ohio for six weeks *he's been telling me all year that he'd get a job back there, anyway, but he's never applied he's just lying again* and so you'll finally draw a line you will make a strong decision you're not some kind of doormat and you think your mom's wrong on this one you'll tell him *get out your resume. You've taken six days off work this year already to get it done and haven't even started it. Do it now. I want to go back.*

He will look at you, amused. Your daughter will be six weeks old, and she'll sleep on the airplane the whole way home. The boys will be so happy to see their Papau *it's been seven months* and the horses will want to be scratched and the toads in Granny's garden will be abundant. The whole hugeness of your extended family will show up to adore your daughter *we're so glad to meet her she's so wonderful, Helen, I'm so glad you get to have a girl, too,* and you'll inhale the love in their breath and your lungs will fill back up so you can laugh again and it won't be long before you and your mom will almost fall out of the car you'll both be laughing so hard. Laughing about that frog you'll just have to catch when it hops in front of your headlights on their dead end road in the night. Slamming on the brakes *Did you SEE that? The boys have to see it CATCH IT!* You'll dive right into the bushes and have that leopard frog but it won't be caught for long it'll jump right away from you and into the back seat you'll both be diving after it and finally she'll have it clutched in her two hands and she'll stare it down for a second—woman to frog—and then turn to you with the full seriousness of the situation. *Them sirens done turned Pete into a hoo-r rrr-ny toad. What're-we-gonna-DO?!* And that frog will be gone again right into the back seat and you'll fall all over yourselves chasing it once more but it will leap effortlessly up and out the back window and be gone *I'm going to pee my pants* you'll be laughing so hard and then you'll remember that you're alive and it will be so beautiful that you won't even realize you remember.

All because you made a decision. And with that will come more strength to decide.

PART II
What it takes to see

05.
MIRAGE

Most people choose words
that match up with
what they mean
and how they feel.
But some people
can say whatever they want,
and that can look like
kicking the dog
as you praise it.
It especially works
if the dog
really believes what it hears,
like people do.

You will spend the summer in Ohio with your toddlers and
baby girl, and in August, your tenants will decide to move out
of your farmhouse you will jump right on the chance to move
back in you won't have any furniture since it's all in Colorado
with Wyatt but your friends and family will drum up two air
mattresses, a card table, a futon, and a whole gob of toys.
Thank you. That's just enough. They will build a giant bonfire will
help you straighten things around they will show up with
pizzas they will travel the farm on their four-wheelers and dirt
bikes they will take quiet walks back to the stream. You will
read books from the library to put your children to bed at
night you will hike around the farm as far as they can go you

will eat peaches right off the trees you will watch the sun set most evenings while you nurse your tiny daughter in a lawn chair you will realize the mind-soothing beauty of living without things you will gain strength in your quiet moments alone on the farm you will decide *I'm not going back to Colorado.*

And then you will go back to Colorado.

But just for the weekend. In September, you'll fly out with your baby girl to help get the house ready to sell. Wyatt will have found another job in Ohio pretty quickly through a frat brother and he will make plans to move back in December and you will feel you were right to draw the line even though no one will ever tell you that you made a good choice. Instead, most people will feel sorry for your man. *She just deserted him out there he only got to see the kids for two weeks out of the last eight. He's broken hearted.* You'll keep yourself from sharing that they should butt out of your business that Wyatt didn't call to talk to the boys once that he's been mountain biking and partying and out dancing with other women. No one will believe you anyway he always talks louder and longer and when you call him and say *how's it going what are you into* he'll say he can't hear you because he's out with friends and when you say *who are you out with what are you guys doing* he'll hold the phone out from his ear and scream *stop yelling at me! What is wrong with you?* You'll guess it's just so everyone around him will think there's something wrong with you *that poor guy, there she blows* so there's just no point in asking questions he'll just keep right on rolling with his show *I told you to lower your voice why are you always YELLING at me* it'll take too much energy to argue against that but sometimes you'll try anyway *I'm not yelling why are you saying that* he'll make you out to be some kind of relentless psycho every time *please just stop YELLING at me* and so you'll just let it go and let him go and not care what anyone thinks of you anymore you were raised not to care what other people say *what matters is who you are in your heart.* That's right.

But sometimes you'll wonder, anyway. Is it normal to wonder and second-guess things? Did you really desert him out there? You will begin again to doubt your decisions you won't want to be the kind of wife he makes people think you are, *are people right that I shouldn't have left shouldn't have made him do the resume thing he did promise after all so maybe he would've eventually gotten around to it maybe I was harsh to force the issue.* You'll wonder. *Maybe people are right* and then you'll call him one day around noon to talk through some of your second-guessing and another woman will answer the phone and she'll be giggling and you'll be startled. *Um, hello. Who is this who am I speaking to?* And she'll giggle some more and put him on the line instead of answering and you'll learn that she's an airline stewardess who sometimes stays in the house across the street and that she's come over for lunch and she'll be giggling even more in the background the whole time. *It's just the two of you hanging out in the middle of the day on a Wednesday? Aren't you supposed to be in Wyoming?* And he'll say he has to call you back but then he won't. Call you back you'll end up calling him six or twenty times which later you'll think might've sealed the deal that this is absolutely going to happen again. So you'll want to get back out there to claim your man and help stage your house to sell and also to see who all these airline people are cycling in and out across the street. And you'll arrive in a bit of excitement, determined to be sexier than before *I'm just not a very sexy person I should get some lingerie or something* and you'll arrive with your sleeping baby in her car seat hanging over your arm you'll take her softly into your bedroom to lay her seat down in the quiet you will have been gone for months you will be looking all around you'll be excited to see your things you will feel happy and all your stuff will remind you who you are. And then you'll see it there on your bedside table, *Another Woman's Bracelet #1.* A plastic-y looking thing you'll feel even worse right away that it's chintzy you'll think *why is there some cheap piece of jewelry on my bedside table? It looks like it belongs to a teenager.*

And he'll suddenly be standing behind you he will sweep it right out of your hands and assure you that he found it in the dash of his golf cart and thought you'd like to have it so he brought it home and put it next to the bed for you. You will stand still and absorb him, absorb nothing, look for signs, look for no signs. You will just stand. He will continue to explain you will pull him from the room and shut the door *let her sleep* and you won't believe him in certain cells of your body, but all the other cells that are lined up with his public image of *cheaters disgust me* will be ready and willing to take his explanation and run with it. *He speaks out against infidelity all the time. He hates people who cheat. I don't want to be a jealous kind of wife. Insecure. He would never cheat. He speaks out against infidelity all the time. He hates cheating.* And he'll be busy reminding you of that, too. *You certainly don't think I cheated, do you, because you know I would never, never do that. You know how I feel about that I would never, never do that.* And you'll decide to be almost flippant will tell him that you don't like the bracelet it's pretty cheap and young and gaudy and you left that phase in pretty much the eighth grade and he'll say *ok you don't have to keep it then* and he'll take the bracelet and throw it away somewhere. And so your last weekend in Colorado will begin. Day One. Just you, him, and your baby—the boys in Ohio with Granny this will be a nice relaxing time there's not much to do to stage the house it's an easy sell.

But then the next day you'll do it all over again when you find *Another Woman's Bracelet #2* on the floor outside your bedroom door. *What's this?* You'll hold it up to his face and he'll snatch it right away just like the day before and he'll say pretty much right off that he doesn't know where it came from so the realtor must've dropped it on the floor when he came through the house last week it must be the realtor's bracelet. This one's a bit nicer still kind of chintzy but at least it's not plastic but you'll swear it must belong to a teenager it just has that look. Wyatt will start in *I'll call the realtor I'm sure it's his you're not going to bring up that girl being in the house now are you because it's not hers and I'll call the realtor because it must've fell out of his pocket. And you know I would never, never bring a girl into this house and you know I'm the most hard-core traditional kind of guy you ever met and I would swear to God and on the Holy Bible that I would never, ever cheat on you, Helen, I would swear to God and on the Holy Bible that I would never, ever cheat on you.* His voice will be rising his arms open wide but you'll be standing perfectly still letting your cells take in these new changes they will ask for a moment to adjust. *You don't think for a second that I would do that now do you because you know—now wait a minute don't cut me off you never give anyone else a chance to talk do you—no, now give me a chance to talk my God you can never let anyone else squeeze a word in it's always about what you have to say isn't it so just listen for a minute just listen now because you know I would never cheat and I'm the most honest person you'll ever meet why don't you go call my sister and ask her because she'll tell you that I've never cheated on anyone, Helen, not even in high school so if you're worried about that girl—now let me talk! If you're worried about me cheating, then you're just insecure which you know is a problem and you've always been so insecure and you can go call my sister and ask her because I would never, never cheat and you know that's true. I'd swear to God and on the Holy Bible, Helen, go get one if you want I don't even want to talk about this anymore are you seriously going to ruin the whole week over this? Seriously. You need to stop being so insecure and don't ruin the week. Don't ruin the week. Did you hear everything I had to say now wait just let me finish here don't jump in all the time now you know I would never cheat so now are we settled? We're settled. See, I told you we can work through things we worked through that just fine it feels better when we can talk things out now doesn't it that's what people mean when they say we can't communicate but it's good to have a decent conversation once in a while there just has to be some give and take. Let's go get some breakfast.*

You will go get some breakfast. You will nurse your daughter at the table you will study the shine of her baby hair you will trace your fingers across her golden forehead and down to the tip of her nose she will flutter her eyelashes and settle in for more you will use all your energy trying not to cry you will be too worn out to fight you will vow to believe that this is real you will take a deep breath and consciously buy the whole package you will pick up your water and swallow the whole pill you will look at his profile and become his accomplice you will pick up your fork and sign for the deal. You will start to make proclamations you will fall out of love with the man and completely in love with the principles he always claims to represent you will recite these proclamations in public for all to hear. *We believe in the power of a stable home life. We are willing to put our children first. We believe in tradition. We believe in healthy foods, fresh air, and a solid education. We believe in unprocessed living. We believe in growing our own. We believe in keeping it simple. Every decision we make every action we take is based first and foremost on whether it benefits our family unit. Family comes first. Family is our everything.* He will stand up proud and tall he will talk about these things even more than you do. You will both be liars you will both know that he's going to leave at 7:00 that night and not come back until dawn you will both know that this idea that he's *working with clients* is a lie you both will know the charade you both will know who's really going home to tuck your children in tight you both will live in denial of what's real but maybe only you will realize later that you're lying. You will be a liar and you will do it for the sake of your marriage you will do it for the sake of everything you will do it for the sake of appearances but you will never really know it at the time and you will not want to admit it later when you do. Know. That you were lying you will lie to your family *I like to go to bed early, he likes to stay up a little later on the computer that's why he's still in bed now, so do you want some coffee* you will cover for him day after day and week after week and year after year you will not cover for him out of a clear and deliberate choice you will not lie for him with any real awareness of your own, conning nature you will not lie for him because you want him to look better than he is you will lie for him because you absolutely, wholeheartedly will want to believe that what you're saying is true. You will hang on to the person he presented and promised himself to be long,

long after that person is gone and long, long after you realized that no such person ever existed at all and long, long after you realized that you married a mirage and that a mirage does nothing but shift and sizzle on the horizon before you get close enough to see it go up in smoke. You will lie because you believed and you will lie because you believe. You will have believed what you were saying you will have watched him act out the truth of your proclamations in every public situation he will have offered a strong arm for the needy he will have readily lifted a small child to the sun if there happened to be a crowd gathered to celebrate his gorgeous golden moment of family righteousness. You will watch him and believe in those moments that he must really mean what he says when he talks about putting family first *people don't just hold up children with delight and talk about family values for the hell of it. No, they don't, why would anyone put so much effort into those words those images those ideas if they didn't actually, somewhere inside, wholeheartedly believe in what they were saying.*

You will believe that people state what they believe.

Later, you'll know that you were just another one of the world's great pretenders. *We just really want our children to grow up with a full-time parent, and it makes the most sense in our relationship that the full-time parent be me. I'm a nurturer, and he's a provider. It's traditional, yes, but traditional works for us. We both know that I'm the nurturer we both know that's best for our kids. We both know how much that means for them growing up. We believe in family. This is how ours works best.* Women all around you will declare *I wish my man was more of a provider.* They will watch Wyatt chasing all their children around the yard at the party. They will wish and they will wish some more. He will sometimes grab one of these wishers and throw her over his shoulder then take off running after her son. Everyone will laugh hysterically. *Yeah, I'm lucky,* you'll say. And you'll work hard every day to believe every word you say.

And it will be years. Years before you realize that people use other people to say things for and that suckers like you often jump right up and chime right in and even after you learn this terrible lesson, you will still have a hard time hearing the lie behind an emotional proclamation. Especially when it's made by someone you want to love.

And then you'll look around, and you'll realize that everyone else does, too. People don't know how to hear a lie. Even people who are trained to hear the truth.

Even professionals. Especially professionals.

Especially professionals who are trained to know, who absolutely should know and who should absolutely understand the consequences of not seeing the difference.

You will learn that one of the easiest things to do on this earth is get lost in a lie follow the mirage to the horizon and wake up there in the middle of your own demise.

In that place where everything goes up in smoke.

06.
BLIND

To us,
warmth and likeability
mean safety
and trust—because
if someone's going to hurt us,
we'll see shifty eyes
and feel a certain coldness,
we're sure.
That is, until we meet
the privately brutal behavior
of a devastatingly warm person.

You will not see what's invisible no one will see what's invisible. You will not see what's lost in the swirling powerful smoke you will not see beyond the sparkles in your eyes when you look with your before-eyes you will only see a grand smile a man living in his body with the ease and self-assurance of a lion and two strong arms sweeping through the air in grand expressions of triumph and dedication and love. Those arms will wrap themselves around every willing and unwilling being for tosses into the air wild laughter and hugs those hands will hold elbows and doors will touch an old woman's nose for a smile will point a finger at young boy with a click *good run, man, you're getting it.* Those arms will carry two kegs at a time they will bulge while changing tires they will fit perfectly into a suit you will admire the way they shift from tossing babies to holding the perfect angle at a dinner party to dancing their way straight to frenzied joy. Your before-body will have fun everyone will always always always have fun they will have the most fun they ever had he will always be the center and the life of every party and you will love to laugh. Your before-ears will not hear any discrepancies in his tales you will not hear the words and phrases strung together like plastic beads and stones and then sold to you as pearls you will buy the whole thing you will tie it right around your neck you will love to listen to the magic you won't hear the ways nothing lines up right to be true. Your before-heart will not notice that his gifts for you won't ever come without a parade for everyone else both before and after, you will not see until later that there will be no private gifts there will be no private praises there will be no private reassurances there will be no private care. There will be no care at all you will not see until later that care is not a possibility. You will not be the only one to consistently miss this huge, life-altering fact, instead, you will be one in a whole crowd of people who can't see you'll be one of many who miss the whole thing. You will work with therapists and other clinicians, prosecutors and other attorneys, victim advocates and other activists, magistrates and several judges, and you will learn that these people are not trained to see. No one will see him. No one will see.

No one will see.

No one will see because when he turns on his smoke machine, kids will leave their nests to climb on him and play they will laugh they will chatter like squirrels and their parents will smile *man, he really knows how to connect with the little ones.* They will not know that his unique ability to connect with people could just be part of a dangerous game they will not see that he always has his eye on a prize. That there's always a reason it will make you wonder what a relationship is after all. They will never see that he's willing to do anything to get what he wants and that if a person stops serving his purposes, he'll either knock them on their back or stir them up into confusion and walk away. Sometimes even kids.

Sometimes just for fun.

You will remember, later, the time he tripped a fourth grader in mid-air and then laughed as the boy flipped head over heels twice before landing on his back. The boy did not get up. You will remember racing across the soccer field to figure out what in the world got into that man you will run straight to the boy *are you ok, do you need anything can I help you up?* You will glare in disbelief at Wyatt he'll still be laughing as he walks away you will chase him down once you know the boy's all right *what was THAT who trips a little boy?* He'll look at you and shrug *I told him not to score on me so if he can beat me then he can take what comes with it. And stop glaring at me anyway he's fine my God you don't even know that kid what do you care just leave me alone he's fine we're never going to see him again anyway.*

No one will see that he has no remorse. No one. Not even you, not even when he flips the soccer boy not even when he lies looking straight into your eyes not even when he works daily to make your kids cry and then tells them that mommy's doing it to them not even when he breaks into your house or threatens your life. He will follow you around in his car, not even bothering to hide. He will ask questions. *You feel safe sleeping at night?* You still will not see that he's a man without a conscience you will not know that he's a man who doesn't believe that regular rules apply to him you will not know that's possible and no one will warn you no professional will pick up on the truth.

They will be blinded.

You will be blind.

07.
SNAPSHOTS

Some people become proficient
at acting
and often show emotion
they don't feel—
appearing intensely interested
in your problems or causes,
thumping their chests and
saluting your flag and
weeping crocodile tears
over your losses,
even while
working behind the scenes
to cause them.

You will go back to Ohio after that week in September and
Wyatt will stay in Colorado until Christmas your furniture will
arrive three days before the holiday just as a blizzard hits so
the semi will get stuck in your driveway and your sister-in-law
will park at the top of the hill to drop off her kids she'll say
I'm not ready for Christmas and our electricity is out the basement is
going to flood and I just can't handle this can they stay here with you?
She will cry you will say *yes* you will plug in the generator have
the whole family over will lean against the boxes and open
gifts you'll think there's nothing to freak out about the kids
are so happy and blizzards just happen and this is a beautiful
snow. *Why do people freak out over every little thing?* You'll love

Christmas you'll love watching your baby girl shake wrappings in her fist love watching your boys scream and bounce around over their Star Wars Legos you'll love the way your parents celebrate taking a shower after living without electricity for a week. After the holidays, you will unpack and begin to remodel *I never liked this house and it's time to change it* you will feel more proud of yourself than you have in a long time when the architect you hired to draft your sketches tells you that you designed the most amazing remodel he's ever seen *your work should be featured in a magazine.* You will smile and cry, and then you'll cry again later in the shower, and even a few more times after that. It seems compliments sting the worst after you've been so long without them.

You will change diapers and teach your second son to read and decide that everyone has to spend at least three hours outside each and every day. Your dad will bring over twelve ewes your sons will feed orphaned lambs with warm soda bottles full of formula your daughter will watch them from your hip and then want to get down and then want to get right back up. Your house will start to change no part of it will go untouched there will be crews of men there every day for months and months. You will feed them sometimes and bring them coffee all the time your brother will manage everything for almost nothing and he will not charge at all for his labor and you will cry over the idea that your brother is building your house *my brother is building my house and I can stay here for the rest of my life.* You will take photos of him standing up high in the beams with his hammer the blue sky behind him will be radiant his square jaw will cast shadows his eyes will be full of concentration you will watch him in wonder.

He will watch you, too. He will also watch your man no one's ever been in the house so much before he'll say *it's an education.* Your man will show himself a little with the laborers he will stand behind them when he's at home and criticize everything they do. Your man will call the stone mason over to review the lines of the firebox again you'll pull him aside with an angry whisper *that man is the best in the region and you have no idea what you're talking about so leave him alone.* He will ignore you and proceed with his thoughts *you see this here, Chuck? The way these three line up on this side here, now I think these three should be more like those there don't you think that line should be something more like this I mean, I just want this thing to be perfect.* His hands will show the proper form the mortar will be almost dry the request will be made for a redo the very next day the mason will look like his head might explode your man will look like he's holding in a good laugh. Your brother will make amends when this mason says he's not coming back *this happens every single day* he's not going to redo every day's work *I'm a master I know quality work I do quality work* he's not going to do every piece of this fireplace two times over again. Your brother will make amends with the mason *no redo* he will make amends with every sub on the site he will make amends again and then he will make amends again and they'll say *I'm only coming back because I've known your grandpa for 45 years. He's a good man, and he helped me through some bad times. If it wasn't for your family, I'd be long gone.* The builders will also include your uncle and your cousin and men who've worked with or for your grandpa for most of their adult lives. You'll watch their backs stiffen when your man comes in he'll stand in the middle of their path in the middle of their space in his favorite position one foot propped up on something so his balls can swing free he'll hold his cell phone to his ear and talk loudly about how he has his doubts about this project his free hand will bounce up and down with every word just for emphasis he will laugh a deep belly laugh and smack the sides of his legs. Your brother will watch him with dark eyes he will take his two-by-four and go around. The subs will all wander to other spaces but once the room has emptied your man will migrate to a new space and set himself up all over again. *Don't you think you should be putting two nails in each of those? Wait a minute now don't finish that there until I talk to you just wait on that a minute don't pound another nail just hold on now I have to take this call.* You'll watch your brother's jaw clench and release. Your brother will be watching you.

Your brother will be watching everything.

Your brother will see. Enough and for the first time ever.

Enough to know.

But of course, no one will see everything but you. No one will ever see you being held up against the wall no one will see him choking you no one will see him shaking you no one will ever see him laughing at you and turning his head in disgust when you cry. Over anything. *You're just crying to try and make people feel bad try and get what you want. Well it doesn't work on me. Look at you, my God get up you're so ugly. Such an ugly person my God look at you! You're insane there is something wrong with you, Helen. There is something really wrong with you.*

No one will ever see that.

What most people will see is a man who loves to take photos of his wife and says *isn't she beautiful* all the women around will stare longingly *I wish my man would talk to me like that would ever take a photo of me* just to deepen the moment he might lean in close to one of them put his face right up to theirs almost for a kiss and then give them the smile of the century. Camera still held in front of him time would pause for a moment and the woman would maybe blush maybe smile, too, maybe take a step back you'll wonder if she feels a rush from head to toe. He'll watch her for a moment with what looks like joy and ownership in his eyes, and then he'll turn back to you. *Let me get one of you in front of the fireplace* his voice will boom in all its deep masculinity every woman around will notice will say *I'm serious. Paul never takes pictures of me why don't you teach him he needs a lesson.*

Over the years, you'll start to walk away from these scenes, not knowing that you're helping set yourself up to be hated. Despised and detested. By the whole big community of women. *She has no appreciation for him she just walks away and she's so flat he's trying to take her photo what a bitch and Wyatt's such a lover there is something really wrong with her.* He'll give them a sorry look that says *I try so hard* they will nearly swoon with affection and longing and sadness all stirred up into a crazy kind of powerful, smoky stew *that poor, poor man* it will be no wonder that by the time you file for divorce a whole flock of them will take off work find a sitter reassure their own men *I have enough vacation days* they will attend every single day of your trial they will fill the benches just outside the courtroom door you'll hear their voices in the lobby echoing off the marble all day long. *I can't believe she left him she has no idea what she had I can't believe miss-stay-at-home would do this to her kids she's so selfish she's so incredibly selfish.*

I hope that judge sees right through her.

08.
OTHER WOMEN

It's a game of making people jump,
and that's what counts.
Because for some,
controlling and winning
are more important
than anyone
or anything
else.
So they will
manipulate with charm
and likeability,
and you think
you'd know if
you were being conned
until you realize
that you were
just the dupe in someone else's
main event.

Your man will have other women. Women wanting him women laughing so hard they almost cry women working hard on a transfer to the closest city women watching you and wishing they were the one. *She has no idea how good she has it.* He will ask them questions and he will know which questions to ask *where can I get the best chocolate in town? Is there a flower shop nearby? What kind of wine's best with truffles?* He will know how to ask these questions will take his pelvis in close maybe two, three inches make it an almost touch but not quite shoulders leaning back head tipped in close and closer but in a way that no one will notice outright no woman will ever think to say *back off* most will look flustered at worst and jittery-thrilled at best and they won't know exactly how close his chest was to theirs all they'll know is that when he's missing a button on his shirt and needs a bit of help that something inside them wakes up and rushes to the scene. *Wow what was that* you will get used to the way women watch him you will get used to the way they long to dance with him at the weddings *teach me how to swing* you will stop trying to explain to him how it makes you feel because he'll just turn it on you *you're the most insecure person I've met in my life* you will only once in a while find a sitter and claim his dancing as your own and then the other women will watch you and sometimes grab your arm *oh my God that is so hot* they'll be watching him spin you and longing for their men to spin them *I wish I had a man like that does he have any brothers?* He will belly laugh at that one will sound like a lumberjack who knows how to dance you will sometimes wish yourself that all those other men would stand up, too, you'll wonder why they stay glued to their seats with their drinks or stand outside for a smoke why don't they take photos of their women or bring them the treats why are so many people in the world who are like a black hole in space when it comes to knowing how to love especially when it comes to keeping on with loving. You will wonder. Why people fight over the details of their two-year-old's birthday party fingers pointed at each other with angry whispers *get out of my fucking face* why people make their lives together with so much resentment even hate it's like a breeding ground for lonely people lonely wives who know in their hearts that you have it so much better than they do. He'll watch every one of them will ask *what should I get her for Christmas? I did make her a little book, here I have it in my pocket. I made it. For her. Awwww, well thank you. I do like the little things and she really likes the little things and I try so hard to make her happy.*

86

Why don't you come shopping with me maybe you could help me pick out something perfect I'm sure you have prefect taste absolutely let's find a boutique why don't you try on these dresses wow you should buy that for yourself, girl, I am definitely getting that for her you look so hot in that now try on this one and I'll wait in this chair here go put that on yourself and show me this one, too, I want to see it with these heels and when you come out make sure you spin around and now look back at me over your shoulder that's right you got it, give me an innocent look like you're surprised now that's it, girl, you look absolutely amazing. Two weeks later, he'll take you to the same store for the same scene but you won't know about the other woman at the time. The storekeeper behind the counter will stare at you with bulging eyes as you explain *I just need to exchange this one it was a Christmas gift but it's not the right fit.* And then Wyatt will ask you to model a few dresses for the first time in your life he'll say he wants to sit in that chair right there he'll want you to try it with the heels he'll want you to spin around and look back at him over your shoulder. *Maybe he does adore me after all.*

I wonder if he adores me, after all.

You will wonder. You will never really know you will never know anything but you will always and consistently try harder to get it right. Maybe you'll be terrible at trying. Maybe you'll be a terrible wife. Flat. Boring. Or bossy. Maybe you won't know how to communicate effectively. Maybe you'll need to be more spicy and fun. More seductive. More feminine. More giving *am I really selfish?* You'll never really know there will be only a few things to see clearly you will only in little ways learn what to do and what not to do. The little things. Like a dinner left under foil in the oven makes him happier at the end of the night than a dinner left under foil in the fridge. Or not to ever beat him in skeet shooting again *that was an ugly scene.* But you will mess up your numbers when you add in your head this will always delight him tremendously *she can't add 10 to 20.* You will be careful to do or not to do all the little things you know how you will want to delight him you will want life to be easier you will want to build a solid family you will want him to come home. In the way that you thought it would be. Before you married. You will do everything you can think of to get him to come home you will serve lunch to the woman he brings to the house *she's new in the field I'm just helping her settle in.* She will watch you at the stove and say *you're nothing like him.* He will watch the two of you at the table and give her a special little smile they will leave together at the end of the day just as you start getting the kids ready for the church Christmas play he will say *we have a client meeting* and you will object *Jim bought all these tickets and cooked a five course meal for us and you said you could go* he will not even look back over his shoulder as he leaves and he won't come home till dawn.

You will ask for couples therapy you will remind him of the appointment at least three times you will find a sitter and sit on the leather sofa and he will not show. You will do this again. And again. *I have to make this work how the hell did mom and dad stay together they were seventeen years old when they had me so if they can make it then why can't I?*

What am I doing wrong?

You will eventually have to break through your well-trained woman's veil of self-blame and start to look at him it will really start to happen when you find *Another Woman's Bracelet #3* in his hotel room when you show up there by surprise. At the luxury resort you will tell him *the kids have been wanting to use the lazy rider pool all week you were supposed to call us so we could come so why haven't you called us why haven't you answered?* This third bracelet will be gaudy and adolescent, too, and it'll be draped over a cigar and some pocket change on the table next to his bed. He will rush in when he finds out you're all there he will breeze right past the kids your aunt and uncle, too, he will snatch up that bracelet will ignore the boys trying to hug him will come straight to you hold it up for you to see. *I found this in my golf bag and thought you'd like to have it.*

And then you'll find more. *Another Woman's Hair Clip #1* will show up in your car after he borrows it. Clipped to the handle on the passenger side. You'll ask him about all the bracelets again and the stories will have changed. *I found that one with your uncle up on the mountain. We were hiking. You can ask him he will remember.* Your uncle will be pretty sure he remembers. You'll watch all that unfold in amazement will smell the smoke in the room will realize that in this crazy world there's no realtor dropping bracelets on the floor there's no teen dropping bracelets on a mountaintop you'll realize there's no truth to anything you'll realize that Wyatt can make people believe whatever he wants and that you're feeling really sick and that you need some outside help. *I need some answers to what's going on. I need some help.* Dipping back into self-blame, you'll pack up your medical file to find out once and for all if something's wrong with you and you will pick out a doctor who's been a long-time family friend you will shake his hand when you enter his office and your body will keep on shaking you'll sit and try to keep still will hold the files carefully perched on your lap will study them closely as you talk *I just need to know you see, and here's where I went to the ER for breathing here's where my heart started racing it used to beat 48 beats per minute but now it bounces all around and here's my blood test from two years ago you see this doctor said my adrenal system is pretty much worn out so maybe it's my hormones and I have one other question, too, do you think my husband could be cheating?* He will sigh and slouch down on his stool he will pause for a long moment before he asks *what do you think?* You will burst you'll dive right into the whole story will tell another human being about all the jewelry and all the abuse and all the details for the first time in your life you will begin to tell the truth. And at the end, he will rub his eyebrows a few times with his head tipped back then he will sit back up and look at you square and say *I don't know whether Wyatt's cheating or not. But you need to know, one way or the other.*

You need to find a resolution. You will start weekly therapy you will invite Wyatt along you will continue alone when he doesn't show. You will secretly call a private investigator and talk to an attorney they will both tell you that *the court won't care whether he's cheating or not but it sounds like he's absolutely cheating I tell people that if they're calling me thinking that their spouse is cheating, about 99% of the time they're right. But I wouldn't waste your $1,200 on some kind or investigation because honestly, it won't do you any good. The court won't care. So unless you need to dump that money to prove something to yourself, I wouldn't bother gathering evidence.*

That will make sense *they should know they're the professionals* so you won't bother with hiring the investigator. Especially when the therapist and the attorney both agree *the court doesn't care. They don't care about all the stories and the drama they just want to divide up your stuff and get on with it.*

And with that, you'll start to think about how good it could be. To divide up your stuff and get on with it.

PART III
The mechanics of departure

09.
FINDING
YOUR VOICE

To traumatize someone,
silence them.
Tell them it's not happening
to them.
Tell them it's their fault.
Then
tell them they can't tell anyone.
Shame controls.
It's terribly effective.

You will begin to open up to people will bump into your brother at the grocery store and tell him that you're thinking of leaving because there might be some cheating you will be standing at the exit leaning over your cart you left your kids at home with your mom you'll expect to hear that you should try harder to work it out your brother's such a traditional man when it comes to family and commitment and then he'll lean over the handle of his cart and look straight in your eyes the air will clear so suddenly your ears will pop *Helen, if you think he's cheating, he's cheating. I watched that man lie time and again through your entire remodel. And I've never seen a person more degrading and disrespectful in my entire life if he treats you like he treated our subs then I can't even imagine. And then he turns around and acts like he's Mr. America to everyone else. I've never known a better actor the man would probably pass a lie detector test. You've done everything you can do, Helen. If you leave, I fully support you.*

You will breathe. Sharp inhale—long, slow exhale.

Someone else can see. Someone else in this world can see me.

And you'll start to think that it's not all your fault and you'll start to know that you're going to leave and every day you will feel stronger and stronger about your decision you will talk to your therapist. *I'll stay through the holidays just to keep everything smooth for everyone else plus Rachel's getting married and my house will be perfect for the engagement party and perfect for the shower and I'm not going to steal my sister's spotlight with my wreckage and by then it will be Christmas so I might as well hang in here until then so the kids can have a normal holiday. And then I'll leave. Unless he makes some major break through. But what am I thinking he's never going to change he doesn't have the capacity or else I wouldn't be here I'm finally figuring out that I really just can't hope anymore.* You'll go ahead and cut off all touch with Wyatt and you will be straight with him *I'm thinking of leaving and I don't want to be with you like that and we have to go to therapy* he will smile at you, always amused it will make you so angry every time and this time will be no different you will feel your throat tighten *do you know how hard I've been trying? Do you know how hard I've been trying all these years? You don't even notice and you know what, I don't believe anything you say anymore you've lied to me every day every single day since I've known you* he will walk away from you into the kitchen without even acknowledging that you're standing there as if you haven't said a word and it will light your fire every time *you always act like I'm not even talking like I don't exist but I'm right here I'm a human being and you know I'm talking* he will keep right on with ignoring you and you will scream at the back of his head *you don't even care!* You'll start running around the house, talking to yourself *I'm sick of him acting like I don't even exist like I'm not saying anything at all when I am clearly saying something* you will gather up every save-your-marriage or heat-it-up book you've ever read will pull out the letters and the cards and the love coupons and even some underwear every loving thing you can find you will storm back to him there in the kitchen he'll be pouring a cup of coffee and you'll cover the table with your things toss it all on until it's piles and piles and piles. He will lean against the sink looking bored will take the cup to his lips for a sip you will yell. *You see all this? You see all this? Every single day I try to make it better and every single day you tell me lies and I know you lie you can lie straight to my face and not even blink and I've twisted myself up into a pretzel trying to love you and trying to make you love me and I so sick of trying and trying and you never try and I am done with this you see all this? Well the ball is in your court the ball is in your court now, Wyatt. I'm done.* He will lean back further into the countertop the cup still at his lips through the steam and the silence you'll see only his eyes they will dilate and blacken with a coldness it'll hit your stomach with a punch will make your toes hurt *you're not going to leave, Helen. You think you're going to leave. You won't.*

I will. You start therapy with me now, or I'm out.

He will stand right up and laugh a deep belly laugh put his coffee cup down on the counter *are you serious? You think you're leaving? You're serious yeah, that's right, you're seriously unbelievable.* He will push to walk past you shake his head in disbelief he will find it funny will laugh and smile with his mouth but still somehow stab you with the darkness of his eyes you will let him walk around you, you will let him walk away. That will be in September you will spend the rest of the fall walking the farm with your daughter on your back and your boys by your side you will move from tree to tree leaning your cheek into their bark for the mix of the cold and the warmth. Your boys will climb and hang from Granny Apple they will chase your hens around the yard they will gather the eggs each one carrying a tiny basket they will carefully make sure that they gather an equal number. You will close your eyes to the sunshine you will stand and listen to the horses chew their grain you will put your nose on their noses one at a time you will lay on your favorite slope below the orchard to the west you will feel the ground getting colder as the night sets in. You will whisper to the rise *I love you* you will spread your arms wide to the wind you will check the ewes one more time before you head inside and put your cheek to the cheek of every sleeping child settle quietly into your own bed put your arms around your loneliness you will wake off and on through the night you will listen to your pounding heart in the silence and you will wonder about life and the meaning of love.

10.
FILING
FOR DIVORCE

The average person believes that
anyone who betrays us
will feel bad about it
at least somewhere inside—
but instead there's sometimes a
childlike delight,
an unexpected joy in
the act of fooling you. And
when you see it in someone,
they'll be looking you
right in the eye
with no distress and

no regret.

You will file for divorce. It will happen in February. You will tell Wyatt quietly on an early Saturday morning that it's now official *please go ahead and move in with your parents or your sister because I want a dissolution and the kids should get to stay in the house* and then you will leave to take the boys to their basketball games and you will stop for gas on the way home and your credit card will be denied for the first time in your life. You will call everyone you can think of your brother's wife will be nearby she will save you with some cash but you still won't put two and two together until you arrive home to find Wyatt's sister in your driveway sitting in his car with one leg on the ground outside, a bottle of beer in one hand and a camera in the other. You will ignore her and go inside and tell him that he needs to be gone that *I'm not going to fight in front of the kids* he and Trent will be on your computer they will have closed every account stolen every file off your hard drive will have photographed everything will have done everything that you didn't think to do in preparation for a war that you didn't think was going to happen.

I didn't think he was like that.

Why didn't you prepare the way he did? Because even though you'll know by the end that he's no good for faithfulness or fidelity, you'll still believe in the idea that this man believes in doing what's right for kids. You'll be stuck on all his key words and phrases. Children. Tradition. Family values. A mother in the home. Stability. You'll believe that he has no reason for vengeance. *He's made it clear that he doesn't want a relationship with me. He'll be happier on his own. He'll be relieved. And I haven't done anything to him. I've never cheated. I haven't held him down. I haven't pushed him around. I've tried hard to grow. I've tried hard to engage him. And he doesn't want it. He doesn't love me. But he loves our children, and he knows I've been their 24/7. And he'll want this process to be as easy on them as possible. Gentle transitions. They need to come first. We can at least agree on that.* You will not know that Wyatt will want to hurt you that Wyatt secretly beats his favorite dog that Wyatt can say *family* like he means it even while he's up inside another woman your brain will not know how to see a person like that. You will not anticipate the way he'll try to move money around the way he'll call all the banks on that very first Saturday of separation all you'll know is that he'll come back on Sunday and tell you that he really wants to work it out and *here's $120 for you and the kids to live on for a while let's give this a try* he will not tell you in his little Sunday speech that he tried to pull $50,000 the day before you will not know until the bank calls the house the following Thursday and says that the Saturday transfer was unsuccessful you will say *what transfer.* You will call your attorney and hear *there's no way to stop him from doing it again unless you file for divorce because that's the only way to get a restraining order* you will start to shake all day and night you will make big decisions you will pull out the entire credit line yourself to prevent any more fancy transfers until you file and then you will file for divorce. You will feel like a criminal moving money like that you will wake in the night worrying about what might happen when Wyatt finds out even though you already put all the money back *I just needed the restraining order in place.* You'll be afraid of Wyatt but you'll trust that the court process will protect you now that you've filed you'll trust that the process will bring justice *I just need to do what's right and if the court knows I'm honest and if I stick to the high road, this will all sort itself out* only later will you realize that you made a huge mistake when you put that money back you'll be so broke you'll be so desperate and you'll be accused so many times in court of stealing the money that the magistrate will forget the truth and start to believe that *he's right, she did drain their credit line after all* you'll want to scream *for the eighty thousandth time, I put it back! I had to pull it because he was trying to take the money can't anyone see that he's the issue here can't anyone hear me?!*

No one will hear you.

You will not expect in the beginning that he will break back into the house every night you will not expect to wake up and find him leaning against the wall in the darkness right next to you, silently watching you sleep you will not expect to wake up on other nights to him shaking you senseless by your shoulders *where's your ring, Helen, where are your RINGS!?* You will not expect that he will forcibly move back in you will not expect that he won't care *I don't care what you do with the kids I'm moving back in on Thursday I really don't care what you all do.* You will move in with your parents immediately will make their

99

upstairs into the best bedroom you can you will sit with them on the back porch after dinner and watch the sunset over the cows in the field. *What is this world like, really,* you will wonder. *What makes us a human being.* Your sons will tag along with their Papau you will watch them hop into the feed lot under the windmill you will wonder to yourself *what makes a good person* you will watch your dad carrying two five-gallon buckets full of grain and you'll wonder whether the really good people are often crabby or impatient from the exhaustion of serving others or maybe they often don't communicate well until sometime when they're older and their grandkids come along and then you will wonder whether bad people are always the smoothest people whether dangerous people are the ones who seem to do everything right.

You will wonder if the world's going to protect your children you will know that nature doesn't love the life of every single baby that some things run their course you will have struggled to save newborn lambs and calves that eventually died in your arms you will have warmed and massaged frozen-stiff animal babies until their legs began to bend just a bit and within an hour those babies would stand in the center of a miracle and then wobble across the kitchen floor for something to eat you will have spent summer afternoons chasing away the neighbors' house dogs gone wild over the blood of your sheep you will have carried their kill away in a wicker basket the lamb's head will have dangled lifeless over the side you will remember later the way its jugular gurgled with your every step *house dogs* you will remember paddling across the farm pond to tow the swimming-in-circles-spring-lambs that escaped the house dogs to shore with the help of your mother and a canoe you will still not understand *why* you will wish you could understand you will watch your two little towheaded sons chase each other in gum boots that clatter across the gravel you will hold your nursing daughter close in your arms in the evening light you will spend a moment

100

gazing at your mother leaning over and pulling a few weeds you will wonder if there's any chance that God could possibly *please, God just please bless them with a steady life I will try so hard,* you will know that you can't really tell God what to do but you will hope that you can buy a little piece of peace for your children *I will give anything I will sacrifice anything I will do anything You say, my God, whatever You say, I will.*

But you won't be big enough to understand God just like your eyes won't have known how to see evil like the three little monkeys in a row you will have plugged your ears covered your eyes and covered your mouth, too. You won't even know that you can't see evil you will not understand that you don't know and you will barely open your mouth to ask questions you will barely open up to anyone at all and it will only be little by little you will begin to peek out and little by little that you will begin to open—first to your very few friends.

You will open to your very few friends.

You will be grocery shopping for your sister's wedding shower with a long-time friend in town for the weekend your children will be at home with your mom you will be playful you will be riding down the aisles and across the parking lot with your feet up on the bars of your carts. Smiling and laughing and out it will come *do you think he would cheat* and she will be stunned into stillness you will be stunned into stillness by her answer your carts will freeze in space your mind will not have expected her to say *I have to be honest with you, Helen, I'm so sorry I didn't tell you before I was afraid you'd start asking him about it and I'd lose all contact with you forever I didn't want to be cut out of your life but here's the thing. This is going to be hard for you to hear but I have to be honest you are asking me to be honest. You know last year when we went for Mexican with your parents and everybody? He was sitting next to me in the beginning. Do you remember? And I got up and moved to the other side in the middle of our meal I said I wanted to be by you do you remember that? Well the real reason I came over there is because he put his hand on my thigh under the table when we were all laughing and he ran it upward pretty much under my shorts and then gave me a squeeze. He didn't even look at me and no one else saw it go on I just came over to your side after that I was so creeped out. But how could I tell you?* How could she tell me. How could she not tell me. What do people do when they're put in crazy binds? *And then when I spent the night with you when I came into town last spring and you had a farm meeting the next morning and left to drop the kids with your mom so early I was sitting in the kitchen having a glass of orange juice and he came in and offered to cook me some breakfast. I said ok and went to pack up but when I came back he stood behind me and started trying to massage my shoulders so I got up and left the room and he followed me through the house and kept leaning into me I was so creeped out I fled your house and locked myself in my car and just sat there and cried and cried and cried. I was really freaking out I had to call a friend for support and that's why I'm not staying with you this weekend I just don't feel safe in your house. But I hope you can understand why I wouldn't tell you I thought later that he might've just been trying to scare me out of your life I'm not going to leave your life, Helen. I just didn't know what to do.*

But yes, I think he would cheat.

This will come to you in the grocery store parking lot. You will still be standing up on the bars of your carts your breath will steam between you in the pause, headlights of other shoppers shining through it. You will step down and over to hug. You will understand. And you will feel the difference in your heart right away it will be racing in the moment but will also start to take on an ache that feels like a lump in your throat except it will be lodged in your big, empty, rattling ribcage and if someone could stab you slowly, you'll think maybe this is what it would feel like.

The feeling will not go away. You will carry around a lump in your chest for years your heart will never be the same it will pound pound pound and then flip once over itself and then race off to the side and then it will be still but for just a moment it will never be invisible to you again you will have spent the first thirty years of your life taking the thing for granted won't even have known to be happy and thankful that it quietly and tirelessly worked without cease you will only know later to be thankful for the way it used to be. Like so many things, you never know to miss it until it's gone. Now some years will be better than others and there may be weeks where you won't notice it beating at all or at least not during the day but it will always wake you up at night pounding itself around in your chest running like a hamster on a wheel it will bounce up and down on your mattress you will want to scream at it like a child *now that's ENOUGH go to SLEEP* and so at some point you'll find yourself in a cardio lab hooked up to a machine they will come back at the end of the test ask *did you notice any strange sensations at all* the tape will show that you had a mild heart attack in the middle of the run they will ask that you wear a monitor taped to your chest for a month. You will be moving to a new rental during that time you will carefully carry the boxes so they don't pull off the wires running everywhere under your shirt.

I'm not having a heart attack.

Still, you won't know how long you're going to live you will start to believe you won't get to have a full life you will tell your mom about Wyatt chasing after your friend she will admit to you that he did something strange to her, too, all the way back on the day before your wedding. But it was the first moment he ever touched her like that and her view of the world just wouldn't couldn't let it in *what just happened*. She was sitting in the back of the car waiting to leave when he leaned in and over her and he put his hand on her leg at the knee as he leaned in to fetch your purse off the floor his body was over hers his hand slid itself from her knee down to her ankle he was staring into her eyes with a smile when he gave her

103

foot a gentle squeeze and then he was gone. She was left with either a secret or a strange and unbelievable truth to tell she will remember sitting still for a moment and watching the joy of her daughter through the window she will remember thinking she must've made it up in her mind she will remember deciding at first that it was indeed a mistake she will remember deciding years later that he must just have a thing for making women uncomfortable a way of touching them that they can't or won't know how to object to when they're standing in a crowd *maybe I just made that up in my mind* she'll think he likes to catch women on the spot make them uncomfortable make them maybe even thrilled or upset, your mom will have decided that Wyatt never actually ever goes through with anything he just likes to send a message *I can touch you like this and there's nothing you can do about it.* He will always look a woman straight in the eyes with a smile and he'll never be smacked or slapped on the scene at most he might make a mother worry about whether or how she could tell her daughter that he ran his hand down her leg with a smile the night before she became his mother-in-law.

She'll hope all those years later that you'll understand why she couldn't tell. You will absolutely understand you'll understand why no one can tell each other anything after they've had a special moment with him you'll wonder why or how certain people collect bonds of lies everywhere they go and with everyone they touch *let's stay out a little later* or *yes, I just touched you* or *go ahead and dance with her* or *go ahead and dance with me* or *you know I secretly want you* and *I know you secretly want me* or *I won't tell if you won't tell* or *just this once, just with you* or *did you feel that* his smoke will create confusion even when it doesn't pull out passion, pity, or love. It will earn him a nice living it will blur the edges between all the people he is in the world he will be a humble, good-old-boy small-towner for some will be an orthopedic surgeon for others will show up as a salesman wearing scrubs at your children's school and give medical advice to the school nurse who thinks he's a physician he will be the most dedicated diaper-changer at the dinner party will be the drunkest man on the beach will be the most prayerful Bible reader in the church he will be the most successful golfer-salesman at the conference he will be the best laugh at the gay party he will run his hand down the back of the gentleman next to him as he stands and turns away the man will be left wondering in a mist of sparkle and smoke *well, maybe he is, after all* he will be the most fun and fantabulous football coach he will connect with the boys like no other he will be the the biggest square-dancing-barbecue-man *you can't put earrings on a pig* he will be the abstinent, mourning, sorrowful man left standing to raise children alone after his unstable wife left him *with nothing but debt and children to raise.* Not one person will think to question his identities he'll be the most real and genuine man they've ever met they'll feel pulled into his vitality they'll feel more alive when he's around they'll love the results he gets they'll love the way he connects with their children they'll love the special attention they'll love the joy they'll love the way he lives in the now they'll love the way he moves through the world they'll fall head over heels in love with the man *he's done more for my son than any other coach on the team.*

You will walk gingerly around their fierce commitment to him and to his righteous character you will move through the divorce like any other flawed but hopeful human being, answering questions with fearful hesitation and trying your best to stick to the high road but finding it harder and harder to understand why the high road even matters when the world puts a scarlet letter on your chest *he lies, and it works. People believe everything he says, every time.* His lies will help him have more and take more and you will come to regret what you did not steal from your farm when you left as if it wasn't yours anymore as if it already belonged entirely to someone else. *The court granted him exclusive use and ownership of the property.* You will regret leaving the stalls full of horses you will regret leaving the barns stuffed with tools he will accuse you of

105

stealing *his* sheep and cattle *she gave them to her dad I think he came and hauled them away that man owes me some money* he will submit the cost of each and every hen you took he will not mention that he threw open the coop doors and let raccoons devour each and every hen that you left behind. He will claim that your father owes him money and that your grandfather owes him money, too, he will claim that your family took advantage of his labor and time. *I put in hours and hours for them, and they never wrote me a check.* You will not have expected this in the beginning you will be shocked at every single lie *what is he saying he is lying I can't believe this he never did anything for anyone to the point where it was embarrassing* and your dad will reassure you *he's just slinging mud at the wall to see what sticks. But when he shows himself to the court, all that will end the court will not tolerate it* you will regret leaving the horses *but how could I take them when they were officially his* you'll more than regret leaving them later when things go badly for them and then suddenly one day, they're gone. You won't even get to know when they go and you will never forgive yourself for the way Princess died you will pray and pray that someone saved the other two at the meat auction you will dream of them in the night their giant, black bodies will cross the soft earth to you through the mist and you will cry to them *Butch, how could I have left you oh Princess oh Bonnie I'm so sorry I'm so so sorry* you'll be sorry for Princess most of all, your majestic velvet black goddess your piss-and-vinegar beauty so strong and proud she loved to show off her kicks and jumps in the field until one afternoon when she found her hooves stuck in a gate and the rest of her stuck on her side scraping off her hide against the ground trying to get free and after the first day or two eventually scraping out her soft-horse eye, too. She will lie tangled in that gate for three days and nights in sheer panic she will lie abandoned and caught in that gate but she will not be heard and he will never notice her until finally a neighbor will see her and come with a tractor to stand her upright when she can't find the strength to rise on her own *you need to call a vet* but Wyatt's first thought will be to lock her out of the barn *so she'll be easier to bury when she dies* you would only find out all these details later, at the time you'll just know she's had a rough time with a gate and is sick and his dad will call to tell you she needs a lot of care *but don't you dare set foot on that property* your own dad will say *don't go over there he'd probably trap you* so you will call and call and you will ask and ask and Wyatt will reassure you of her care you will never have dreamed that there was no care at all because he won't tell you that they let her sit in rotting bandages for two weeks only the neighbor will figure it out too late and give you a call and you will have never dreamed that he'd let a horse go like that *Oh Princess please forgive me for leaving you there I should've gone back for you I should've checked on you myself I shouldn't have believed a liar please forgive me Princess I never dreamed he would be so cruel I never dreamed he would let you fall to your knees on the earth oh how could I have left you there to die.*

And Princess will fall to her knees, and Princess will die. And you will feel responsible for her death and you will mourn even as you sit on the stand in court to be accused of taking everything of value from the farm this accusation will become the court's truth this accusation will become the world's truth and your arguments will not be heard because no one will hear you talking your voice will never be heard. Reality will state that you took everything from that farm though you will spend the rest of your life regretting what you did not. *I should've taken everything.*

You will know shame.

You will lie awake at night stewing on your own mistakes you will listen to your heart pounding and racing and bouncing around you will ask it to stop *I just want to sleep, please calm down* and when you finally do fall asleep, you will wake suddenly over every little sound you will grow tired of Wyatt following you around you will grow tired of his threats to your life you will visit the Victims Units at two local Prosecutor's Offices

107

you will go through the screening you will be told by the advocate that you need a protection order. *He is obviously stalking you and threatening your safety and he has a clear history of domestic violence. He's a batterer.* You will prepare a request for a domestic violence protection order you will sit with the victim's advocate in front of the magistrate *here comes help at last* you will be told by the magistrate that there will never be a domestic violence protection order without some very recent emergency room records of broken bones or something along those lines you will withdraw your request you will leave with your head hanging low. You will wonder why the advocate would lead you on like that and you will find that the advocate wasn't well trained and didn't make much money you will discover this particular victim's advocate freshly employed in a cosmetics shop in the mall not six months later she will stop you as you walk by *this is where I work now and I'm so sorry I should've had you request a stalking protection order we could've gotten that one without X-rays and I don't know what I was thinking but now I'm not there anymore but you could try again you should go try again.* You will be too exhausted to try again *I'll just rely on that letter you sent him from the Prosecutor, thank you for doing at least that much. I don't feel hopeful enough right now to ask for a protection order again.* The letter she sent to Wyatt was quite official and reassuring and basically told him to leave you alone *you cannot come within 100 feet of her* so you'll believe it must offer some protection. But later when you show that letter to the cops the day Wyatt threatens that he's taking the kids and won't bring them back you'll tell the kids to stay inside you'll shut the door on him but he won't leave and he won't get off your front porch and he will start with his threats so you'll pull out your letter and call the cops and two squad cars will pull up and leave the lights flashing while they have a 45 minute sociable chat with Wyatt on your front lawn the kids will try to peek through the curtains they will be petrified and then one cop will come inside and glance at that letter and tell you to stop being such a *crybaby* and then take your kids out the door to Wyatt. Wyatt will load the kids right up and drive away and your children will know exactly who has the power in the world and so you'll give up on the Prosecutor's Office you will decide that it all means nothing. You will think *there has to be another way to get some support I have all this evidence on tape what can I do with it I'm tired of being squashed down* you will call the guardian again *you know, I know I'm not supposed to talk about abuse without evidence, but I have evidence I have tapes and tapes of his tirades on record here at my house and I think they're very telling and if a man abuses his spouse you know the research shows that he's also more likely to abuse his children* the guardian will question you *the tapes are at your house? What exactly do you have on tape?* You will tell him about the rants and the choking and the name-calling and the threats to your life *I have evidence of him following me and I have accurate dates and times* you will hang up feeling the first bit of heard in a long time but within two weeks the guardian will have informed Wyatt of your dangerous vault of evidence and your house will be mysteriously broken into and all that evidence will be gone. It will be the only thing missing.

You will call the police and a new young officer will come to your house for possible fingerprints *if you think their father took this stuff, it's going to be impossible to prove because his fingerprints could be all over their things I don't think you're ever going to prove this but let me tell you I really think you should invest in a gun well if you don't want to keep a gun by your bed you should at least have a taser that'll stop someone and if your kids get ahold of it at least it won't be a bullet.* You will thank him when he leaves and wish for the money for a taser but then imagine what your kids might do with it and so you will put that out of your mind you will call the guardian *yeah, now that I told you I have evidence, my house is suddenly broken into and it's gone and it's amazing that no one in the world knew I had that stuff here before I told you isn't that a stunning coincidence* the guardian will change the subject *you know, I never did do that house visit for you maybe I should arrange one now just to check in on how the kids are doing at your house I want to make sure you're meeting their needs.*

You will be angry you will fantasize about punching the man in the face.

You will be frustrated all your efforts will be frustrated you will be lost you will always have more bad news to share you will feel like a burden to everyone who knows you and you will be ashamed of who you are you will be ashamed of what you've done you will be worried about your parenting you will be guilt-ridden you will be sick you will be full of remorse and self-blame. But he will be happy. He will be very, very happy and people will flock to him for his happiness and he will never, ever be sad. He may be angry. He may want sex. He may care more about his reputation than anything in the world. He may have a passion for the game. Of making people feel what he wants them to feel. He may love the thrill of making a woman jump. He may love the power of standing way too close. He may lust after other people he may risk everything in his life for a thrill. He may feel satisfied when he makes you struggle. He may smile when people cut you out of their lives. He may love to push your buttons until you freak he may be angry when you leave. But he will never, ever be sad. Later, later, later, when you finally figure that out, you will wish for and want him to be sad you'll want him to know when he's hurting you you'll want him to feel sorry for Princess stuck in the gate you'll want him to feel guilty when he's hurting your children but he will never, never feel guilt he will believe wholeheartedly that he has never done anything to hurt your children at all and he will believe wholeheartedly that getting rid of you would solve every problem they have and he'd like to do them that favor *they hate her anyway I just can't get them to go over there anymore I try so hard to make them* and so when he knows he's hurting you he'll believe he's doing what the world wants him to do. *Some people deserve to suffer.* He will make his own rules for right and wrong and will follow them when he wants to and will expect you to follow them, too. And when you don't follow his rules, you will suffer. And when you dare to break his rules, you will die.

And someday, you will die. And you'll fight it the whole time, but that just makes it more fun. Nothing better in life than to manipulate and control an absolutely worthless moron for the sheer joy of watching her struggle.

11.
ON BECOMING EDUCATED

The one who lacks empathy
is the easiest to like, and even more,
to feel sorry for.
Because people who hurt you
often get you to sympathize with them
just before.
And so we often
drastically underestimate the
pathology we're dealing with
and choose to bond with
absolutely the nicest
person around
just moments
before and after
we get nailed.

After you file the divorce papers and after he moves in with his sister your man will return to haunt you in the night *this is my house, I can come in whenever I want* you will try to stop him you will be shoved out of the door frame you will be pinned to the wall you will be shaken by your shoulders you will be held in place by your throat you will be choked you will be threatened you will be laughed at you will catch his spit you will scramble to your phone you will call your dad because

113

Dad gets here faster than anybody. Your dad will come right over at midnight your man will hear his truck climbing the rise your man will meet him in the driveway and when your dad rolls down the window your man will lean right in toward his face *I know you're here because you're scared of me.* Your dad will say *you need to leave, we called the sheriff* your man will laugh and step back and lean over a bit to laugh some more and your dad will simply repeat himself *you need to leave* he will sit in your driveway on the phone with the sheriff deputy he will tell the deputy *we just need your presence if you could just pull in or drive by there's no report to make right now but we don't want one and so please just keep an eye on this place when you can we've been having issues over here pretty much every night for the last few weeks* the sheriff deputy will start driving by every night the sheriff deputy will sometimes pull in to talk to your dad and you will stay inside to protect your three sleeping kiddos from any bad ideas your man might have you will start to live on guard you will stop sleeping much at all your dad will sleep sitting up in your driveway for weeks he will insist *it's ok, I don't need to come in. I don't want the kids to see me and wonder what's going on if they wake up.* Your man will come whenever your dad's not there *how does he know* he will wake you on top of you shaking your shoulders yelling in your face or he will lean against the wall and watch you sleep when you don't know he's there you will wake suddenly to find him standing in the shadows and staring so you will start to stay up at night watching for him you will guess that he's sleeping it off all day long but with three children to care for each day, you will run out of sleep. He will call you on your birthday he will tell you that he's moving back in to the house you will protest *the kids need to stay in their home it's best for them to be here and there's no way we can live here together you know that and they need some peace please think of them this is their home* he will say *I don't care what you do with the kids but I'm moving back in so you can do what you want* you will go numb you will think fast you will call your attorney who will say *you should all stay there, too* you will say *I can't stay here with him he's abusive it's not safe for us to live together can't we keep him out of here can't the court stop this* your attorney will say *no, the court's not going to do that the court typically keeps both parties in the house so just do what you want but if you leave take everything you think you might need because you won't be going back* you will move right into action you will call your parents you will call all your family and friends you will hire a couple extra hands to help you pack and sneak out you will be careful about what you take you will leave all the expensive pieces behind *I don't want him to go crazy over this* you will take the furniture your family gave and you will leave the furniture his family gave and you will leave the hundreds of thousands of dollars worth of tools and equipment in the barns *that should keep him happy even though I took the pots and pans I guess maybe we'll auction off the farm stuff later and divide it up there's no way I can do all that now we've got to go* you will take your parents' sheep back to their house you will take exactly half the chickens, too, you will take one cat you will sell the geese you will want to take the horses *who will deworm them if I leave them here who will pick the burrs out of their manes* but you will leave them because you know they *essentially* belong to your man *his parents bought two of the three of them I can't just split the team because I feel like it* you will leave every last paperclip that you believe *essentially* belongs to him. You will say goodbye to the home that your brother built for you, there will be no time to say goodbye to the land to the orchards to the barns and the coop and the worn out windmill *I wanted to get that thing running so it could supply our water* you will drive by it on your way out and a family of quail will scurry by its base and the giant star your grandpa made to decorate for Christmas will be still hanging at its top but there will be no time to get it down now there will be no time for lingering tears you will need to be gone by five you will go hollow on the inside on your way out the drive the horses will come to the fence to watch you leave. You will try not to look into their knowing, dewy eyes. You will move in with your parents your attorney will say *you can't stay with them or else the court will lower your support they will assume that your family wants to take care of your kids* so you will move into a rental in a neighboring town *I guess I need some space from him, anyway* you will cross the county line you will feel it snap back into place behind you *that's my favorite county that's the best place to live in Ohio* you will stare straight ahead while you drive *this new town will be good for us there's a carpool to one of the best ranked schools around I can't imagine that the court will let me homeschool them anymore so I'd better get them tied in somewhere solid and that school is a beautiful little community I don't want this to ruin their lives I want them to come out better than we are I want them to know some peace and have some neighborhood friends maybe living in town won't be so bad I can do this we will take their bunny hutch they can still have their bunnies.* You will move into a rental owned by family friends you'll figure it's destined to be yours since it's empty and freshly painted and ready to go and best of all there will be no strict lease to worry about so you'll be free to move into a home of your own as soon as the divorce is over your attorney will tell you *the courts rarely, rarely let divorces go on for more than a year once filed. You can make it through one year.* You will move forward you will throw yourself forward *I'm going to build my own life there's no time to second guess everything now* you will start work as a childbirth educator in a hospital not five minutes from your new house and your aunt will volunteer to let you use her education fund to help pay for that perfect little school for your children she'll tell you *we established this fund to help out any member of the family who's getting an education, so your children can use it for this indefinitely. We're really happy for them it seems like a really special place* you will be so thankful you will also receive a financial aid package from the school you'll be even more thankful you'll know it's at least one dream coming true *I want the best education for our kids I will do anything to have it and I know it will make Wyatt happy, too—we always talked about going private if I wasn't homeschooling* but your man will protest in court he will make it clear in the parenting plan that he will not ever pay a dime for that *ridiculous and unnecessary* school, even inadvertently. He will moan and complain loudly to everyone around and people will feel sorry for him big hoards of people will start to feel sorry for him *she's making him drive all that way to their school from the farm and how is that good for the kids she doesn't think of anyone but herself* but none of the hoards no one in the crowd will feel sorry for you being chased off the farm no one will even know it happened because he'll always talk more than you do so what they'll know is that *she abandoned him and took everything why should she get to decide where they go to school* you will get so sick of hearing the general community complaint you will object *if they knew what was happening, I'd care about their opinions but no one knows the truth I'm so sick of nosy people who probably just talk about my life to avoid looking at their own* you will wish for a podium and a microphone you will make a little speech in your head sometimes while driving in the quiet of your car your hands will grip the wheel as your imagined anger grows *you know, what makes any of you think that I wanted to leave the farm or leave the house my brother built I'm the one who actually lived and loved the farm life not him and didn't you see that and what makes you so interested in passing judgment on my life, anyway, and if you're going to be so obsessed with my dealings, you might as well get your facts straight I didn't want to leave he ran me off the place and he's getting scarier and I had to escape. And you know what? Now that we're over, he has no right to live some prolonged elevated lifestyle on my equity so he needs to leave the farm, anyway. Yes, that's my equity and I want it back because in spite of your patriarchal assumptions that he owns everything, I actually bought that farm with my own independent assets, and I'm the one who had to move away. You know that? No, I bet you don't know that. I bet you wouldn't even guess it because I'm a woman and I bet you have no idea that I worked and bought and built and sold places all through college so I could have that equity I bet you don't know that I've been working my ass off all my life and so there's no way in hell I'm going to linger around wherever he wants to stick me to make it as easy as possible for him to sit like a fat king on a piece of property that I bought because he has no right to hold my equity hostage and I'm not the only one who's going to have to adapt and make some changes in this process. No, I'm not the only one. And he can shut up all his whining about how far the kids' school is from him because I'm 22 miles away and the school is 27 and he needs to move, anyway, and he's supposed to be at*

117

work most days within ten minutes of that little school so if he goes to work he'll actually be closer to them every day than he would be anywhere else and it's the best school around and he doesn't have an alternate suggestion so at least I'm moving things forward in a positive direction instead of sitting on my rump and complaining so you can all just shut yourselves up and worry about your own family issues. You will imagine every face you want in your audience but you will never get a podium the truth will never be told it will be nearly five years later by the time he leaves your farm and you will have been stuck in a rental the whole time. Waiting. Throwing money away. But no one will ever have conversations about what you're losing financially no one will ever even imagine that you bought the farm and you won't know why people make the assumptions they do but you'll become very familiar with the fact that no one including the court will ever acknowledge that you contributed anything to anything in your entire adult life. You'll get used to them making false assumptions in the face of clear and convincing evidence you will say over and over *we have a paper trail how can they ignore that* you will get used to the hundreds and thousands of humiliating questions you'll have to answer on the stand *have you ever contributed to society in any meaningful way did you even contribute to Social Security look at this statement here. Zero zero zero. And so you never contributed and now it seems you think that this man is supposed to pay your way?* You'll get used to the court doing whatever it wants regardless of any factual evidence you'll get used to the court feeling more like a dramatic soap opera than a house of justice you'll get used to the smoke your man spreads around on everyone he meets you'll get used to people falling for his humble charm you'll get used to people feeling sorry for him you'll get used to him feeling sorry for himself you'll know his techniques *no, I can't afford it, she's absolutely wrecking my finances I can't afford anything and you know what I saw around her neck last week? Jewels. New jewels like every week* you won't even own a *jewel* but you'll get used to his strange language you'll get used to the mockery and the anger that comes from people who listen to his woes *she won't let me keep the farm the kids want to stay here more than anything in the world but for her, it's never enough. She doesn't care who she hurts as long as she gets what she wants. And as much as she's moved, I don't even think she knows what that is.* You'll get used to people blaming you for everything. *You made him drive all that way to that school for all those years and you tortured your kids because they had to make that drive, too, just because you can't decide now that is absolutely pathetic you're so selfish how could you make him lose the farm on top of everything else you should have been paying for his gas all these years and he's right. You are unbelievable.*

You will spend a lot of time trying to place your children in neutral environments where people aren't pointing fingers and choosing sides. It will take an enormous amount of effort. *They need to focus on being kids they need a stable daily environment that's not about their parents that's not about our divorce.* You will continually sweat over the cost of their school and you will try to plan for the future *I want the best for these kids and my childbirth education courses don't bring in much and I need to support my family* you will think about going back to vet school or med school *I would love it but I don't think I can handle it with three kids under the age of eight they need me and I've been their most present parent and they need to rely on some things not changing overnight* you will look at your resume *the only thing I really know how to do for a decent income is build and sell houses, but I can't buy or sell anything until this divorce is over. My hands are tied and I don't have a resume what am I going to be a union laborer again or a vet tech on minimum wage I don't think so I've got to come up with some alternatives what can I do what do I want to do* your answer will come to you quickly *I want to help people heal* you will naturally become more and more engaged in psychological research around trauma *I want to heal, too, I want to make change.* You will think about the difference your therapist has made in your life you will decide that's what you want to do *I want to be a therapist and I want to be an activist somehow I want to change things and two years is all it should take to earn a license at OSU* you will complete an application to the College of Social Work that first winter in your new home and you will be accepted for the following September.

You will be accepted.

You will thrill over the thought of a graduate degree you will take a deep breath *I have a path* the relief will be enormous *I get to move forward I get to build my own life I get to make a difference I'm going to be good at this I'm going to kick some ass* you will take out giant loans you will pore over diagnostic manuals you will pore over clinical texts you will visit campus early to browse the college bookstore you will buy a sticker for your car and a T-shirt for each of your children you will love the smell of all the books you will pulse with the anticipation of what's next. *I am making my own life.* You will arrive early for orientation you will cry in your car before you walk across campus and you will break down again when you hit the oval all the green grass will welcome you and there will be people throwing frisbee in the sunshine *these people are happy* you will keep walking and with each private step you will feel the energy and the life and the thought, every building will glow with things happening *people are making things happen* you will realize how much you missed this buzz of life you will climb the stairs enter the ancient stairwell you will push open heavy academic doors you will find relief in the possibility that you can make things happen, too.

I can make this happen. I'm going to be a therapist. I get a chance at a new life.

I am breaking a family cycle that needs to be broken I will not raise my children to watch their mother being devastated over and over again by their father like his mom was I will make my own life I will protect them will help them rise above their parents and our ways. You will drive them to school in the morning and then cross the giant welcoming bridge over the river that will separate your school from theirs. *This is so perfect we're so close and life has so much possibility* people will comment on your appearance *you look spectacular* and *you're so beautiful* and *I haven't seen you look this good in years. You are flat out intimidating, girl.* You will work to say *thank you* instead of shrugging it off in disbelief you will learn to try this at a three-year clinical training program in Gestalt psychotherapy you will enroll in and complete that program on top of your graduate coursework *I've always been a go-getter* you will take all it on to learn more because you will love learning more.

You will learn more.

You will work to become educated you will begin to change the way you are in the world. You will work to take your head out of the sand you will work to be more aware *I thought I was aware I guess I was wrong* you will work to balance out all the feedback it will sometimes be confusing and you will have to decide what to keep. People will tell you that *you're so articulate* people will tell you that *you're so small and contained your voice is so low you need to be more clear and direct you need to speak up.* Your therapist will tell you that you're like a billboard for other people's projections and that people could believe anything about you that they feel inside themselves in any moment in your presence and others will tell you that you're stoic they will tell you again that you're contained. *That's funny, someone else told me that, too.* The guardian ad litem will tell you that you talk too much *you need to be quiet and sit there and listen* others will tell you that you don't say enough and you're hard to read *you keep so still and you're so quiet* you will hardly ever cry anymore in front of anyone you will wish that you could and will even try but you'll duck your head when the tears come will sit quietly until the urge passes by. *He used to tell me I was ugly when I cried. I want to cry.* You will tell your therapist about some recent tragic experience with dry eyes and a strained expression and then you will sob in your car all the way home. You will sob in your shower several times a week. You will run, run, run will squeeze running in the cracks of your life will run off the negative energy will run a marathon by the end. People will tell you that they don't know how you do it and when you run the path around your son's football field during his practice one evening a few women will approach you and one will say *you know, I'd like to exercise like you, but I don't have time because I've actually dedicated my life to my kids.* People will tell you that your voice is incredibly soft your attorney will tell you one hundred times that you're going to have to speak up in court *your kind of a weak little thing you need to work on your self-esteem.* Your friends will tell you to talk louder *I can't hear what you're saying* your parents will tell you that you're outspoken and that they're proud of everything you're doing they will listen to your rants about the injustices of the world the injustices that were so undiscussed so unmentioned so invisible before you engaged in *social work* your professors will know you quite well you will contribute in class and they will be mostly patient when you're late for their 7:30 am courses *I had a hard time getting my children out the door this morning* the other students will tell you when you're feeling like a slob that your quiet nature makes you *hard to read plus you're always so put together.* You will be surprised *I feel like a wreck* you will speak up in class some more you will love every class you will wish for more time to spend on the reading your whole graduate education will feel like a midnight to 4 am scramble. You will try as hard as you can during the wee hours and your aching, tired heart will cry when you do well. Your professor in your first clinical class will watch a tape of you in session and then write you a personal note *I want you to know that you have by far the best clinical skills of any student I've worked with in my career.* Your whole body will cry when you read it you will cry over this gift of taking classes you will cry over the beauty of the wisdom and the service of social work. *This is a perfect fit.*

You will cry you will never cry and you will always cry. You will cry and not cry. You will redirect your thoughts to a plan. You will plan. You will take a Women's Studies course and fall in love with the work you will plan to add it as a graduate minor you will plan your thesis with fingers trembling over the excitement of it all you will *prepare* you will complete several independent studies on domestic violence, the role of a guardian ad litem, nonlinear research models and therapeutic communities. You will earn a scholarship for excellence in domestic violence and child welfare. You will earn it again the next year. You will take every child welfare and family policy course available. You will take psychopathology and deviance. You will learn to assess and diagnose using the DSM-IV. You will work with marginalized and traumatized women who just found shelter after time on the streets. You will serve lunch in a settlement house you will lead wellness workshops for women who hope to learn the basic skills of self-care that might help in hard-core survivalist situations. You will meet other students who are broke you will meet other parents who are incredibly rich you will feel equal to all of them you will reaffirm your core belief that *we're all so much alike* you will begin to develop new friendships you will be invited over to dinner your children will be included and they will play with the other children no one will be talking about your divorce no one will know what is happening behind the scenes no one will know how hard he'll be working every day to unravel everything you're doing.

He will be working every day to unravel everything you're doing. He will go for your job first he will suddenly start making sales calls on the hospital where you teach he'll have old relationships there to build on he'll have lunch with a gay nurse who's been in love with him for years he'll pull aside a few other nurses he knows *let's meet for happy hour, invite the surgical team it's my treat* and within three weeks you will lose your job by surprise and your replacement will call you on the phone *could you sit in on my first class could you make sure I get all your keys?* No one at the hospital will have called to let you know that you've been replaced and yet you will have a pile of positive evaluations at home in your drawer.

You will let it go. *I wasn't making much there, anyway, and who needs such a negative environment I'm so sick of gossip I just need to focus on getting a good internship.* You will work every day to ignore him it will have been months and months since you left you will be focused on all the positive parts of building a new life *I can't spend every day mourning you know so even though I miss the farm and the horses and hiking around with the kids but there's no going back now and I can't spend every day crying over every little thing that I miss and I can't have those things right now and I have to be a hard ass and I have to build a life I have three kids to raise I have to be thankful for what I've got.* You will be determined to do things the way you want *this is my life* you will be cooking eggs and toast you will be shopping for used uniforms you will be writing a little every day. You will settle in to your little rental you will have a wonderful neighbor who will drive you to the eye doctor when you can't and who will let you know whenever the private investigator is parked just down the street. She will approach him and ask him to leave. *You can't just sit in there on this street all day long.* The investigator will ignore her and you will ignore him. You will instead listen to motivational speeches on tape you will focus on the reading for your policy course you will focus on the project for your clinical course you will learn everything you can about mental health. You will meet healthy parents and families at your children's school *these people are so smart and so kind and so giving these kids do their own fundraising just last week a boy was gathering toothbrushes and toothpaste for a group he found who needs it that's such a great example I love this school and my kids are settling right in they already have several solid friendships and the school set them up right away with a buddy system and they're so happy and that school is worth whatever it takes.* Your children will be adored by their teachers they will slap high-fives with their senior buddies your children will participate in special projects that blow your mind they will ski every Friday with their whole school they will make art that is out of this world you will be so thankful for the friendships they develop with these children you will

124

have the mobile phone numbers of every teacher you will promise to do everything in your power to protect the stability of their every day you will be so determined to make their lives better than yours you will be determined to give them every opportunity you will be determined to make your own life.

Your ex will linger in the background of every place you go, watching you. You will get used to noticing his car. He will hire people to watch you when he's busy. You will get used to noticing their cars. He will hire lots of people to analyze and follow and attack you he will spend every ounce of disposable income he has to go after you in court. And he will have a huge amount of regular cash flow to spare.

You will have none.

He will hire a vocational expert a forensic accountant a private investigator an appraiser and the nastiest attorney in town. People will groan when they hear this man's name. He will request a guardian ad litem he will ask for full custody he will drag out the required mediation he will act like he's on the verge of coming to agreement through every meeting but he will walk out without signing every single time. He won't show for the last session his attorney will call and say it's all off and he'll see you in court. You will sit in stunned silence with the mediator *so he's not coming I really thought we'd both sign* you will walk down the grand staircase and back across the marble floors slowly you will make it to your car you will cry the whole way home. He will send your stolen journals to every expert he hires and he will submit them along with your hacked email into evidence. You will protest *those are my private journals how is it ok that he has them why are you admitting them when he stole them and that email came from a new account I set up since I left and I change my password every month so there's no way he should have his hands in my private emails that should be unacceptable to the court.* The court will want to decide for itself and your journals and your email will be admitted into evidence. The court will note *indeed, she has emailed a man since she left, and she was friendly.* You will attend a meeting for temporary orders and will suddenly and unexpectedly find yourself on the stand for hours. You will attend pretrial and sit on the stand again. You will attend the hearing for his objection to the temporary orders. You will sit on the stand again. You will work through mediation. You will meet repeatedly with the guardian ad litem. You will attend depositions. You will attend days and days of depositions nearly every day will be focused on you. You will meet with his vocational expert. You will drive to these meetings you will need to meet again later on the phone. You will be evaluated. You will meet with his forensic accountant. You will spend months gathering the information his experts want from you. They will lose it. You will gather it again. *I'm trying to go to grad school I can't do all this gathering and prep for my own attorney and his experts and also go to all these meetings and still go to class. I need to go to class.* Your dad will meet with Wyatt's appraiser your dad will meet with his very own attorney your dad will be subpoenaed and then your dad will meet with his attorney again *Wyatt is trying to say that I owe him money.* Your brother will spend weeks gathering family papers for your grandpa's attorney your brother will volunteer to speak for your grandpa in court *he can't leave his house he has Parkinson's and he cannot represent himself he should not have been subpoenaed in this case* your brother will spend months gathering papers to prove that your grandpa doesn't owe your ex any money your brother will be consumed by the preparations. Everyone will be consumed by the preparations. They will prepare answers. You will prepare answers. You will meet with your attorney at Wyatt's forensic accountant's office. You will meet with the guardian ad litem. You will meet with him again. And again. And again. You will ask him to contact your children's teachers. He will ignore you. You will submit character letters from doctors, dentists, school friends, and long-term family friends. He will ask you *what's your point.* You will discover that the guardian held secret meetings with your ex and your children on multiple occasions. You will object to your attorney. He will tell you not to raise a fuss *it will only make the magistrate angry*. You will attend trial. It will be continued. You will attend trial again. And again. And again. And again. And again. And again. You will miss class. You will miss internships. You will extend your graduate program by a year to make up for it. You will not complete your thesis, after all. You will cry. You will sit. You will sit on the stand for hours every time. You will drop your minor in Women's Studies when you can't arrange your schedule for the classes. You will sit in your advisor's office and try not to cry. You will go back to court. Your ex will object to the decision. He will object to every decision. He will object to or appeal every single item throughout the entire process. He will drive you into debt. You will live in a rental. He will live on the farm. You will be ordered to stay off the farm you will not be permitted to set foot on your farm ever again. You will not get to go back for your jeep or your bow and arrows you will not get to wash a dish in your extra deep sink you will not get to visit Granny Apple tree you will not have any power to stop him from bringing in industrial agriculture the farm will be sprayed and tilled against your wishes for the first time in thirty years no one will even ask you no one will even let you know *but I wanted it to go organic*. You will not know when they chop down the trees you will not know when he lets Princess rot to death you will not know when he brings in the rented cattle you will not know when he sells Butch and Bonnie off for meat. You will not be permitted to rehang the giant barn doors when they blow off and land sideways over and across the crushed fence. They will stay where they lie. You will not have any say about the growing junk piles *why is he hauling in junk*, you will not be permitted to trim the torn and ragged branches lying across each other in the orchard you will not have access to your garden you will watch it each time you drive in to pick up your children you will watch the weeds they will grow six feet high you will not be permitted to dig up and move your grandma's clematis you will not be permitted to mow the grass it will never be fully mowed again. You will not be permitted to save the chickens you will not be permitted to save the ducks you will not be permitted to save your grandpa's star when it blows off the windmill you will not save the house from filth and decay you will not have access to anything you own you will lose the money you spend on rent every month for five years. And you will never be cradled by that slope to the southwest again you will not see the stars you will not stand in the breeze and inhale the sounds and smell of the meadows. The meadows will be no more after the spray and the beans come in. He will collect the farm income he will be permitted to keep all the farm income for himself. He will be awarded every part of every payment ever made on the mortgage. You will own the land, but you will lose your power and your equity. And the longer the trial, the more he will control.

He will tell other people that you're holding everything up *she keeps coming after me I just wish this could end.* He will reject every offer you make he will reject every attempt to settle he will reject you after three days of constant deliberation he will play on your hope every time say *I think this just might work* but then he will reject every single offer you make on the very last day *she just won't work with me I don't think she'll ever settle* he will do this again and again and again and again and again.

You will fight to stay on top of things you will fight to stay in school you will fight your way to every class against the chaos of crazy schedules and endless atrocities. You will meet with your therapist you will meet with your children's therapists they will push you to settle they will say *can't you work something out this process is really hurting your children* you will say *I'm trying so hard to settle I'll keep trying as hard as I can and I can't believe the court will let it go on much longer* you will say that to the therapists during the first year and again during the second year and again during the third year and you will eventually sit on the stand to talk to the court about *therapy* the opposing counsel will stretch the numbers *she's cost him twenty grand in the last two years in therapy appointments for those kids* you will protest *that's impossible our insurance covers 80% of every appointment and we'd have to meet thousands and thousands of times to add up to twenty grand that's impossible* the magistrate will look down at the evidence and sneer *yes, it looks like she goes twice a day* you will protest again *I'm not going to therapy twice a day. Ever. When I have a parenting consultation with my children's therapists you are looking at times I've met with my children's therapists and that is incredibly rare maybe three times a year total and can't you see I'm trying to help them get through this terrible process* the opposing counsel will start to speak over you *no one asked you a question we're going to have to strike that from the record can you strike that from the record the question is a simple yes or no now did you see therapists more than once in a day yes or no* you will say *yes but they weren't appointments with my therapist and it wasn't a regularly scheduled thing* the magistrate will tell your attorney to take you out of the room and remind you about the rules of the courtroom *it's yes or no* the bottom line will be decided the court will declare that you owe your ex $9,000 and they will also deviate your child support below the minimum standard as a result of your insistence on taking your children to therapy. You will not bother to object *what's the point I don't want this to last yet another year and what's the point when there is no truth or justice* but you will continue to deliver your children to therapy you will dedicate a full three hours to the process every Thursday afternoon for years you will see the positive results directly so you will stand your ground and then you will complain to your dad after a day of trial *the therapists are the only professionals doing any good for my kids and here I am punished for taking them why doesn't anyone else care about what the kids need* your dad will grind his teeth in silence you will walk down the giant stone steps side by side, he will drive home to do chores and you head down to campus for class you will sit that night for a discussion on the ways society constructs what it means to be a woman you will find yourself both exhausted and on fire *this has got to change I don't want to be this idea of what I am I just want to be what I am this is so limiting our whole world is holding women down and it's so ingrained inside me I don't even notice when I do it to myself* you will want more courses you will study gender and policy you will rant about the way the system owns your life *the court process itself is a violation of my rights I just want to be free and they are giving my battering ex the full power to control my life and drain my assets and benefit from my equity and all they do is humiliate and degrade me one question after another and I'm stuck sitting there taking it I can't even choose to leave unless they say it's time and this whole thing is a violation of my liberty in fact it's a violation of my right to pursue happiness and as long as I'm caught in this snare, I can't pursue anything I can't buy or sell a single thing I can't establish a home for my children I have to rent and I can't even live and what kind of mother can I be if everything I do to build my family strength is degraded and violated and punished. Meanwhile they ignore the fact that he's stalking me and threatening my life and ending my jobs and interfering with my ability to develop relationships he slanders me everywhere I go he makes it impossible to find a peaceful spot he even goes after my family and I'm the one who gets degraded in court for wasting money on therapy. Therapy, of all things. As if hiring a bunch of forensic experts is a great way to spend your children's college fund as if going back to grad school is some kind of a lazy way out what the hell do they think I'm doing every day my program requires a big internship for a year and a half on top of everything else and now I can't even do my thesis because the professors think the court process takes too much time away from my work and I can't even keep my minor and it's taking me three years to graduate now because of all this time spent in court and all I want to do is move on.* The court process will hold you back the court process will hold you down and as time goes by, you will invest more and more of your time doing the foot work for your attorney to cut costs. You will be busier than ever you will spend long nights preparing documents and gathering information your graduate studies will falter and you'll return to the court room for yet another day of trial you will find yourself once again on the stand instead of attending your daughter's field trip to the post office instead you will cross your ankles inside the wooden box and the opposing counsel will stare you down *so*

130

you're taking three years at OSU when you said it would take two. It says right here that you stated under oath that it's a two year program so can you answer me did you lie to the court Ms. Beverly just yes or no did you tell the court that you're in a two year program yes or no. You will say *yes, I did say that it's a two-year program.* He will continue *well then it must be obvious to the court that you're not completing the requirements of your program in a timely manner it's certainly obvious to me and it must also be obvious to the court that you're trying to drag it all out so you can live a leisurely lifestyle while in fact, Ms. Beverly, our vocational expert has finished his report, and it's clear that you don't even need to complete your education to make a decent living. In fact, it's quite clear when you read our expert report that your family has a business that you could join in less than six weeks with a real estate license. And when he testifies here shortly, I believe it will become very obvious to the court that this is the most likely and sensible course of action. My client is asking the court to recommend that Ms. Beverly discontinue her graduate education and join her family business starting immediately.*

After days of listening to this on the stand, you will go blank.

It will be an education.

12.
SELF-DOUBT

Since you can't steal
the best in others,
like their character
or their success,
some simply
smash them to bits. Then the
trauma of those losses
becomes a stronger force
in that person's life
than their own
amazing strengths.

In other words,
certain types of people do enjoy
cultivating dissociation
in anyone they're close to.

You will remember the things you used to do. Before. When you were very young, you did things that showed you were destined to live a successful, creative life. You won't tell anyone when you're thinking about these things because you won't want to seem boastful, but in the privacy of your mind you'll examine every strength and weakness you ever had as a young person. Secretly and with some shameful embarrassment you'll focus on your strengths *you'll need to feed your own fire*. And to figure out what went so wrong to figure out who's hands you're examining when you look down at your own. *Who am I? What have these hands been spending their time on? What were they doing before are they the same hands? How did I get to where I am?* You'll remember reading reading reading as a child and spending whole summers alone at the pond when your mom said *go outside and don't come back in until lunch.* You'll remember yourself as Pocahontas with braids and feathers, paddling in complete silence across the water at sunset. You'll remember being incredibly stubborn once you hit 13 you played your music too loud yelled at your parents snuck out at night on the 4-wheeler and got caught you'll remember fighting about little freedoms and about control and even about vulnerability and protection. Once you could drive you'll remember feeling absolutely terrified of your family's big empty creaking pitch black unlocked house in the woods when you drove yourself back the long drive after dark and no one else was home yet *can't we lock our doors?* Your parents would say *No. Nobody's going to come back here and if anybody did want our outdated stuff then they can take it.* Your parents hardly ever worried. About accidents or incidents or failure. *It's going to be fine.* Sometimes their *it's fine* attitude made you worry and you'll remember taking your fear of the unlocked house into your own hands, vowing at least to never watch a scary movie again. *I don't want that in my brain when I go home alone at night.* The next one you watch will be 21 years later, and you'll be shocked.

You'll remember skipping school in sixth grade to sleep after staying up all night to finish *Gone with the Wind.* You'll remember writing dark poetry in seventh grade that you took down off your walls and hid away in the ninth. You'll remember that when you were 15 and 16 and 17 you tried hard to walk and talk with confidence even when you felt like ugly worthless mush. You'll remember clearly arguing that you should be allowed to make all your own decisions because you didn't smoke pot and your grades were perfect. *You'll need to feed your own fire.* You'll remember that you were

134

the president of your class every year that you were also voted Best Personality, Most Sophisticated, and Best Legs. You'll remember those awards as some kind of ancient argument against the present when you hear that no one likes you *you have no friends for a reason* that *you're so weird and selfish and that's why.* You'll pull up your memories for an internal debate. *Am I really an unlikable person? Do I actually have a good personality? I just could never stand cliques. But was I too bossy? Did I not see myself clearly? Or have I changed? Do people like me?* You'll remember hanging out with whoever you wanted in high school even the wildest group quite a bit and you'll remember pushing for a later curfew and pushing for more school spirit and sometimes yelling at people when they were mean. *Jeff, seriously. You want me to say that stuff to you? Leave him alone.* You'll remember that you never liked Jeff again. *Who does that stuff.* But maybe you were too much you did not hesitate to leave class and pull out another person to take care of these things if necessary. *This is an emergency,* you'd explain to the teachers. You did not hesitate to write a long and probably insulting letter to a coach you felt was being too degrading. You did not hesitate to tell your girlfriends when you thought they were violating you in any way. Sometimes maybe you were inappropriately offended. But you were young, right? You were involved. You were in the honor society and won awards for your paintings and cheered for the football and basketball teams and ran track and even went out for soccer your senior year just for fun and it was the best team time in your life. You will remember sitting in your first college class in your high-school-to-college program, a nervous wreck until you realized at the first exam *this is not that hard, after all. I can do this.* You'll remember blow-drying your hair upside down for extra, extra volume and drinking too much at a Fourth of July party and getting caught *I really pushed my parents I was so stubborn maybe my adult life is some kind of karma pay back.* You'll remember that you were smart when you hear that *you have no sense your brain obviously has something wrong with it* you'll wonder *am I still smart* you'll remind yourself that you were the only

135

person in the history of your school to receive a perfect score on an AP English exam *why did I burn all those journals and all my work and why did I stop writing?* You'll remember that you were the one who received the state scholarship for academics and test scores you'll remember to yourself that you somehow got all A's in college and you'll either feel better about your smarts or you'll wonder whether it really was you who did that after all. *Whose hands are these? Where is that person now? Am I a complete weakling? I shouldn't be living like this.* You'll remember things you did that took strength *you'll need to feed your own fire* physical strength like baling hay the night before cheer camp and showing up with scratches all over your arms that horrified your girlfriends. *I can't believe they make you DO that. You're a girl!* You'll remember hating your parents for it at the time. *I can't believe they make me DO that. I'm a girl!* You'll remember things you did that showed endurance like getting into vet school after an undergraduate degree in History of Art and how hard it was to take things like physics and biochemistry and still hold down a job and how hard it was to pay for your undergraduate education yourself without taking any loans and how lots of things were hard and how serious you were about working and trying *I was so grown up by the time I went to college I pretty much partied myself out in high school and besides college is supposed to be about learning* you will love all the learning *I love learning.* But then you'll remember that as a young adult you were put in situations where you had to make strange choices. As if your learning actually hurt the people around you and once you were convinced to think of your schooling as a disadvantage to your children, well then there really was no other choice that's just how you were raised *people mean more than things* the tricky part will be understanding, later, how vet school got twisted around into something that looked like a disadvantage to your future children. Maybe you're not so smart after all *is everyone so open to influence? Am I weak?* You will become defensive *you'll need to feed your own fire* you'll remember that no, you haven't been a weak-kneed little wimp all your life you've been brave. You've been brave. Not afraid to say no but also not afraid to jump when the stars line up and God offers a perfect opportunity. *I'm not going to falter. I'm going to go with it. This is a gift and I'm not afraid to take a flying leap.* And then you'll wonder whether God was tricking you with the way things lined up over Wyatt. Or whether you're being tested, like Job. Whether you have what it takes in faith. Faith in what? *Why is my life like this when it really could be joyful when I really want so badly to make it joyful or at least useful or at least ok. Am I stupid after all? Do I somehow deserve this? Is it happening because I'm a terrible partner and I just haven't figured it out or maybe I can't see myself clearly? I'm really trying hard what am I doing wrong? Is it me?* And that very question will be the foundation of your doubt. A weak spot that will take over your psyche for years and maybe even for the rest of your life.

Is it me.

Yes, it's you. This answer will come in waves, never really landing anywhere but never really not. Back and forth. Back and forth. You'll spend the last part of your marriage coming to believe that it's not about you. *It's not me. He's actually lying and twisting things around. I'm not selfish. Crying is not ugly. Anger is not a sign of borderline personality disorder. Grief is not pathetic. It's ok to expect honesty and get upset when people lie. It's ok to hand this suitcase of shit back to him. I don't have to carry it around. I don't deserve to hear these things.* This will come through therapy.

Is it me.

You will spend the first six months of therapy asserting that *it's not me.*

It's not me I didn't deserve this. I am just a normal human being. Not the best, not the worst. But I don't deserve to be degraded. I haven't done anything wrong.

It's not me.

I don't deserve this.

And then you will start with a different therapist, and this therapist will change your direction.

It is you.

She'll say it's you because no one can impact you if you're well put together and you don't let them. No one. Not if you don't have weak spots for them to push. If you don't have those buttons, it won't ever, ever, ever matter what any human being says to you or about you. Ever. If you're whole, you'll just shrug off insults with a *what's your problem.* She will call your weak spots your introjects. *I have an introject/project system.* You will explore all the ways you're weak and open to someone like Wyatt pushing your buttons. You will explore your part in the whole thing. You will.

Have an epiphany.

You will learn that *it is you, after all.* That there is something inside you that attracts this and takes this in and pretty much makes you deserve it.

It is me.

And you'll spend the next two years working through that one. That there's something wrong with you or this wouldn't have happened. Your seven-year twisted pretzel marital position of carrying all the responsibility will perhaps set you up well to take ownership of your therapy situation and open your eyes to your weak spots, but it will also tell you that you're entirely to blame. You'll defend yourself once in a while. *I think I was tricked. At least in some ways.* But the therapist will turn that right around. *That's you being defensive.*

You're being defensive. He didn't trick you, you just didn't see him clearly like we see him clearly. You'll swallow this whole on the spot but wonder much, much later whether the best kind of therapy for you at the time was really about taking apart your defenses. Did it make you stronger? Did you find validation or clarity or enhanced self-esteem or a strategic safety plan? Is it possible for a therapist to help someone who might be dealing with a sociopath if they don't know that they're helping someone who might be dealing with a sociopath? If the professional has no training in identifying sociopaths or the symptoms in their systems or any idea to even suspect?

Who suspects? Who sees him clearly? You will never meet anyone who does. And therapists have just enough training to make them dangerous. When they meet him, they'll make their own decisions based on what's inside themselves. Professionals or otherwise, the worst anyone will say about him is that he's a flake, but most everyone in the world will think he's one of the most dedicated, solid, genuine people they've ever met. *He may be upset that she left, but he's got a good heart.*

You won't see the good heart by the end. What you'll see is power burning in his core—burning so bright it lets off his seductive smoke, his subtle-sparkle smoke that introduces him to a crowd and then lingers in the corners after it's over and he's long gone. You'll know his way of stepping in close and even closer, leaning in so fully it'll be ear to ear the smoke will fill lungs and skip heartbeats and even explode in crazy laughter. The smoke will do the work for him his mind may be in another place but the smoke will stay right there in your eyes you will feel that you've captivated him you will feel that you've captured his soul you will feel that you've finally found someone who wants you for you, who gets you for you, and who can share more joy and adventure and love than any person you've ever met before. All wrapped up in a flannel package of sparkling smiles and deep laughter. All tied up with a humble piece of string.

He's so powerful, you'll say.

He's powerless, the therapists will say. We all saw right through him. That's just you in your head, making him powerful. *He's nothing.*

He's so tricky, you'll say. *Hard to see clearly.*

Oh, we see him all right, they'll say. He's nothing. He's nothing. You're the only one who's lost on him no one else falls for that and you need to leave the conflict. Step out of the conflict. Stop talking about him. Worry about yourself. And follow the formula. Here it is. You need to start by apologizing to him for anything you've ever done to hurt him. In fact, we'd like to watch you do it we think you should apologize to him and do it as soon as he gets here to pick up the kids. And mean it. Go out to the parking lot and do it right now. We'll watch from the front door. Trust us on that one. It doesn't matter whether you've ever done anything wrong or not. The apology will help. So you have to apologize and then give, give, give to him as a parent. Consistently. That's what works and it works *every single time* we've seen thousands and thousands of parents here and it works every time. You just haven't been doing it right or it would've worked already. You need to empower him as a parent.

Ok, you'll say. *I'll try harder to be more empowering.* And you'll mean it.

You will try harder. To be more empowering.

Most of this *you're not trying hard enough* will come after two or three sessions of co-parenting counseling. Because just after

140

you file for divorce, Wyatt will hand pick these therapists based on a friend's recommendation *they'll help you guys work it out. Worked for us.* But during the second session, he will rage at the therapist when put on the spot with *you're not doing what I told you.* Full out rage it will shock you that he's showing himself in public. Shock you. You'll sit in stunned silence as he marches from the room. Later, he'll email everyone present and apologize and say that he's just hurting so, so much. This is all so hard for him to take he's so incredibly sad. But he will never go back to therapy again.

It's him. It's me. It's not me.

You'll find books that help you see that he's hard to have a conversation with the way he'll always redirect it right back to something that's wrong with your character. Or else divert it to another topic completely. You'll direct it back. He'll redirect it. Round and round and round. You'll say *you're changing the subject.* And then he'll come right back at you. *You want to change the subject you don't make any sense you want to talk about hard stuff? How about you being so selfish can't even put your children first for five seconds it's all about what you want out of life, isn't it. Miss Princess always first on her own list. Ask anyone. Why don't you ask your mom. Go ahead.*

Then you'll go back to therapy. *I can't talk to him even if I'm just asking him to bring Gabe's shin pads to his practice it'll come back around that I'm so irresponsible I can't take care of anything not even my own kids and if he's around me he'll yell across the parking lot that I'm a slut mistress bringing men in and out of my house like a revolving door he hopes I'm at least getting paid for what I do and I'm not even with anyone and it's like other people don't hear what he's saying they don't react at all in the moment. But I know they do. Hear. People are starting to keep more distance from me all the parents on the team are having parties for all the other parents and kids and I'm the only one not invited. So my kids go with him and they act like they have to hide*

141

something from me and so I know he's doing something there. I just don't know how to change it.

You need to stop worrying about him, the therapist will say. *You know, you just spent all your time so far today talking about him. He's going to do whatever he does. You have to focus on you. Are you going to spend your time talking about him?*

And you'll wonder, *am I?* I don't want a life based around him anymore I just want to tell someone what's hurting right now and that it's so wrong and so confusing and *I don't know what to do* and our kids are hurting and I'm hurting and there are new things every single week and I'm so scared that I'm losing my kids and you will say that last one out loud but then the therapists will all tell you that it's impossible to lose your kids if you have an emotional bond with them that *it's absolutely impossible to alienate any child from a parent they're connected with so if you lose them it's just because you don't have a good connection so let's talk about how you can connect with them even more and better.*

Ok, you'll say. And you'll ache inside you'll worry you will want to have the best connection with your children *what if I'm not doing it right what if I'm not connected with my own children? That's so scary I'm so wrong can you tell me how to do that so it's stronger I really don't want to lose them and people always used to say that I coddled them too much with my whole attachment-style approach and they said I needed to get out more and now they say I need to make sure I'm more connected and that's so confusing and I want to make sure I'm doing it right* the therapist will reassure you *you're a good mom, just be curious about their emotional experience. Ask them, what's that like for you? And let them have their own feelings about a situation the facts don't matter so just let them talk and believe what they believe.* You will worry some more *but what if their dad connects with them better and then uses that connection to get them to believe whatever he wants even if it's with evil intent? Uses his connection to twist things around?* The therapist will reassure you again *he can't touch them if you have a connection with them. He's nothing. You give him too*

142

much power in your head the guy is a nothing he's a total flake. Saw right through him the first day he walked in here he's completely powerless and your kids will see that it's so obvious to everyone but you. We need to talk about you. Because if you change, it'll be like a baby's mobile hanging over the baby's bed. Touch one piece and the whole thing shifts.

Now that will make sense. You will know *I can change* and you will believe that maybe that's enough to change everything. *I can only change myself. I am a lifelong learner I am open and my path is to grow. I will grow.*

And all that will come *after*. After you leave. You will dedicate yourself to personal change. Another thing that will come *after* is a lot of questioning about how you got into a relationship like that in the first place. It must be a personal flaw. *Otherwise, why would I not see the signs?* Surely, there must have been some signs, the therapist will say, just after. *You can probably see them now that you're looking back, am I right? And you can question yourself for the rest of your life, but I think the best thing you can do is work on yourself—your introjects—so that you never have a relationship like that again.*

Yes, you will think, *I know you're right. I never want to be in a relationship like that again. And maybe I should've seen the signs what are the signs that someone's going to beat you down? What should I have looked for? What was wrong with me what were my weaknesses what did he do what did I do? Was he jealous? Did I move too fast? Did I not know him well enough?* You'll remember him when he was twelve years old. *Everyone loved him.* He was such a popular and likable person *such a charming guy* and even if he was arrogant in some ways, he could still hang with the salt of the earth. Everyone he ever met seemed to love him. So in tune with people. So connected and so pure of heart... like some kind of masculine hero sitting in a cabin in a flannel shirt playing the banjo and ready to take you in *come, sit down, I just baked a pie so let's talk and I'll pour you some tea* when you were dating he really

143

did everything. Cooked beautiful meals. Kissed his dogs. Helped his parents and held your hand and loved to look under rocks in the creek, just like you. He was so in tune with the way you looked at the stars and the way you felt about the birds living in the fencerows. You'll wonder what you should've seen. But no one will be able to tell you. No one will be able to tell you. They'll either tell you that they're so totally shocked *you seemed like the perfect couple! I'm so shocked! You can't just give up like that! You need to sit knee to knee and work this thing out. You need to go back over there and sit knee to knee. Did you ever sit knee to knee? You need to go back over there and sit knee to knee.* Or if they're a therapist they'll tell you that you can't see because your weak spots are keeping you from seeing. Until you get stronger and get rid of those spots. But what were you missing did he push your weak buttons back then? You will wonder. What weak buttons were pushed when we were dating? *Maybe I am insane after all. Maybe I have a victim mentality maybe I'm a sucker maybe I'm sadistic maybe I asked for it. Because I didn't see it at the time and I didn't know if he was pushing my weak buttons unless maybe love is a weakness or maybe I'm naive or maybe I'm being defensive but no one else I knew told me they had any major alarms going off before I got married, either. Not that I knew of. He represented stable and still does, to most people. He represented genuine manliness and good-old-fashioned, dedicated love. So, no, I didn't see it coming. I didn't see it coming.*

There must be something wrong with me.

And so you'll doubt. And the doubt will grow. Because when you think about it and remember really hard, you'll know that you knew something was wrong two weeks after you said your vows. And so you'll cry. You'll cry at 25 and 29 and 33 and 39 that you've been tied up since 24 to someone who spends every day trying to use you or destroy you unless there's a better distraction. And then you'll wonder if you're paranoid *am I paranoid? No one would spend that much time trying to hurt someone. No one would waste their life on such a fruitless endeavor*

I'm just not that interesting why in the world would I think that he's so focused on hurting me I left him at 33 that was so long ago now but then you'll open another typical email from him that says you're going to have to cancel your summer vacation after all because he doesn't care what he agreed to, before, and your whole extended family is just going to have to change flights and find some other time to go. Because he's just following your lead here so that's what you get. Have you ever heard of karma because he's just following your lead. And the papers say that it's his month for vacations and so it doesn't matter what he agreed to based on your parents' anniversary and so if you don't change it *you can count on being held in contempt of court.*

You will be preparing for your final exams when you open that email and you will wonder what in the world you've done to bring it on you work so hard to cooperate with everything you will have just given most of your birthday time to his mother in an effort to be cooperative you will not know what you've done wrong you will be exhausted you will lay right down on your basement floor in front of the washing machine and cry into the cold, painted concrete and then you will turn over and lay there on your back a while, after, wiping away your slobbery tears and staring blankly at the floor joists above you trying to figure out whether you did something to bring this on trying to figure out why every single day has to bring another Wyatt-drama why he has so much power to ruin things recklessly and why you're even surprised or hurt at all. *This is who he is. It shouldn't even upset me.* You will admire his consistently perfect timing *he knows how to strike in every weak moment* and even though you'll know it's just the way he is and even though you'll know everything he says is a lie, his email will sink your soul, anyway. Because you'll be exhausted of ruining everything for your family you'll be tired of the drama that goes with anything you ever try to plan you'll be tired of the way he makes it your fault even when you haven't done anything wrong and you'll be exhausted because you know

145

he'll take you to court and the truth won't matter. Get ready. Because when he says things over and over, *everyone starts to believe him. Especially the court. Even your kids.*

Sometimes even you.

And he will lie to you about your own actions, with what looks like full confidence in his ability to convince you that you've done something you didn't do. *You keep the kids from me.* Just after you gave him your Saturday time because his nephew had a birthday party. Or he'll tell you that you failed to do something. *You never show up for their games.* Even after you just left a game. The facts won't ever matter. He'll say *you always do these things always violate our agreement have no respect for the system have no respect for the courts.* He will tell everyone else how hard it's been all these years with you constantly pushing the limits and everything's always a take, take, take with you *she was never satisfied even a big fat house and a farm wasn't enough for her she would walk away from anything doesn't do anything for these kids I work so hard and it all goes to her she really drains me and it's just so hard. No, I finally lost the farm the kids were devastated absolutely devastated by that one. They wanted to stay that's their home but no, she just wouldn't let that happen. Yeah, the kids bawled and begged her. But she just doesn't care you know how it is with women like that. You know, she just has these whims where she gets and idea and runs with it like the man she left me for I think he was feeding her drugs and she wanted more who knows what happened there and yeah, he was her gynecologist isn't that sick and yeah, if she's angry she goes absolutely ballistic and then she tries to blame it on me tells the whole world I was abusive can you believe it? Yeah, she's just a bitter, angry person. No one understands her I've given up trying I just want to get the kids to practice and then cook dinner that's pretty much what I do. No, she pretty much does nothing for them and even if she tries she's late every time and there's no food at her house and no, she never did have much of a relationship with them. She wants them to be Amish or something and they're freaked out by her they've never been close I've been reading about Borderline Personality Disorder so I can figure out ways to cope. No,*

146

they don't really want to see her. She's too busy with her men, who knows what goes on there. I know, you just never know a person she acted like an Amish woman or something but we all know how that turned out and yeah, it really breaks my heart. Yeah, all I can do is hang in here for the kids I just want what's best for them I keep asking her where she's going to settle down I really want an open door policy so I'm willing to move anywhere for them but she really doesn't she's so determined to block me out of their lives yeah she's one of those I hardly get to see them can't get a straight answer from her. Yeah, the kids really cry about it and she's forcing them to play soccer right now and she never shows up for anything on time she just doesn't understand sports and she hardly goes at all no she's never there, really, and they can't stand how she wants to push me away and she practically stalks them and they're so tired of her moving she can't even have a home she calls herself a therapist but she doesn't even know that her kids need a stable home and I have such a strong relationship with them I don't know how else I could go on. No, I'm ok. It's ok. I just need a moment. I'm sorry. Yeah, if you have a tissue—thank you it's just so hard I just feel so bad for these kids I just want what's — best — for — them — this is all just so hard. I'm sorry. No, I'm ok. Just gotta look on the bright side, I guess. That's what I do.

And in the moments when that tirade comes right at you, even after years of therapy, your shoulders will start to slouch and you will wonder. *Maybe it's all about me after all. Maybe I'm making him feel this way. Maybe I'm making the kids cry maybe I'm crazy what if his perspective is right? Am I making everything difficult? Am I pushing the kids away not meeting their needs? Are they scared of me? What are they scared of?* Levi's spent the last three years scared that there are snipers hidden in the trees, that his dad hired snipers to shoot me and so I should always stay in the car. That's heartbreaking and what am I supposed to do with that and I'm not crazy and no I didn't leave him for another man no I wasn't taking drugs why is he saying these things? I left him for myself I was saving my self and our children I was breaking a cycle and I want the world to know that's the truth and the kids are mostly scared that someone's going to kill me and he's just trying to make them scared of me but even Grandma says I'm the *sweetest mom she's ever known so this is crazy. I'm not crazy. I'm not violent and I know what Borderline is and I'm nothing like that why does he keep bringing that up? I hope he finds a girlfriend soon or something else to think about he really needs a distraction but what am I supposed to do differently is there something I can do differently? What if it's really me? Am I doing this all wrong? No, it's not me. Well, maybe it's me.*

What if it's me?

PART IV
What leads to despair

13.
RAISING CHILDREN IN THE SYSTEM

Children are open to manipulation
because they have no way of knowing
whether affection is genuine—
and if harm comes to them,
most will never disclose. At the time.
Instead, they will live a confused existence
in which the people they love and depend on
also bring them pain they can't talk about.
And so while we went to the moon years ago,
we still haven't figured out how to see, hear, and heal
our own hurting children.

Today, professionals regularly fail to become anything but hostile toward
children and their advocates. Sometimes, it's fatal.

You will leave the playhouse your parents built nestled under the orchard apples you will leave the arbor full of your grandma's purple Clematis arching up and over the garden gate. You will for years see remnants of the five-foot tunnels you created for climbing cucumbers and zucchini and beans, and when you drive by them you will remember shady picnics with the boys at the tiny sawed-log table and chairs underneath. You will think of Gabe's own little garden trellis and how much he loved planting carrots and corn. You will smile over photos of the boys at two and three, standing on the bright yellow straw in nothing but tennis shoes and Buzz Lightyear underwear. Picking cherry tomatoes and eating them on the spot. You will long to raise another orphaned calf together, remembering when Abby felt safest strapped to your back and the two boys argued over who got to hold the bottle until the calf's tongue reached out and wrapped around Levi's wrist. *Stay focused*, he reminded them, *feed me*. Wide-eyed and silent for a moment, the boys then broke out in crazy giggles and got back to the work of feeding a baby bigger than they were. *Hold it higher, Levi. Tip it up.*

You will not think of these things most days, later, because life's too busy to sit and stream tears all day long. But you will know longing for the rest of your life. You will resent your divorce *I had no idea that divorce meant I was going to have to give up everything. I thought we'd have a house I mean I had all that equity so having a house wasn't just some pipe dream and I thought we'd keep some parts of our lifestyle.* You will fight the changes for a while you will fight them for years, actually, first with a tiny chicken coop in your city back yard. *Gabe loves chickens, and I'm going to make sure he gets a chance to have some.* When he joins 4H, he will bathe his tiny bantam rooster in a tub of warm water before the fair, and every kid in the neighborhood will come to help. You will keep a rabbit hutch along the side of your house, and you'll buy a tiny rabbit for Abby named Hop who will grow into a giant and live for years. And years. A rabbit who can beat up the cats if he wants to. Inside in the winter, outside in the summer. You will plant a tiny garden in your side yard. Tomatoes and rosemary and basil, at least. You will buy a puppy you will put in a sandbox and a donated swing set, you will keep your yard tidy you will do your best to make it a warm, family kind of place. You will even raise an orphan kid goat in your dining room one winter until it's big enough (and warm enough) to go back to your parents' farm. Your

152

new neighbors will stop by to introduce themselves with a plate of cookies and you will love the looks on their faces when little Goaty goes bouncing by in an all out crazy goat run he will twist a bit in the air and kick up his heels to say hello you will explain *he lost his mama so we keep him in that dog kennel over there when we're gone but he runs around with the kids when we're here and they're having a ball plus I figure our floors are hardwood and he only weighs maybe fifteen pounds, so what can it hurt?* The neighbors will smile in wonder and they won't come to hang out with you again. But they will send their kids over all the time.

You will mix warm bottles you will clean up after the goat you will sit with Gabe and Levi to pick out chicks from a beautiful color catalog and Levi will have one very specific favorite breed but Gabe will circle and re-circle most every colorful kind. By the end, the catalog will be nearly torn through with pencil marks. You will place your order you will rush to the post office when they arrive you will carry home the warm, peeping box and in the car on the way back the boys will take turns sticking their fingers in the holes to see who gets pecked. They will both get pecked every time, then laugh hysterically at each other and then gingerly poke a finger in again. Abby will lean forward and peek around the side of her car seat to watch them, and each time a boy yanks his finger back out of the box she will laugh and clap her hands and bounce herself forward and back in her seat. Then she will quickly lean forward and crane her head around to watch it all again. You will smile the whole way home you will raise these chicks in the corner of your kitchen under a light in a water tank and your cats will sit on the chick's screen roof to study the little peepers all day long.

You will live in that little rental for more than three years during your divorce, and when you leave you will still be married. You will not be finished with grad school, and you will still be looking for a way to make things easier. Gabe will

153

be eleven years old, Levi will be nine, and Abby will be six. By then the boys will be less interested in raising animals and more interested in spending time with their friends. Their school, your school, your work, and all their friends could be closer if you moved, and so you will move you will find a place even smaller than your first rental but this time in your favorite city neighborhood *we can afford this it's even cheaper than the last place and we can walk to get ice cream we'll be two miles from their school and the boys can ride to their best friends' houses on bikes.* They will be delighted Gabe will hop in the car with his best friends after school and not come home until six. Levi will ride beside you on your runs until he knows the neighborhood well enough to take off for the pool or the park he will cheer you on the whole time *good job, Mom, you're a fast runner good job* you will feel safe letting the boys go for ice cream on their own and every parent will reassure you *these kids get the run of this place and don't worry, we're all watching so here, give me your cell number so we can stay in touch* you will be ten minutes from the OSU Recreation Center you will run a car full of kids over there nearly every winter weekend for basketball and swimming they will get to meet OSU football and basketball players they will run right up to them they will pose for photos and those big huge guys will even invite your boys to join in their pick up game of ball you will watch them adjust their pace and passes for the young ones they will make you fall in love with OSU all over again and Levi will beg you to buy Gatorade so he can treat the big guys you will watch him pass out the blue bottles with pride and on the way out you will all run through the scarlet tunnel it will be Abby's favorite path she will hold her towel behind her like a cape and take off at a run *the whole world looks pink!*

And those will be the good times you will be three quarters from graduating your internship will be an hour north but you will make it happen on the days your kiddos are with Wyatt you will make it happen by studying after everyone else is in bed. Your boys will take roles in their school plays they will perform in the poetry slam they will play monopoly with fierce competitiveness they will pick on each other they will pick at each other they will miss each other when one of them's gone. Abby will tour a pumpkin patch she will do a back flip into the pool she will ask you to paint her bedroom walls pink she will ask you to paint her bedroom ceiling green she will fall for American Girl Dolls you will do everything you can to help her have a life that looks something like every other little girl she knows. You will stress over the cost of their school and when your aunt pulls her education fund out unexpectedly *we didn't really mean that the fund was always available we didn't mean for the long term* you will vow to keep things going on your own you will strain to reduce your groceries and eventually, when your divorce is final, you will pull some of your retirement to cover the balance. *I will make up for it later right now I need to keep their life stable they have strong relationships they have caring teachers they have the best curriculum they have diversity they have best friends. And going back to court over changing schools would cost more than keeping them here. I have to try.* You will vow to hold it together you will vow to make things work *I'm almost there now I'm almost to graduation our life is going to move forward our life is not going to go down.*

You will freelance as a writer for a branding agency you will learn to distill the authentic stories of major corporations you will write in the cracks of your life you will blog here and there just for fun you will burn your light at both ends you will drink bold coffee all day long. You will fiercely move forward you will work every day to stay fierce *maybe I lost my farm maybe I lost my assets maybe I have no idea how I'll make this better but by God I'm not going to let some stupid group of assholes ruin my life I am going to keep this all together for my kids and I will persevere.*

You will fight for stability you will fight for friendships you will fight for education you will fight to stay in the middle class. But your children will not have a stable life. They will know chaos they will know betrayal they will know confusion and they will know pressure. They will watch their mom's finances going down the drain they will watch their mom's daily fight to rise. No words will need to be said about the differences between before and now. They will know transition. They will know indulgence. They will know disappointment. They will know alienation. They will know violence. They will know bullying and battering and brainwashing and abuse. They will live out of a duffel bag with two days here, two days there. Five days here, five days there. They will live in one house that has art supplies stuffed into packed bookshelves in the dining room. They will live in another house that tells them *art's for weirdos and freaks*. Because if you like art or music, then *you're a geek*. If you support them in chess, then *chess is for the biggest dorks in school*. If you take them to their 4H meetings, then *4H is for losers who can't fit in*. This will come from a man who would stand in public and talk about how he supports the boys in any activities they choose. A man who participated in 4H for years. But no more. Because today is a time when bookshelves aren't just a sign of someone who likes to read. Instead, they will become a clear and shining symbol of *oddity*. Instead of shopping for books with excitement, your boys will decide that they never want to buy a book again. And so one by one, you will watch them drop every interest they've ever had outside of traditional sports to align themselves with the man who's approval and attention they crave the most. Because dads have a natural power to influence their children. And he will exploit it. He will use it to end everything that's ever had anything to do with you. Even hiking. Even camping. Even snowboarding. Even travel.

Even your extended family.

He will go after Papau. He will go after Grandma. And their aunts. And their uncles. And all their cousins, too. When they're young, they'll be so confused that when they step out of the car after a weekend at their dad's, an older cousin who runs out for a hug will be greeted with a smack, instead. *You're a weirdo loser, Thompson. You're a fag.* Then Gabe will run upstairs and slam the door and lay on the bed and sob. Your whole family will be upset you will go up to figure out what's going on and Gabe will choke on his tears *Dad said Thompson's a fag.* You will rub his back and comfort him you will wonder what the hell Wyatt thinks he's doing. *But what do you think, Gabe?* He will lay silently for a while, calming down. You will ask him, *has Thompson been mean to you or has something happened?* He will say *no* he will slowly bring his eyes to yours *I like Thompson, Mom. I don't think he's a fag.* You will hold his hand. *It's ok, sweetie. It sounds like you're confused.* He will cry some more with that, but then he will eventually run downstairs to tell Thompson he's sorry and they will hug and rush outside together to throw the ball.

You will worry you will stay up at night worrying. You will protest when they're mistreated. You will look for help. You will learn that the court doesn't care about their well-being as long as no one's whipping them with an electrical cord while the film's rolling. You will learn that the court couldn't care less when your ex takes your recently weaned and potty-trained daughter right off your hip after he never spent a full day with her in her life and then keeps her and her brothers from seeing you for 35+ days straight through manipulating his vacation days and parenting time. She will cling to you like a baby monkey when she finally gets back she will not let her feet touch the ground she will not be smiling anymore and the boys will be a wreck, too, they will start punching and pushing each other more aggressively and they will be angry most all the time. You will protest while they're gone you will object you will ask the court for the right of first refusal *they're not even on vacation they're sitting at his sister's house while he works and I'm only five miles away* you will tell the court that his sister shouldn't be keeping your kids for weeks while he's working and out of town and you're right there and available for them

157

but the guardian will say *shut it we're not doing that because this is divorce and kids have to adjust.* You will ask *why, why do kids have to adjust so much so quickly when it's not necessary and they're suffering and he's not even around* the guardian will tell you that *you're the one who left if you didn't want them to suffer well then you shouldn't have taken that step.*

You will study this guardian for a while with deep, darkened eyes. You will wonder who he is and where he came from and why he plays this role. You will research this guardian and find almost nothing at all he will not have a record there will not be any record of any guardian there will be no governing body watching over any guardian ad litem at work in the United States. You will learn that these ultimate representatives of our children's best interests are free to make any decisions they like about custody and visitation and a parent's ability to parent and that these ultimate representatives of our children's best interests might have a few newspaper articles that pop up on the internet which describe their recommendations in famous or infamous cases but otherwise there will be no clear way of determining whether the guardian is slanted or biased or has some personal agenda against people of a particular ethnicity or people of a particular gender. In your case, you'll suspect and then feel quite certain that your guardian does not like women one of his first statements to you will be *some people are just too sensitive so don't even start talking about abuse and don't you ever bring that up again or I will assume that you are trying to keep your children from their father like every other typical woman, and you won't like how that turns out* and you will listen as he tells you that *if you think the children should have a gentler transition into equal time with both parents then why don't you go ahead and give more time to their father now and then wait for a transition into the equal time with you.* You will tell him that you would absolutely do that if the children had ever spent any time with their father if he had ever been their primary caregiver and you will listen to him tell you that *you're on a slippery slope here* and that he's *not going to listen to you badmouthing fathers* and you will wonder *how am I badmouthing fathers by stating the fact that I've been their primary caregiver* you will look up any articles you can find on the man and find very few but you will see that he likes to recommend full custody to the father. You will want to complain to the magistrate but learn that she appointed him and he's consistently one of her favorite choices so *complaining will get you no where with this magistrate* you will want to demand that some organization track these Guardians who may be helping or wrecking the lives of the children they represent *no one can know either way and that's not right!* You will grow tired of the man you will start to glare at the way he picks the skin on his arms you will label him *fat-shark-eye* in your head you will get sick and tired of listening to him talk about his sons' sports and how he likes to punch coaches in the face if they don't play his kid when they should and how he used to be a power lifter back in college and how he was quite the champion and your attorney will shuffle his papers and change the subject a bit will ask whether anyone's still playing basketball at night *anyone still involved in any sports these days?* You will volunteer that you just ran your first full marathon the five men in the room will not hear you they will go right into a big talk about baseball. This will be during a break from your depositions, when you will spend day after day after day sitting in a small conference room at the court house answering any question that these five men want to ask you and they will be particularly interested in whether you now have a sex life and what exactly that might entail. Fat-shark-eye will stop picking his arms and lean his paunch forward over the table on that one. You will learn to hate that man he will not hesitate to yell at you whenever he wants he will not hesitate to threaten you over Children's Services when your son's therapist calls them with a mandatory report he will tell you *don't you dare call them I don't care if you have more information to report don't you call them I mean it now Children's Services is a wreck of an organization it's an absolute worthless pathetic mess I would not call them and if you call them they will come take your children right away from you those people are idiots I would not call them if I were you.* You won't call. You will be afraid. He will scare you, and it will take many months and a couple child welfare courses at OSU to make you realize that he made you feel afraid for his own purposes. Because without Children's Services involved, he maintains total control. You will wake up to this fact some time later and your head will burn over being tricked into withholding supportive information so you'll decide to go ahead and call them but it will be too late. *We can't investigate a case unless it just happened.* The guardian will find out that you called and will call you to scream *you're really on a slippery slope NOW!* He will then reassure you a few days later that he will take care of things concerning your children *if you just sign these papers, I'll maintain contact with their therapists to ensure their safety and well-being. If you don't sign these papers, well then the entire Parenting Plan deal is off, and you'll be in court for years. And let me tell you, the court does not care. And I make the recommendations. The magistrate's decision is based on my recommendation, and she can take away your kids and you can lose custody entirely. Or you can sign these papers.* You will call your children's therapists to ensure that they will work with the guardian they will reassure you and add that any agreement is better than a continued fight so you will sign and that guardian will never contact those therapists again he will ignore your requests for follow through and he will ignore their calls he will never honor his protective role for even a moment. Your children will never be protected from the cause of that mandatory report your children will never be protected from that older cousin who held them down and did things to them that made them cry and that made one son cry again later to his therapist. What *will* happen when the therapist makes that original report to Children's Services is that Wyatt will get the same calls you receive and the therapist will tell you both *I just wanted you to know that I am a mandatory reporter for Children's Services, and I've made a report based on the following information...* Once Wyatt talks to this therapist, the lid will come off and your son will be shamed and scolded and embarrassed and blamed by his father's entire extended family they will have a strong need to protect these cousins they will not appear to have any need to protect your son. Because in these situations, it's often more about protecting the family image than it is about honestly dealing with hurtful and embarrassing situations. So your son will be ripped apart for talking he will have a swarm of angry adults on his head *what are you doing?! You KNOW that never happened did your mom make you say that did your mom make you do it yes your MOM did it, didn't she, well you know, you're mom's just trying to make sure that you never see me or any of your favorite cousins ever again ever again in your life do you never want to see your dad or your cousins ever again in your life* your son will cry to you he will cry to his therapist he will apologize to his dad and you will agonize over his losses *he just learned that he can't tell the truth* you will toss and turn all night long over the grown-up bullies who are circling round your second-grader's head. You will worry about how to help you will worry about his cousin's well-being *what has happened to him that he would do these things* but no one else will worry all they'll do is say that you're trying to label the cousin as a sexual predator *I didn't say he's a sexual predator I never used that phrase once and I don't think he's a sexual predator what I want to talk about is who's going to protect that kid who's going to protect my SON?!* The therapists will tell you to keep him in therapy the guardian will reassure you that they're taking this cousin to see a psychologist who will immediately declare that *he's not a sexual predator so case closed* you will realize that it wasn't about helping the boy when you find out that the psychologist and the guardian are chums you will learn that it was only about getting a psychologist's signature so that the entire situation could be swept under the rug you will despair you will lay in your back yard in a sleeping bag and cry silently, looking up through the trees you will wonder why no one cares to make sure these kids are actually ok *this issue is not about whether that boy's a sexual predator this issue is much larger and more complex than that it's about what might be happening to that boy it's about what's happened to my son* you will ask that the guardian do more he will respond *that boy's not your kid so you need to back off their*

161

business and stay out of it you will keep your own son in therapy and you will wonder why the court scolds you for that *nonsense* later you will be astounded when they lower your child support below the minimum standard because of your *ridiculous and costly insistence* that your children stay in therapy you will wonder about the goodness of the court but you will absolutely *not* wonder why your ex's entire family points their fingers at you. *It's all her. She's evil.*

You will worry about your children until you're sick. They will start breaking two or three bones a year at their dad's house and they will come home with bruises and third degree burns. Wyatt will rarely call you when it happens you will find out the next day when you meet Levi at his 4H meeting and he's sitting at the table with his arm in a cast. *Hi, Mom, I broke my elbow yesterday and do I have to keep doing 4H I changed my mind.* Levi will also tell you that there's going to be an appointment with an orthopedic surgeon to discuss the possibility of surgery. Wyatt will not tell you anything himself he will not answer your questions or your calls so you will call orthopedic surgeons all over the city trying to find out where the appointment is but the doctor's offices will not tell you whether your son has an appointment or not *I'm sorry, we're not permitted to share that information over the phone.* On the day you think there might be an appointment, Wyatt will finally answer your mom's call when she tries to help you track him down and he'll tell her at 10:10 that the appointment with the surgeon started at ten she will hang up with Wyatt and call to tell you immediately you will rush to the location you will ask to join the discussion you will be very late and look frazzled after hours of driving around and Wyatt will laugh when you walk in the surgeon will smile he will be a friend of Wyatt's he will be someone that Wyatt knows through medical sales and the entire staff will give you a silent eye up and down when you walk by. Wyatt will slap high-fives with all of them you will make it through the appointment with a smile and after it's over you will sit in your car and cry.

162

You will still want to complain to the Guardian. Not because you think he'll care, but because you won't have any other hope. Asking other attorneys will never help. You'll meet with ten or twelve of them in your search for answers, and each of them will gladly take your $200 for the introductory appointment and tell you that *there isn't anything else you can do. Your attorney is one of the best. A real bulldog. Stick with him, because unfortunately, there's nothing else you can do.* So you will stick with your attorney you'll go back to the Guardian. *Isn't it his job to guard my kids?* You will tell him that the boys came to you with bruises all over their legs and arms from their dad playing some smacking game with them and that it's the fifth time it's happened and that Levi started crying and said that his dad sits on his chest until he can't breathe and he won't get off even when he cries and Levi hates it and when his dad finally got off last time Levi actually threw up and Wyatt called him a crybaby and smacked his legs some more. The guardian will ask *do you have any pictures of these bruises? I have to have pictures because it's clear when I talk to these kids with Wyatt that they absolutely adore him and are very attached to him so I'm not going to stir things up without some kind of proof.* You will say *no, I don't take pictures of their bruises I thought that was invasive and traumatizing and the wrong thing to do.* He will tell you to call him back if you ever have anything real to talk about if you ever have any proof so when six-year-old Abby comes to you with big rope burns across the fronts of both of her biceps you will take some photos *how did this happen, Abby?* She will tell you that her brothers and older cousins put her on the four-wheeler at her dad's house and had her drive through the yard while they chased her with ropes and tried to lasso her off the thing you will ask where the adults were *Dad was having a party they were up at the house on the deck and we were out in the barnyard so I don't know what they were doing but they were so loud* you will picture in your mind just how far the house is from the barns and just how impossible it was for anyone to see them so you will call the guardian again *I have photos of these rope burns and that four-wheeler can go 60 mph and she's six years old and they could've snapped her neck with those ropes and those kids never wear helmets* the guardian will tell you that *you should never, never, never take photos of your kids' injuries like that you are going to traumatize them and make them afraid and what is wrong with you, anyway, you are a serious headache, woman. You have got to leave that man alone.* You will say *it's not about the man it's about our children's safety* but he will have hung up on you by then.

And yet you will try again with the guardian. You will ask him to contact your children's teachers you will ask him to finally do his home visit. You will watch him pick at his arms you will tell him that you're not sure whether your children have health insurance anymore *Wyatt changed jobs and he won't let me know whether he carried over their coverage so I have to do something it's been two months can you please tell him to answer my emails and calls will you please tell him to let me know he has a legal obligation to let me know.* No one will let you know you will end up standing in line for Medicaid at the Department of Job and Family Services you will miss a day of your internship to do so. You will fill out the paperwork for an appointment you will watch a stale-smelling man sit in mutilated work boots to fill out a job training application you will wonder if he's out of money and just how long these processes take whether he might lose his apartment in the meantime. You will be assigned to a case worker they will send you the date for your appointment in the mail. You will not be able to make that appointment because of your internship, so you'll call to see if you can connect with the case worker to shift it to another time you will find that case workers are not available by phone so you either take the time they mail to you or else you go back and stand in line for another letter in the mail. *How archaic.* You will realize in just a few calls how much harder things are for people who need a little help you will go back and stand in line to request another appointment they will send it to you once again in the mail and their new appointment time will be at the same time as your *Group Therapy* class you will have to miss class to make the appointment you will have a professor that quarter who does not tolerate absences. You will take a point hit for missing class but you will go meet with your case worker, anyway, and she will be nice and she will try to get you to take some food stamps, too, *you do qualify* but you will be surprised by that one and you will be highly embarrassed, *no thank you, I'm doing ok with groceries* and you will realize just how poor you are *I can't take food stamps away from needy people*. You will sink further into debt in your denial because your image of yourself will not readily adjust to poverty. But you will go ahead and accept Medicaid for yourself and your children just in case there is no insurance you will find out months later in court that they were insured by Wyatt the whole time you will find that you wasted your time you will complain to the court *he's supposed to show me proof of insurance when I ask and I've been asking him for months* the court will tell you to stop complaining *of course he has insurance for them will you stop harping on things you are wasting our time and you give us such a headache.*

You will also have a headache. You will have worse than a headache you will be giving Abby a bath one Monday evening after a weekend at her dad's and her genitals will be flaming red you will ask her if she's feeling ok she will say *what?* you will say *I just noticed that you're kind of red down there, sweetie, and I wanted to make sure that you're ok, that you're not uncomfortable* she will look down toward her toes for a few seconds with some sad sort of tension in her face her mouth will be pinched and then she will look up and right into your eyes and say

I never want to go to Daddy's house again.

Your stomach will wretch you will hold it back and stay calm you will want to wrap her in a towel and run away to Canada you will want to wrap her in a towel and make everything in the world right. You won't know who to call you won't know what to say. *Really? Well, you do look kind of sore, so maybe we*

165

should go see your doctor just to make sure you're ok. You will have been told not to ask children questions about molestation you will have been told that the best thing to do is to read them books like *My Body Belongs to Me* and then to let them talk if they choose to you will panic about what to say you will ask her *is there anything you need to tell me?* She will say no. *Do you want to go see your doctor?* She will say she doesn't know. You will take her and there will be another mandatory call to Children's Services and when you go there with Abby for her appointment you will walk right by the line you stood in for Medicaid and into a side room where an underpaid 23 year old will sit with your daughter and show her some diagrams and this young woman will be perfectly nice when she updates you, after, *you know, if she doesn't disclose to me in our first interview, there's nothing else I can do so if you're worried about her, just stay open to her without ever trying to bring up molestation yourself. I'd say just to you that it does seem like she's been abused, it really does. The hard part is that I can't do anything about it unless she tells me directly that something happened. And she's not going to do that here today. And we can't ask her straight out and you shouldn't do that either, you know.* You will know you will absolutely understand you will have read and studied and reported on the four volumes of Child Welfare in your graduate courses by that time you will know the complexity and the difficulty of these situations and you will look at your daughter and want to take her somewhere safe you will feel trapped in a world that will never let you do what you need to do you will fantasize about flying away with her *I can't take any chances* but you will ultimately be trapped by a system that would hunt you down and jail you for such an outrageous act.

There will be no way to present these occurrences to the court you will ask your attorney and he will say *no, the court will just think you're trying to keep her away from her father. Badmouthing him. Without clear proof, there's no way to bring it up.* Over time, Abby will have repeated incidents of inflammation and irritation not caused by or correlated with an infection, and

166

every issue will come after time with her dad. *Maybe it's her grandpa even, since he just started living there who knows isn't there anything more I can do?* You will talk to more attorneys. And therapists. And attorneys. You will take her to more therapy. You will read books and work to maintain an open, safe relationship. She will never disclose. You will never pressure. *What if I'm wrong?* She will have to adhere to the schedule, and you will never know.

You will never know.

And there will never be anything you can do to prevent the possibility. Unless she discloses. But for many children, being asymptomatic is actually a symptom. These children cope by becoming more perfect. More silent. More hidden. And there will never be any of the acting out that could bring some help because lots of hurt children turn into the wallpaper and disappear. As a mother, you will never know the truth of your children's experiences. But you will worry. And you will feel alone. The system won't support your concerns and you will never be able to discuss anything with Wyatt. Not a single parenting conversation. Not one. Ever. Even if you're worried about something more neutral and assume that he would want to know, if you share with him, it will be held against you. You might text him, *Wyatt, I'm concerned because Gabe's new friend is living with his grandma because his dad is in prison and his mom is an addict but she's in the picture sometimes and I guess she runs with a somewhat dangerous crowd and I just found out that all the kids living there have been pulled from school the third time this year for lice so please help me keep an eye on Gabe I want him to be safe.* But Wyatt's only response will be to share your texts with them, and they will immediately stop looking your way. In fact, Wyatt will reject every parenting conversation you initiate he will reject everything you offer he will reject everything you stand for he will reject everything he said he stood for, before. He will make it impossible for your children to live in peace with any part of you with any decision you make with any ideal that you've ever hoped to represent. He will reject their clubs he will reject their friends he will reject their teachers he will reject their school he will teach them that only dorks and spoiled rich kids go there he will tell them that you are torturing them to have them in attendance he will instill in them that the only way they can have a happy life is by agreeing with him that their mother is a weird, psycho freak he will convince them that they only way they can have a happy life is by agreeing with him that their mother spends every day trying to stalk, control, and torment all of them that their mother is inherently bad *I know she drives you crazy, guys, but that's just how she is. She doesn't need to look at your Facebook pages she's just obsessed with you she's a stalker she's just like that and that's why she doesn't have any friends. She doesn't have any friends and don't you think there's a reason why she doesn't have any friends? Except that one city slicker friend who must be some kind of lesbian on the bubble didn't she shave her head or something I bet someday she will shave her head she's probably a lesbian and so your mom really doesn't have any friends and maybe she's a lesbian, too, and I tell you guys, that's exactly why you don't want to grow up to be like her do you seriously want a life like hers with no friends because no one can stand her look at the way she's acting all friendly with the Rochesters they have no idea who she really is they have no idea she's faking it she's really desperate or something and she'll probably stalk them like she stalks you because she's obsessed and bitter or it's even like she's scrambling to get people to like her she always has to try so hard because anyone who knows better doesn't like her at all because she's like a stalker artist lesbian type which is why she gets on you about what you're putting on Facebook she doesn't understand sports or guy stuff at all she doesn't get you like I do she thinks you guys are bad that's why she's a stalker control freak but I know you're not bad I think you guys are the best and I'm so proud of you guys I will always be here to stand up for you. And tell me about it I know how difficult she can be you should probably block her or delete your account so she can't stalk you and I can help you do that I'm here for you guys I love you more than anything in the world you guys are the best.* He will talk to them every day of their lives he will pull them out of school more than once a week he will take them late and pick them up early he will keep them at home when they're supposed to have camping overnights with their classmates he will tell them what they're missing at other better schools and he will tell them this every day and every available moment of their little lives. But then he will not even meet their basic needs, and they will cry. They will call you from school. *Dad made me wear too small pants again so he could keep the new ones and they are killing my stomach mom please bring come to school please bring a different pair to school.* You will learn to leave extra sets of clothing with the school nurse you will learn to take deep breaths you will learn to surf the wave of a chaotic lifestyle you will do a lot of extra running around to cover all their bases you will spend a lot of time at their school you will try you will never stop trying. You will enroll them in activities and encourage them to meet friends. He will hate their new friends he will end all new friendships *you're hanging around with the nerds? When are you going to get some real friends? How about you let me invite some real country friends over to my house this weekend, and we'll have a real party. With kids who are actually nice. You can hang out with the spoiled whiners on your mom's time.* He will sabotage their chess tournaments *you sure you want to do that tournament? I'm having all your cousins and their friends over today we're having a little party and playing video games all day you sure you want to go to that geek tournament no I didn't think you did just another thing your mom's trying to make you do she's so controlling, I know, it's like she's on a personal mission to turn you into a dork but you can come to my house and we'll just hang out it's all about work hard, play hard in my world, you know.* And they will jump at the chance to join the big party and only cry about missing the tournament to you, later, *dad didn't even actually have anyone over, at all. It was just us.* And they'll swing back and forth and back and forth until they both just quit entirely and say *I hate chess* and you will let it go because reacting to anything will just add pressure to their lives and make Wyatt happy, all at once. So you will let it go. They will still somehow manage to have some best friends at school and they will love their best

169

friends and they will take turns staying at each other's houses but Wyatt will refuse to arrange play-dates with *those kids* he won't allow a single play-date with *those kids* in the five years your children attend that school. Instead, he will be intently focused on enrolling the boys in his hometown district where neither of you live now. He will pull all of their sports activities north to his alma mater. *If you want to be cool, hang with these guys.* Every friend of your children's at either place will of course be a perfectly decent child, but only half of them will be approved of and permissible by Wyatt. The half he chooses, the half that has nothing to do with any part of the daily lives they're trying to maintain at their school. This will continue for years you will try to wait it out you will hope he can adjust but he will not adjust he will never tire in his efforts and you will finally realize that he will never, ever stop working to divide that he will never enroll them in any activity with any school friend they make and you will protest to the guardian *shouldn't at least some activities support their lives at school* the guardian will tell you that *it's not your choice so please shut up* and Wyatt will make friends with the parents on their teams when they play on teams that have nothing to do with their school and he will buy a big tent and fold up tables and benches and people will practically squeal with delight he will bring it to every non-school game he will have them all over for a party and another party and another and he will tell them all about you and then you will never be invited to any of their parent parties again. Team parents will stop talking to you and team events will never again be a part of your life. He will talk to your boys about why no one likes you *I told you she's weird that's why no one ever invites her see it's not just me, boys* he will convince them that you never call them on his phone. *She's probably off with some man for the weekend it's amazing the way they just roll in and out her door.* You will call them each day that they're with him you will only get through 10% of the time and when you see them on Monday they will be in a state of complete anxiety they will be angry, very angry *where did you go all weekend, Mom?! Why didn't you call us Dad said you were out of town why didn't you tell us you were leaving where did you go why didn't you call?!* You will tell them that you were in town after all and that you called them every day they will look at you in confusion won't know what to do with all the anger built up inside. Mostly, they'll stop talking to you when he's around and you'll realize that it gets bad for them when you call and you'll realize they can't answer even their own phones when it's you because he gives them such a hard time for talking to you or even will tickle them through the entire conversation and confuse the entire moment by yelling *talk to your mother, talk to your mother* and when they go to say a word he will tickle them like crazy all over again until they're gasping for air. When they're younger, they'll eventually cry and he will scream at you *now you made him cry! You made him cry, Helen* he will hang up on you and won't answer the phone again. You will feel the hair falling out of your head you will feel the edge of the hot knife that has landed for keeps in your heart. He will be relentless. If they happen to sit with you at a game instead of with him, he will throw skittles or even paper wads at them over and over and over again until they get up and sit with him. He will then toss them up and down will turn them around and around he will tickle their sides shake them back and forth and then plop them down on his lap *now you sit still* tickle them all over again toss them around and then plant them again *now I said you sit still.* They will be gasping they will stand up to leave he will pull them right back on to his lap and start the whole process all over again. People around him will smile *now that guy really gets into his kids.* He will never leave an event without tossing them into the air he will never leave an event without rolling around with them on his back he will never leave an event without deep belly laughing so loud that everyone within 50 yards will turn to see. He will tickle them he will rub their heads he will grab other kids and pull them in most of them will not know how to play like that with a grown up most of them will laugh out loud. He will glance around constantly to see who's watching he will never stop being aware. He will notice whether any parents sit with or talk to you he will make a mental note to warn them later *just want to make sure you don't get hurt I hate to say it but she's a dangerous person yeah pretty volatile I think she's Borderline. Just want you to know.* His sister will help him campaign will call everyone she can think of in that town where you both grew up so you will worry about his campaigning and your parents will reassure you that he can't impact the way people see you when they've known you all your life. But his sister will stay consistent she will just be another concerned citizen making some helpful calls she will simply want to protect the masses from someone who's *unfortunately surprised all of us even though she's complained of mental issues for years we never dreamed that she'd do all this. I just want you to know so you can protect your kids and your family.* She will even call one of your closest friends who will tell you later that she kind of got sucked in, too, she say *I almost believed some of it myself. Then I was like what am I doing this is Helen they're talking about she's not dangerous and this is crazy I'm not jumping on their crazy wagon.* His sister will keep your kids every time he's out of town neither of them will ever tell you that she has them and they'll stagger his parenting time and vacation days to keep your kids away from you for more than a month at a time, three summers in a row and when you bump into your own children in the grocery store with her, she will see you before they do she will try to jump out of line and hide from you a few cashiers over. Your kiddos will spot you and Abby will sob and they'll all want to come with you. Because of the court orders, they will not. Come with you, not without his sister's permission because you weren't granted the right of first refusal because the court said it just makes things too messy and so she will get to keep them even when he's gone and she will insist that they leave the store with her and you will wonder why the world's gone crazy why your sister-in-law gets your kids for a month while your ex travels when you're less than five miles away crying about how much you miss them and bringing home two kittens for company in the night. His sister will help him at every moment she will make sure their favorite colors are the same as hers she will make lots of loud and repeated exclamations *isn't this the best night ever* and *aren't we the best family on earth* and *you guys don't need to cry! We're going to have the most fun you've ever had in your life! In your life!* And then she will use her spare time to make some more concerned citizen phone calls she and Wyatt will call hundreds and hundreds of people and you'll feel the impact when you move back to that town a few years later and only the elderly will meet your eyes with a genuine smile will say

I used to live next door to your grandma and grandpa do you remember when we took you to pick peaches you were just the sweetest little girl I bet you sure do miss your grandma she was a wonderful lady.

You will surely miss your grandma you will miss both your grandmas after spending thirty-six years with them and then losing them both within six months of each other they will have been like second and third moms for you, your librarian grandma will have exchanged titles with you all through your life starting in the fifth grade *you're going to love this one. It's called Secret Garden* your other grandma will have traveled with you on almost every single trip you took since college and when she passes, your ex will cause a fuss with your children during the funeral proceedings and will keep them up until 3 a.m. the night before which is actually what he'll do for every holiday or event when they come from him to you and later you'll hardly remember a family party where your kids didn't fight, cry, or fall dead asleep on the sofa before anyone else arrived only to be carried into the bedroom for a long nap. The sleeping child would miss the whole thing. But when you lose your grandmas, you will be determined to ignore Wyatt's antics and by the time your grandmas pass on you will have worked some language into the parenting plan that keeps him from preventing your kids's presence at all which is exactly what he would do before the language changed he would say something like *sorry, but it's my day and they're not coming to your little family funeral thing why are you always trying to ruin my time with our children they're my children, too, Helen, you and your family need to remember that you're not the only people in their lives.* He will tell other people that you always keep him from his children he will tell your children *you guys should stay with me because after the summer I won't get to see you all year* your children will come back to you crying *it's not fair for daddy he never gets to see us he's not going to get to see us for the rest of the year why are you doing that, mom, that's not fair* you will try to comfort them try to explain to them that their time with each of you is exactly equal and fair but they will never take it in because it's not the facts that matter it's the smoke. Your children will spend their lives thinking that you always took more than their daddy. They'll spend their entire lives thinking that you've been following him around and beating him down with a giant stick *it's really hard, guys* and so when your grandma's funeral comes he will have them all worked up about the good time they're missing at his house he will have invited their cousins and friends over to play video games and have a little party *too bad you guys can't be here I sure wish you could be here but you know your mom* and they will be furious with you and operating on three or four hours of sleep and when it comes time to mourn, you'll stream tears silently and keep your giant sunglasses on you will stand like a deflated balloon absolutely expressionless you will want to go lie down on the grass next to the marble bench your grandma chose for a headstone you will return to see her later when you're alone and do just that *Grandma, I can't believe you're not here anymore Grandma, I miss you so much the kids won't know how to travel without you without bickering over who gets to push your chair* you will cry about her to yourself in the car and in the shower you will wonder what keeps you from losing your mind. And your grandmas will pass. They will pass both slowly and quickly and somehow Wyatt will show up behind the scenes for a few items he'd like to have from one's home even though you'll have been split at least three years by that point he will manage to pull strings through the one uncle still caught under his spell he will take your grandma's very own mattress and bedding he will take a couple pink swiveling armchairs and you will wonder why the hell he's showing up for pink armchairs but then you'll know it's just because he loves to make you upset so you will never say a word you will never show a sign you will wish quietly that you could get him out of your life *I know we need to raise our children together but I just want us to live separately I wish he would find himself a distraction I wish he would find himself a girlfriend.*

He will eventually find himself a girlfriend about four years after you leave and they will be pregnant in the first month they will lock all their combined kids out of the car in the city park where they met, your son will call you and tell you *come get me it's all dark here and they're sitting in there making out and they won't let us in and I have homework and I want to go home it's getting cold I hate Dad so much I hate him, Mom, can't you come get me or something? Wait a minute, they just turned on the lights I gotta go talk to you tomorrow.* They will have three kids each already she will be smothered in smoke and ready for a new life she will lay across his lap at your sons' football games her friends will sit next to you at practice will tell you that *some people are just made for each other we should all be so happy for them that they found each other I've never seen a more perfect couple. I mean perfect it's really amazing.* Her children will attend school across the street from your children you'll be so happy when you find out you'll call your mom right away *well this might make life easier maybe he'll stop pressuring them to change schools all the time.* He'll take her to look at houses when the farm sells after four years of divorce and it's time for him to buy a new home with his profits. They'll look at 50 houses in her neighborhood will spend all spring doing it will drag all their kids around the city and in the very end, he'll ignore all the houses they looked at together and choose to leave her there in her rental and move 45 minutes north to that town where you both grew up to the town he's been pulling the boys to all these years he will move there and invite the boys to come and stay forever and he will expect her to spend the night with their baby whenever she can. They will stay together for years and she will continue to live near you in your matching rentals her mom will live with her to care for her first three so she can transport herself and the baby back and forth to him he will fracture their family with his move and his constant pull to the north and you will feel sorry for how stretched out his new partner is and you will feel sorry for the split your own children must feel and so you will begin to think about moving out there just to relieve the pressure on your kids *he's been working on it for four or five years now* you will have tried so hard to avoid that community entirely *it's a fine town and I grew up there, too, but my God there's so much hostility toward me all the parents he's friends with out there put their chins in the air and look the other way when I walk by and that one mom actually took a swing at me and you know that one dad told the boys that they should be living full-time with their father I can't fathom telling another person's child where they should live yeah I told him I was angry and disappointed I've been friends with that guy my whole life he always comes running up to me for a big hug and wants to catch up and how can he say that to my kids now how could any of these parents think it's a good decision to cut any child's mom out of their lives some of those mothers attended every day of my trial as if I was some kind of fascinating criminal and I'm not a criminal but I might as well be and all that's not good for the kids to see they're going to live in the midst of a conflict for the rest of their young lives this is exactly what I've worked so hard to avoid but it's all over now they'll be submerged in a group of adults who think I'm bad or something and they'll think there's a reason why everyone hates me I want to keep them in a neutral environment no one down here cares about our conflict he hasn't tried to rally them for a witch hunt probably because he plans to get the kids out of here entirely but in the meantime the kids get to go to school and play with friends where no one's talking about me or their dad all the parents love our kids and besides that they've had best friends down here for five years now that's the whole reason I moved closer this way look at this photo of Gabe with Luke and Ty on the last day of fourth grade you know they love riding their bikes to the pool on their own and Levi's so excited he's old enough to ride to Jared and Barth's houses now and Abby's never known another school she's been here five years since pre-pre-K this one's a perfect fit it's absolutely perfect for her nature and so why should we shake all that up why couldn't he just've bought a house down here to make it easier for all these kids to stay settled in their lives why can't they have an easier life?*

They will never have an easier life.

As long as you are in it or have any influence over it. So one February night when your oldest is sobbing about it all for maybe the hundredth time after a weekend with his father you will decide officially to make a change you will decide to follow their dad back to your old town *I can't believe I'm going back out there but they can't take it anymore* your parents will reassure you *there are enough people who have known our family for generations the kids will see that, they won't only see the parents treating you badly and you just need to stick to the high road keep a smile on your face always be social with all of them they'll come to see it in time.* You will have your doubts but your boys will be so excited to make the change you'll go ahead and let them start school out there while Abby finishes out her year in the city and their dad will take them on a shopping spree to celebrate he will throw party after party at his official bachelor pad and the boys will stop staying with you almost entirely and start staying with their dad to finish the school year at their dream-come-true school district they will have no pressure from their dad for the first time in five years you will be happy for them for that *they'll finally know some peace* but they will not know some peace their dad will round up another conflict pretty quickly he will feel threatened that you're moving out there he will start to become more hostile to you in every interaction and he will start holding hours-long evening hate sessions toward an official indoctrination against you and against their old school and within six weeks he will have rewritten history for them they will cut off every old friend they ever had they will refuse their texts or calls *I hate those kids* they will openly despise their old friends they will openly despise their old school they will openly despise you they will be certain that you've ruined their entire childhood *you ruined*

177

my entire childhood, Mom, you ruined it and I hate you I hate you so much all you ever do is lie you're just like Grandpa and Grandma and your whole family is a bunch of liars I'm not staying with you ever again so stop calling my phone I hate all of you and I'm not talking to you so don't call they will not remember one good moment you will look at photos of their smiling faces arms dangling around their old classmates you'll know it's pointless to argue *they'll remember it someday when they're older and they'll remember who I am, too.*

That will be the spring. When the summer comes, you will say goodbye to Abby's friends as well and you will say goodbye to your neighbors and you will pack up and move north you will be nervous you will not know how the other parents will react you'll begin to feel a little hopeful when your boys show some excitement over your new rental you will smile to yourself *maybe this was the best thing to do* Gabe and Levi will stop despising you for a moment and they will ask to stay with you again one day to help unpack and paint *this is so awesome, Mom* you will be surprised they will have hardly stayed with you in weeks you will be happy to have them back around *this is going to be a wonderful life, after all* the boys will immediately have five friends in the house at every moment they will help you move in so you will take them all to the lake they will smear mud on each other at the cliffs they'll ask you for the photos you will be so happy to get to know all these fun adolescent guys you will label toothbrushes for each of them they will spend days in the creek next to your house you will have eight pairs of muddy shorts drying on a line at any moment. But this paradise will not last more than three weeks. Something will flip within your ex he will cut out nearly every other part of his life completely for the rest of that summer he will stop working and will dedicate every moment to courting his kids but especially the boys he will lift weights every day of the summer with them and there will be lots of smoke and they will not have friends to your house again. They will instead play paintball and video games with their dad he will help them build bonfires and they'll have a celebratory burning of any item they have from their old friends or their old school. They will take lots of pictures of the charred items and will use them for screen savers on their phones. They will stop coming to your house at all and all those toothbrushes will sit dry in the cup *you're nothing but a trickster, Mom* they will build more fires to burn most anything you've ever given them they will target shoot at their iPods with a B-B gun or maybe a 22 and the damage will be irreparable when you see them you will gasp they will say *we don't want your stuff, Mom. Dad is sick and tired of supporting everyone Dad is tired of paying for you and your boyfriend so stop trying to buy our love we know all the money comes from Dad anyway and why should he have to pay for everything in your life and Dad doesn't want to support your boyfriend and why should Dad have to pay for you guys to go out to eat* you will start to object and they'll escalate *Dad gives you $975 dollars a month, Mom, we're not stupid, that's just shy of $1,000 Mom that's a ton of money a TON of money and Dad's sick of paying for everything for you and your stupid boyfriend you totally live off of him so we don't want your stuff, Mom. You use Dad's money to buy everyone's love that's the only reason Abby stays with you. Because you spoil her she's so spoiled and we know Dad's really paying for everything Dad shouldn't have to pay for you to spoil Abby and you can't buy our love, Mom..* Their Dad will tell them they never have to stay with you again and he will help them block you and your entire extended family from access to any part of their social media and that will make you worry and so when you find they have Instagram accounts you will sneak to see what they're into and you'll find squished frogs and chopped up snakes and wrestling figures posed for anal sex by their cousins and then lit on fire and handguns pointed up someone's butt through their shorts it will be titled *Punishment* you'll see a video of their oldest cousin jumping on someone's bed as if to attack whoever's in there (who appears to be Levi) and the lights will go out and someone will be screaming and screaming *rape, rape, RAPE* and then the lights will come on and the camera will zoom in on that cousin's

179

fingers and he'll smell them and say they smell like shit and they'll discuss using a metal tool next time and you'll be horrified and you'll ask them next time you see them who did these things *it's inappropriate* they'll tell you that you really are a psycho stalker that Dad was right and their Dad will tell you that *it's your fault they hate you and it's your fault they don't want to go to your house I try to make them but they don't have to* he will decide that the schedule should be up to the kids he will decide this after five years of such intense rigidity around the schedule that he will have at one point insisted that his father pick up Abby in a Level Two Snow Emergency when she'd stayed home with you with the flu and even when he himself was out of town. Again, without the first right of refusal, you won't have any more right to "watch" your kids on his time than her grandpa and it won't really matter if she's sick if he doesn't believe she's sick, anyway, *did you take her to the doctor, of course not, I'm not buying it you always lie about these things to try and keep her* you would argue by text all afternoon *the roads are horrible can't she just stay here you're not even in the state* and he would respond *you can either send Abby or I'm calling the cops* so you will call your attorney and he will say *she has to go* Abby would cry in anticipation she would cry all the way to the car she would sob as her grandpa buckled her into the seat she would press her red-cheeked face against the window and yell for you as he drove away. You would go back inside and sob, too, you would hate the system that keeps you from doing what's right you would lay on your floor in a puddle of tears you would call a friend who would declare that she would simply refuse to send her you will explain *if I don't send her, he'll call the cops and file charges that I'm in contempt of court and they'll fine me or send me to jail and I hate this stupid system they won't protect my kids and they make me powerless to protect them, too.* So after five years of using and manipulating the schedule to block your time in the summer with his vacation days and after absolutely insisting that every second of parenting time should be exact *it's 9:04 are you keeping them from me they should be out the door and when you pick them up next time, I'm not sending*

180

them out until 9:04 either so go ahead and mark your calendar after all that rigidity he will suddenly decide that they should do exactly what they want and then he will pick them up at practice when it's your night even after you tell him not to come you will text him *I'm going to pick them up and have my time with them we're putting up the Christmas tree so don't show up it's my day* but he will ignore you completely and you will object and the boys will begin to attack you *Dad's always trying to be flexible and you're always ruining everything we should be allowed to choose where we go each day you've always been so ridiculous, Mom, you always take Dad's time you make everything impossible just let us decide for ourselves* they will stop coming to your house entirely you won't see them for weeks and then months and they'll change in such a short time from boys who used to leave sobbing messages on your phone *please mom, please answer your PHONE but don't call me back because Dad will hear if you call and he will totally freak out so please just answer when I call you back please mom please he's yelling at us so bad it's so bad here right now please just pick up your phone when I call you back but don't call me back please mom* and they'll choke on their tears and hang up and that was just last year but the guardian said there was nothing you could do about messages like that *so don't contact me unless you have something real to complain about* and so now they'll have changed into boys who stop answering their phones to you at all and when you try to make them come with you for your scheduled time they'll simply lock themselves in his house and play video games in the basement and Wyatt will come out and tell you to get off his property or he's calling the cops *because isn't that what you do how's that for karma you need to get off my place now and I mean now or else I'm calling the cops how's that for karma.* He will teach the boys to hide and to lie *just tell her that we have bigger plans it doesn't matter what just make something up* and he will teach them that everything's your fault and if they happen to come out of his house to swear at you or to scream at you, he will stand behind them and smile he will smile and look glowing happy the whole time. Other people will give you advice *I'd call the cops myself you know you have a right to be a parent you have a right to have your time* or they'll say *I'd make them give you back everything you buy for them if he wants to keep them there then he can start paying for some shoes at least I think you should take all those fancy shoes back to your house* or even *I'd set them free there's nothing you can do about this except wait for them to realize you're a good person and don't worry, they'll come back to you someday.* You will start to shrink into yourself all your emotions will hold a piece of sadness in them you won't be frustrated without also being sad you won't be happy without also being sad it will hang over you the longing for your children will be with you in every moment you'll be watching a comedy show and suddenly feel tears streaming down your cheeks. You will realize that you won't get to be a parent to your teenage sons and that their friends will never come to your house their friends will stop waving at you after they hear that you're psycho and besides *your dad is so fun.* Your heart will be so worn out by then it will have beat itself into exhaustion it will be sick and tired of waking you up every night but it won't know how to stop itself when the rest of your body's still telling it *this is an emergency, be ready.* Your daughter will watch her brothers choose their time and will decide that the rules should be the same for her so she'll run crying from her dad when he tries to put her in his car after a basketball game and he will yell at her from across the parking lot *you going to play that game, Abby!?* You will be getting into your car she will be sobbing and clinging to your coat the boys will be glaring at you from behind their dad and they'll yell *Mom, you're just trying to make Abby hate Dad, and Abby you only like going with Mom because Mom spoils you and you are so spoiled* they will yell at her *what are you doing, Abby, you're hurting Dad's feelings!* He will pat them on the back and say *thanks for sticking up for me, guys. We gotta be a team. I appreciate you guys.* They will climb into his car will start to drive away and your new boyfriend Matt will not be paying attention as they take off because he'll pick up a call from his mom when she needs to talk about his dying Grandma so he will be standing at the tailgate of your car all absorbed in his conversation on the phone and Wyatt will pull right up close behind him and skim the back of his coat with the side mirror and then stop his car on the spot and Matt will turn around in surprise to find Wyatt about eight or twelve inches away from his face and Wyatt will yell right through Matt *you seriously going to do this, Abby?!* Abby will start buckling herself in won't look up at him and you will do the same and Matt will turn away from Wyatt and look at you with narrowed eyes and you'll know what he's thinking *I want to punch that asshole in the face* he will step into your car quickly and apologize to his mom for the noise he will ask to call her back and this will be the scene nearly anytime Abby decides to come with you she will be eight years old at the time and the pressure of a man and two boys yelling at her will be just the beginning. You will let her get in your car when it happens you will reassure her that she should have the same rights the boys have and the rules should be equal and you will shut the doors the other parents will be coming out of the gymnasium the boys will continue to yell *oh, that's it, Mom, just shut your window like always you never let anyone else talk, do you. Dad's just trying to talk to Abby you shouldn't lock her in the car like that* your ex will shake his head *come on, boys, it's useless, you know how your mom can be* Abby will keep her head down until you've all driven away then she'll sit silently for a while and she will answer all your caring questions with an *I don't know* if at all then will eventually turn on the radio and sing like a bird.

But as I said, that will only be the beginning. Abby will be hesitant and even afraid to deviate from the regular schedule like her brothers and this fear will grow when she gets off the bus at her Dad's and finds them burning her clothes in a bonfire. She will cry to you later about it *they told me that if I'm not going to come there more that they'll just get rid of my stuff and let Gabe have my room.* She will cry to you again and again and again *Dad gave me three empty boxes and told me to pack up my stuff because he's giving my room to Gabe since I don't come there enough* and *Dad made me stand in the garage by myself when you were coming to pick me up he totally freaked out because I was leaving he wouldn't even let me come in and get my other shoes it was so freezing out there and he wouldn't even turn the lights on.* You will ache you will worry and she will also tell you *I don't like it when he leaves me in his house at night and goes to the boys' practice but I can't call you there's no phone* and when she's at his house and they're all there she will sometimes call you on FaceTime on school nights at 11 p.m. you will watch her on the screen she will be fully dressed and laying on a bare mattress with her lights on she will say *Dad is going to totally freak out but can you 'please come get me please I don't want to sleep here I don't have any sheets I want to come to your house Mom they took all my sheets and blankets because they're going to let Gabe have my bedroom but don't call Dad and tell him that you're coming until you're pulling in the driveway because he's going to totally freak out on me don't call him or he will totally freak out.*

You will want to stop the craziness you will go pick her up *why is she awake at 11 p.m. on a school night* you won't bother to ask Wyatt because he wouldn't hear anything except an opportunity to make it somehow your fault. You will wish for co-parenting you will wish for your old schedule *why can't we just accept the rhythm of that schedule and move forward with our lives why can't we just leave each other alone* instead he will text you repeatedly through the evenings will try to get the boys to do the same you will be able to tell through their messages that he's been stirring up an imaginary conflict from 6:30 to 10:30 p.m. You'll mostly ignore your ex but will respond to your sons back and forth and if you happen to be on the phone you will hear Wyatt in the background telling them exactly what to think and what to say. You will know *I shouldn't even text with Gabe and Levi their dad is just using them to attack me but if I ignore them to save them from being caught in the middle like that then he'll just tell them that I don't even have time for my own sons that I can't even muster up the decency to answer my own sons* so you will text back and forth with them and try to skirt around their aggressive questions and remind them that you love them your oldest will respond *I hate you* or maybe *why do you have to*

184

lie to Dad all the time until you finally say *I'm not going to talk to you about this right now we can talk tomorrow when I see you and you need to do your homework and go to bed* he will text you back that his homework's done and that he won't be talking to you tomorrow at all so don't bother because you're such a liar you lie about everything so he is going to stay with his dad. You will text *Good night, I love you. I'll talk to you tomorrow.* His response will be simple. *No you won't.*

All this will come after moving to live near Wyatt all this will come with the changing of schools. You will comfort them and struggle with how to best help them and some professionals will tell you that you shouldn't hide the truth *if you pretend their dad's perfect and doesn't hurt people then they'll be confused by their own experience of him.* Other professionals will tell you that you should work hard to point out everything good about their father that you should always give him more time with them than he asks for that you should bend over backwards to help them build a strong, positive relationship with their dad. They'll live for years through a start-stop mess of *you don't need to worry about these grown up issues and no, I wasn't out of town last weekend with a man and yes, I did call you every day I don't know why he would make you think those things why do you think he would tell you those things?* Your seven year old will volunteer *Dad hates you and he wants us to hate you, too* you will wonder whether to say *now, that's not necessarily true* or *yes, you're absolutely right* and you'll be even more confused by all the experts and professionals involved who want you to hide nothing who want you to hide everything who want you to set up a pretend life in front of your kids who want you to let them experience the reality of the situation there will be no clear and consistent advice you will try to follow your own intuition you will rock them when they cry you will make mistakes and apologize and through the years and years of their crazy tumultuous childhoods it will be impossible to not make mistakes but you will want to drive a stake into the heart of chaos you will want to make it stop you will rage at the system that keeps a divorce alive for four years you will develop a deep core of hate for every part of the world that works against children and keeps you from protecting them *there's no emergency brake this whacked court system needs an emergency brake the parent who wants to stop the conflict should get to drive not the parent who wants to accelerate.*

In the year following your move north, the boys will start to forget who you are. *This is normal* you will tell yourself and everyone else *boys this age need to grow away from me but wow do I miss them* you will tell everyone this over and over you will show up at every game play the role of Team Mom will do anything you can to see them you will hardly ever see them and when you do, they'll try to walk by as if you're not there they'll try not to meet your eyes and if you do happen to snag them for a quick chat after a game, Wyatt will come stand close by and stare at them intently with his arms folded across his chest and his stance spread wide or else he will come right over and put his body in between yours and theirs and he will hijack the 20 second conversation and put his arm around them and walk them away. You will realize when most team parents also try not to look at you that you're being pushed off the edge by a charismatic leader you will realize you're experiencing a social death you will realize that coming back to this town was a mistake your oldest will say *everyone hates you because you're psycho, Mom, you're a crazy psycho bitch why are you making me come with you today* you'll break down you will be too exhausted to respond the right way all the time so you will respond the wrong way you will not even know what the right way is and you will say *fine I'm not doing this I'm not going to fight with you like this I'm so tired of these scenes, you wish you didn't even have a mom and here your friend cries that his mom died and you act like you wish I would die you just want me to go away* you will go to turn around and your son will try to grab the wheel will try to grab and hit your arms he will try to jump out of the car you will tell him that you're calling the cops if he keeps twisting the wheel that he's going to cause a wreck he'll explode *you're a psycho bitch why would you even talk about my friends you're so psycho and I hate you, you ruined my whole childhood you lied to me all the time you're a liar I missed my whole childhood with Dad and you never let us spend time with him you ruined my whole life making us drive to that school and I know all about you I know why you left Dad and I hate you I hate you!* You'll pull over into the ditch, stunned. *I'm sorry I said that about your friend, Gabe, I'm so sorry I really am do you hear me I really am.* You'll sit silently for a moment. *And you can't grab the wheel like that we could've wrecked. You can't ever grab me like that again.* Abby will be in the backseat all bug-eyed you will cry when you see her face in the mirror you won't be able to help it the tears will just run down your cheeks *your dad and I had equal time with you,* you won't know what else to say except *maybe we should see a therapist* he'll say *I'm not seeing a therapist just because you're psycho don't even try that you're not going to trick me again what kind of mom says she's going to call the cops on her kids you are so totally psycho.* You will know that this is not the normal kind of drifting away from mom at thirteen after all and you will read about alienation and you will tell your mom *it's a textbook case* you will tell your boyfriend Matt that you're so thankful he hasn't run away screaming by now he will have never expected a year like this *our first year together was relatively peaceful and wonderful but who could have expected everything that's happened in year two* he will tell you that all of this will never, ever change *there will just be some times when he's a little less engaged* you will sense Matt's hopelessness *why is every good part of my life driven away even my friends drift away from the chaos and if I don't figure out how to contain this, I bet Matt will leave, too.* He will cry with you over missing your boys *I can't imagine what you're feeling I miss them myself and I only had a year with them before it changed* your ex will work diligently to eliminate any relationship your boys might have developed with Matt they will stop looking at him, even, or if they do talk to him they'll tell him *you're so weird you're a loser, Matt.* Abby will come home from a weekend at her dad's to stand in the doorway and yell *Matt, you're a weirdo!* And then she'll run to her room and slam the door but later that day

187

she'll ask him to push her on the swing and by the next morning she'll be completely back to normal *Matt, watch this Matt, watch this* and when she hears her dad telling her brothers not to *pull a Matt* when they do something stupid *don't pull a Matt you don't want to end up a total loser* she will come home and ask you why he would say that. You'll ask her what she thinks she'll say *Dad wants the boys to hate Matt. He wants them to hate everybody like Grandpa and Thompson and everyone in our family. He tells them to never, never be like Thompson that Thompson's a total weirdo loser and that they never, never want to be like that. Why does he hate Thompson?* You will not have an answer you will have to tell her that you don't know and she'll come up with her own reasons *Thompson's only a teenager I think Dad hates him because they like him and he's in your family. Dad wants Gabe and Levi to hate everyone in your family.* You will nod at her you will wonder about taking him to court for parental alienation but you will be broke and scared to death after losing everything the first time around even your parents will tell you it's pointless to go back to court *his attorney is too chummy with the judge and the magistrate and Wyatt gets whatever he asks for every time he files and you'll just lose more and more maybe you'll lose all of your visitation rights including Abby I know it sounds unreal but look what happened the first time around* but they'll also be confused and desperate and so at times they will change their minds and head in the opposite direction *maybe you should go to court after all this just can't go on I just don't know what you should do.*

No one will know what to do. No one will ever know what to do. You'll talk with your therapist friends about chronic developmental trauma and what you might do next but your history will tell you that involving professionals and specialists will only increase the risk and the trauma because your ex will either charm and smoke them over to the point where they'll align with him and come after you for ruining everyone's lives or else he'll manipulate your children's feelings about the process of therapy so that they'll accuse you of trying to turn them into a weirdo *you're not taking me to some place for psychos you're the one with the problem Dad said you used to try to blame him for everything and now you're blaming me just like him I'm not going to your stupid appointments if you try to come and get me I won't get in the car.* You could negotiate with them or you could ignore the comments and try to make them see someone at least once or you could simply care about how they feel and let them know that you love them and respect their feelings *so let's figure out some solutions together what do you think might work here* and while all of these approaches might have some positive aspects in another human system none of them will ever work while their dad has any influence over any aspect of any decision. It won't matter what the decision is, really, whether it's about therapy or who likes vanilla ice cream he will work day in and day out to be sure that your children are perfectly aligned with him on every point and he will absolutely align himself as the opposite of anything you are or present yourself to be and so they'll parrot their father and despise every detail of your life. Every aspect of being a normal human being will be twisted into something negative. If you're nice *you're too freaking easy on people* if you're artistic *you're not like other parents your stuff is so weird* if you wear work clothes to a weeknight game *you don't dress like a normal person why do you have to dress up in a white shirt like that for my game you're not a normal parent you don't even understand sports* if you like sweet potato chips *you always have to try and impress people can't even eat normal potato chips* if you have a diverse group of friends *you don't even know who you are.* He will work and work and work until they'll look at any of your very natural human tendencies as some kind of major, deep flaws they will hear and say these things every day of the week they will come to see you as a dark force as an *other* as a person who is at the core of any and all suffering they've ever endured in their lives and they'll know by experience that no one will have peace until you're not around.

There will never be peace until you're not around. He'll stir them up and point their anger at you. Stir them up and point their sadness at you. Stir them up and point their losses at you. The worst part is that he'll never stop stirring them up you'll tell Matt *they have to live that way talking about me every day when they should be talking about dirt bikes and girls or I don't know what but they shouldn't have to live so stirred up all the time.* Every night they'll either refuse to take your daily call or they will text you angry messages repeatedly about make-believe issues and other sorts of lies their father will have constructed about how their mother is hurting him now. He'll tell them *your mom keeps asking you to come to her house but she's the one who started keeping Abby away from us so she gets what's coming to her did you see her text from last weekend? Look at this it says she's pulling in the drive to get Abby well you guys don't have to go to her house ever again I will stand up for you guys I will be there for you I tell you someone has to protect your rights she will just do whatever she wants and then lie about it.* So you'll text your sons and invite them for Sunday family dinner and receive texts back from them and from their father for the next three hours declaring that you're such a liar it's unbelievable and no one's coming to your dinner and if you didn't lie to their dad all the time maybe they would come but they don't want to talk to you and then their father will throw in something about karma. Chaos, conflict, chaos, conflict, chaos, conflict, chaos. This will be six years after you left, and you'll be completely exasperated and you'll know you ruined their Sunday by your dinner request *now they have to be all stirred up all day* and you'll know by now that it's never going to end and so like the mother who would give up her baby rather than cutting it in half you will wonder *should I just leave this town and try to have them in the summers* Matt will remind you *they won't come see you in the summers, he'll make sure of that no matter what the court says* and you'll know that he's right when Levi and Gabe start sneaking to call your sister if they actually do want to see or talk to you because Wyatt won't let them call you directly they'll say to her *can you have my mom come get me please call her or can you come get me* they'll hang up quickly and your sister will call you and you'll know when this behavior begins that if you're not living close by and if you're not sitting at their games then they'll never see you at all and Matt will continue *plus the court would never let you take Abby with you and there will be no way you could leave her behind and if you leave their lives, they'll be told that you abandoned them that you left for another man that you never loved them like their dad loves them that you only care about yourself. They will lose any chance to see how you live they might lose any chance to be who they really are. If they haven't already.*

So you'll be left to wonder *where is the emergency brake? Does every parent go through this? The feeling that they've lost control of everything I feel like my chance to make an impact is long gone or even to have a connection and there's no way to stop this downhill roll there's no one to turn to for help I've exhausted my family and no one can make it stop the court just makes it worse there's no help there and I feel so alone in the world my kids are suffering and my friends drift away from my sadness and I know Matt is on the edge of leaving, too, it's just too much pain to take it's too much for him and then these other parents make a wide path around me it's like I'm too dirty to touch only a few of the bravest and kind-hearted will dare sit and chat with me after they've heard who I am. How can I stop this from happening? They won't even look at me they act like I'm invisible my kids see them doing it at every game at every event is this what racism feels like? Is it bullying? What else feels this way? It will kill a person it's killing me I keep fighting and fighting but my God I'm so exhausted I need a revolution I'm so tired of losing no matter what I do whether I pick up the fight or let it all go. And then when I screw up I don't get any chance to repair with them because I never get to see them and I'm a human and I screw up and I need a chance to repair with them just to sit with them and say I'm sorry and they can't be expected to understand that my heart is broken by what's happened or that I don't know how to be a mother to boys who don't want me to be their mother anymore. They can't be expected to understand any of that and they aren't here to fill any of my needs so I don't want them to feel that way at all and I just miss them, I miss them so terribly there's this whole huge part of me that is gone and it's not just a teen phase this is different because they hear terrible things about me on a daily basis and now they believe terrible things they think any good thing I do has a bad motive they think I'm just faking it how could he hijack their memories how is that even possible and what am I supposed to do and how can I sit with this maybe I'm supposed to try and find zen peace become enlightened so that all of this is just a matter of being too attached and once I figure that out I'll fall into the bliss of some non-dual reality where it all sits together and I'll be suddenly filled with deep peace in the face of suffering but I don't know anyone who can watch someone hurting their kids over and over for years and just let it go as some part of a greater thing and is this idea of 'walking the high road' going to lead me to my grave is it some sort of guarantee that I will die at the hands of another, more aggressive being? Will my children? Is this the way of the world? Who's going to save my kids? How did it come to this place. How can I make this different. How can I begin again.*

Where is the emergency brake.

14.
THE ENERGY
OF LIES AND
EXAGGERATION

Most identified criminals actually
do have a conscience.
Those that don't are the ones who
rarely get caught or
even if they do,
prosecuted.
Partly because they're so good at
deception and
we all think
we can tell when someone's lying.
Professionals especially.
The result is that
we very often
get duped.

You will go to class. You will study gender and policy you will study gender and violence you will study gender and poverty you will get on everyone's nerves when you read about anti-welfare propaganda and start ranting against the media against the system of giving voice. *No one knows the truth about welfare none of us know the truth it is suppressed everything we learn and see is a twisted lie the only people who get to talk are the people who have money and power it's all propaganda there's no honest media there's no balanced portrayal and it's destroying people it's strangling people and it's hurting children it's hurting people who care for children here's the real research here's an amazing book of case studies can you believe we've been misled in this way who is going to stand up for these people who is going to care about these kids?* People will not be hooked, intrigued, or inspired they will not want to read the book they will not care about the author's incredible body of work they will have the image of a *welfare queen* seared into the flesh of their brains there will be no budging it the image will serve their needs and it will not go away. You will be furious over the betrayal *everything I thought I knew and believed in eventually trips and falls over its own sham of a self and why can't we just hear the truth* but you will also want to be invited to pleasant dinners so you will quickly learn that it's your job to keep these thoughts to yourself because people don't like talking about deception what they like talking about is the sale over at *Anthropologie* people like talking about their new earrings people like talking about their mother or their work or their latest journey people like talking about the deep peace of meditation people like talking about deep peace.

You will wonder about yourself *who am I to care so much about these things? Things I'm not sure how to help? I'm in such a mess of my own.* But your own mess will not stop you from watching Martin Luther King Jr. speeches over and over, sobbing the whole time. When your kids are young, they will pat you on the back and you will wipe your eyes and when they are a little older you will find yourself ranting about violence and about inequality that people either can't or don't want to see anymore and so your therapist friends will eventually suggest that it's really about your own trauma and not about the bigger issues and that it can even be a diversion from your own life and you will wonder *is that true am I selfish or something that makes me feel selfish but I also feel like I'm just angry that no one ever told me the truth before. No feel-good until we're equal. Is that a diversion?* You will wonder about your own trauma you will

194

decide that *I'm not going to spend my twenties and my thirties being beat down by some man who's out to get me I am going to persevere I'm going to beat this so I have some power to help other people I want to help other people but as long as I'm sitting starving in the desert I'm not going to be a whole lot of help to anyone I need to rebuild myself I need to get my hands on some resources.*

You will not have many resources. You will have lost most of everything you will have been fighting your losses the whole time, starting at 24 when you married and took up the fight for your dignity and for the truth but along the way you will have lost your ability to see it and say it you will have told one million lies in some confused pursuit of stability and family you will have been focused the entire time on what you felt in your heart to be real but you will have lived as a partner in your own betrayal. You will remember the John Mellencamp quote that spent twenty years pasted up on your parents' fridge: *An honest man's pillow is his peace of mind.* You will lose your peace of mind you will lose your self-respect as you work each day to patch together the image of an All-American family you will learn to experience shame all through your marriage for Wyatt's choices as if his actions were your own. You will work to cover up that shame. You will work to not see his lies. And in doing so, you will lose your energy. You will have children and you will fight for their education and their ability to be their own people and to make their own choices and to live a balance of interests and to appreciate all kinds. You will fight for their right to stability and safety and love. This will take energy, too, everything will take more energy than you ever imagined. You will fight the loss of energy you will take extra vitamins and go for an invigorating run you will go back to school you will sit in therapy you will read books you will practice you will become a licensed therapist. You will work. You will work as a freelance writer during grad school you will work as an intern in a college counseling center you will love the writing you will love the clinical counseling you will want to pour yourself

195

into the work you will drive all over the place to get there you will take out more loans to make it through. You will fight. You will fight for your freedom you will go more than $120,000 into debt to your attorney so that the government will finally set you free from your bonds to them and to your ex. *When you marry, you also marry the government. No one sees that there's a third party standing there at the wedding.* And when it's over, you will still owe money to this attorney and his firm, and he will take your very last leftover asset. A piece of your grandpa's family farm.

He will take the last piece.

You will lose energy. But you will keep moving. You will remember the truth you will fight to tell the truth. You will know the basic facts you will study the Revised Code you will be fully aware of the law. You will know that you bought your own farm land with more than $250,000 of your own cash you will know that the law states that this money will return to you in divorce if you can trace it on paper as your own separate asset that has not been commingled with his and you will show the court the evidence and you will have a clear and easily traced paper trail that makes the source and separate nature of that cash investment very obvious and clear you will know that you're not only entitled to your own separate assets that you're also entitled to any passive appreciation on these assets you will know that these facts are the law you will know the truth of these facts.

You will summon your last bit of energy you will fight for your rights in court. You will fight for the application of the law. You will find that the court can pay attention to the law when it chooses to pay attention to the law but that the court is also permitted to make subjective interpretations of the facts and that sometimes the court can ignore the truth and choose instead to believe its own lies especially if one party spends $40,000 on a forensic accountant who's friends with the magistrate and if that party also gives the forensic accountant false information so that this 'expert' then creates false reports that muddy the truth you will find that even if your attorney carefully points out each incorrect detail behind the false nature of these reports to the court that the damage will have already been done and that the court doesn't really care if people commit perjury you will learn that clever lying is actually so much the name of the game that it not only goes unpunished but that it instead is an expected part of the process and that it works. You will find that the court can ignore factual evidence you will find that the court can make false statements to the contrary *this property has been hopelessly commingled and not only does the husband get half he actually gets more than half because he's the one who's been gainfully employed so he gets all the payments back on top of his half* you will object *I object. If you look at the property you can see what I showed you in Exhibits C and D that it was purchased in two parts. I bought all the land with my cash. No mortgage. We bought the house and five acres together with a mortgage and the land just sat there and it's traced on paper and so the value of the land is wholly mine I want my assets back plus my passive appreciation and I worked all through college to make that money I didn't party I worked and yes contrary to what the opposing counsel had to say I have contributed to society I made investments and I need those investments back so I can build a new life for myself and my children I need my assets to pay my bills and fix my credit and put money down on a new house you can't take my assets and give them to that man he didn't even own a car when we got married and I had a brand new Tahoe with no loan and you already gave that car to him, too, and you know what he did? He gave it to his dad and his dad trashed it as a work vehicle and I had to have it hauled off the farm on a trailer it couldn't even be driven anymore and you can't give him everything you can't give him more of my clearly separate assets it's not right it goes against the law!*

The court will say *we can do what we want to do and we own your things and when you married us you gave us all the power. It doesn't matter what you say it doesn't matter what your papers show us because*

197

we have the power and don't get too mouthy because we can make it even worse for you.

And so you will lose your assets. And you will sit on the stand while the court negotiates over whether you should be permitted to finish graduate school or whether you should be forced to quit and engage instead in your family's business immediately. You will insist on following your own career path and the court will show their disgust for your choices by cutting off all spousal support and deviating child support even further (two times) below the minimum required standard exactly one year before you're scheduled to finish your graduate program. *If they want to cut me off, then fine. But give me my freedom, too—my freedom to buy and sell things. My freedom! Don't pull the rug out from under me while you're keeping my hands tied. I pay for everything the kids need I'm not sure how I'm going to get through this.* You will sit in court and listen to these decisions for years and years and by the end you will have been married for more than twelve and a half years but you will have left him and started in court at barely nine. Years. You will request that the court record the divorce date at twelve years *because we've actually been married for twelve years and I haven't been able to move on to buy or sell anything to make my new life* so you'll believe that the very least the court can give you is full credit for the whole twelve especially when you'll lose any marital Social Security benefits if you're not married at least ten. *If you're married ten years, you'll receive $1,200 per month in social security once you turn 65. If you're married less than ten years, you'll receive nothing. You'll have to start over completely.* The court will ignore you and the court will back-date your marriage to the date you filed. Nine years. You'll receive nothing from Social Security at 65. You'll say that if they're going to back-date the marriage, then they ought to back-date the unpaid months of child support to that same date. You will make the request. The court will say no.

You will take more vitamins. You will take a long walk. Your family will ask to take you on vacation. Over the years, your parents and aunt and uncle will spot for some trips they will feel so sorry for your kids that they will want to sweep you away to the beach they will want to sweep you away to a state park for the weekend you will be so thankful your kids will be filled with joy. *We can't always swing these things, but you guys have been going through a lot. So we want to do something nice for you.* The court will find out that your family has done something nice for you, and they will rub your nose in it. *You're going to sit here and claim that you're struggling through graduate school and yet you took trips? Ha!* The opposing counsel will state that you've taken seven trips you will protest *it's only been four and they weren't all big trips a weekend getaway at the local state park is a lot different from a full vacation* the court will note *seven extravagant trips* on the magistrate's yellow legal pad and your voice will always and absolutely remain consistently unheard.

When a woman files for divorce, she's supposed to suffer.

You will fight against expectation and your parents will wear out they will work to fill in the gaps help you get the kids to school when you have to be in class they will buy winter coats and bigger muck boots and they will teach your children all the skills of living on a farm. They will try to be normal grandparents but they will also want to show up for court *she can't be there alone when he's there with his whole little party of women* they will become completely and utterly exhausted they will work to hide their despair they will work to stay positive you will come to know that your presence in the world is a burden for everyone around you *I'm a walking package of daily bad news. I'm just too much for everyone* you will wear out your sister and brother the opposing counsel will put your brother on the stand the opposing counsel will put your father on the stand the opposing counsel will put your brother on the stand again you will grow weary of driving to the courthouse with your family you will grow weary of the worry you will become

199

angry when your dad's forthright testimony is mocked openly in the courtroom you will become exhausted of keeping your mouth shut when grown ups act like bullies so when you're on the stand yourself you'll speak right up and ask the magistrate to please tell the opposing counsel and your ex to stop laughing and giggling and gasping at all your answers *it's so distracting* the magistrate will become infuriated *this is not your court room. Counsel, can you take your client into the hall and talk to her about respect I am not moving forward until she knows when to keep her mouth shut.*

You will listen to your counsel you will try to remain absolutely expressionless when the opposing counsel lies about documents you've given him he will complain to the magistrate *they never gave me full discovery their obstinance has made this process incredibly difficult that's why we had to hire all these experts so we believe that she should have to pay for all of them* you will have time-stamped copies of every document they asked for which means you will have clear evidence of every copy you delivered and when you delivered it you will show the court your proof you will point out the court that *this man is lying* and the court will act like you haven't said a thing. You will want to blow up you will be forced to sit quietly. You will sit quietly. When the opposing counsel begins to question you on the stand in 2009 about your medical records *did you begin a prescription for anti-depressants in early 2007?* You will not know what he's talking about you will say *what are you talking about? I haven't been on any anti-depressants.* He will hold up a copy of a prescription you will say *where did you get that let me see that oh this is a prescription the doctor gave me back in 07 just in case I wanted to start these because he knew that I was coming into some really hard times and I already seemed depressed but I never filled it I had forgotten all about this and it's just an anti-depressant, anyway, what's the big deal and why are you asking me about this in a court process that's supposed to be only about dividing up assets at this point everything else is done and so where are you going with this and how did you access my medical history that's supposed to be federally protected information* he will tell you that they can follow your medical history because you're still covered under your still-husband's insurance and so Wyatt has access to every medical move you make and Wyatt has the password to the insurance website you will ask but *where did you get that actual prescription* and you will ask the court for the password so that you, too, can review your own and your children's medical transactions and the opposing counsel will object *she can't have the password we're not going to give her access to Wyatt's health information* you will protest *but he has access to all of mine how is that just* and the court will remind you once again to *please just sit there quietly, and counsel, she's not getting the password and you're going to have to take her to the hall again I am not going to tolerate her today I have a headache.*

You will have a headache, too.

You will keep trying. You will call Legal Aid and hope to change your attorney once you start sinking into debt. *You have non-cash assets? Well I'm sorry, ma'am, but that means there's nothing we can do for you.* You will try to change attorneys you will visit more and more of them and they will say *I don't take a case like yours mid-stream. Your attorney is doing everything I would do, and if you wanted me, you should've come to me in the first place.* You will think about going to court without representation. *You can't do that or that asshole will eat you alive.* You will be stuck. Trapped. You will watch your car begin to rot *I need to sell this thing and get something more gas efficient but I can't buy or sell anything until this is over I'm so frustrated* you will pour a glass of wine your hips will start to ache when you run you will need to pick up more hours of work you will feel your age setting in you will exercise less and less you will work more and more you will pick up weight. *I thought I'd build a new life in my thirties. Now I'm closer to forty and I'm still married and everything's gone. That man has owned my whole life. He has owned my whole adult life.*

I just want to be free.

You will learn that no one knows freedom unless they know they don't have it. You will fight for it you will insist on your rights you will be told that you're disgusting you will be told to shut up. Your words will be exaggerated most of what anyone comes to know about you will only contain a morsel of the truth. You will try not to care how anyone sees you and you will insist on your right to live you will insist on your right to parent and your right to an education and your right to date. *He's been dating since we got married. I'm not going to let him own every part of me until the divorce is finally granted because that will be years and years.* You will start to date. You will date determinedly you will shocked by the kindness of the first person you go out with he will be one of the kindest men you will ever know you will be in shock in his presence you will be in shock when he pays you a compliment you will be in shock that he finds you attractive you will be in shock when he says *you are the most graceful person I've ever known.* The first kind thing he will ever tell you is *you write beautifully* and you will cry when you hang up the phone. You will never forget the sound of those words. You will be eight months into the divorce process when you first go out, and you will insist on your right to do what Wyatt does but you will still be too fresh and naive in the process to know better you will tell yourself *Wyatt can scream around all he wants if he finds out but I can't let him own me I can't let him manipulate me I just have to be careful and not do anything to hurt the kids.* But Wyatt will instantly tell the kids he will tell them that mommy left daddy to be with another man he will block your calls to them and tell them that you don't call them anymore because you don't love any of them anymore now that you found a new man. They will come back to you after a weekend with their dad in crazy tears and anger and chaos *why don't you love us anymore why don't you call* you will think *what is happening why would he do this to them this has to stop* you will meet with their therapists you will ask *what can I do to make this better I wasn't ready to tell them that I was dating but now I have to do something to make this better for them what can I do.* You will make yourself sick with worry you

202

will work harder you will try to stay positive you will tell yourself a lie *Wyatt will stop getting the kids so worked up pretty soon because he won't want to make them hurt like this* you will wonder *should I not date at all maybe I shouldn't date at all* you will talk to your children's therapists again they will say *it's ok to have adult relationships you just have to be careful so just don't start eating dinner together every night and don't spend the night together when your children are at home* you will take that advice to heart *Ok, I won't* and you will lie awake at night and worry about whether your children are doing ok you will sit by them at bedtime for long conversations you will work to be open and curious about everything they feel and you will tear yourself up when they parrot their father *you hurt Daddy you don't love anybody you only love Miles*. You will work to remain open and welcoming to their perspective and you will also be so frustrated because their perspective is coming straight from their dad *I'm trying to be an open parent because I want them to be who they are I want them to trust their own experiences but then their dad jumps in their and creates their worldview for them, and that worldview involves hating me or believing lies about me and they think I follow their dad around and beat him down with a giant club all the time and I just don't know how good it's going to be for me to do nothing to be nothing but open because they'll become completely hypnotized by their dad but I also don't know what else to say because arguing back and forth about the facts doesn't do any good and I want to help them and not make things worse. How can I handle this?*

No one you know will ever have a good, clear answer, just like no one you know will ever anticipate that he will keep up this game for years. In fact, Wyatt will never wear out. He'll poison the well every single day of the rest of your life and after a while you will watch in some kind of numb and horrified awe. Sometimes you will even laugh in despair. But mostly you will ache that no one can make the man stop. Ever. But that will be later, and forever, and right now we're talking about the beginning, or sort of the beginning, near the end of your first year of trial when you very quickly find yourself back in the court house over Miles, this new man you're dating, circled in close by five men in suits who want to hear your deposition.

You will make a deposition.

You will be questioned for two and a half days solid you will sit in a small room with these men in suits they will ask you whether you drive your children to school *did you drive them to school on September 23rd* they will ask you how much you spend on groceries *let's review these numbers* they will ask you where you were on December 19th they will ask you everything they want to ask you they will ask you about your friends they will ask you about dating they will ask you about sex.

They will all lean in for the sex questions except your attorney. He will lean back he will clear his throat and make a couple notes on his yellow legal pad. He will flip the page. You will shift in your seat at first you will glance around the room but by half way through the first day you will sit straight-still and stare back at the opposing counsel with the same cold contempt he has for you. *You want to hold me here day after day just to show me that you can, well fuck you. Fuck you. Is this really what you do for a living you hold housewives for questioning make you feel like a big man you little weasel faced worthless leech on society. Go ahead and ask me another pointless question. Talk to me like I'm a criminal. Pretend you're master of this sick little game, your time clock running the whole time. You have a pathetic, worthless life.*

They will spend a lot of time asking questions about your new relationship. Your answers will tell the story. *Yes, I've had dates with that man. Yes, I've met his children. No, their mom died of cancer five years ago. No, I don't spend the night there with his kids. No, he doesn't spend the night with my kids. Yes, he's a physician. Yes, I went to see him when I wanted to talk to someone about leaving Wyatt. No, he never became my regular physician. No, I went back to my regular midwife for my annual care. No, it was that summer. No, he sent me a letter of termination of care. No, we didn't have a date until more than ninety days later. Yes, our families are friends. No, we didn't date right away. Yes, we met with a psychologist first. No, it was just to make sure it was ok. Yes, I know his business partners. Yes, he delivered my sister's children. Yes, I was a doula. Yes, I wrote a book. Yes, he read it. No, he's not helping me publish anything. No, I'm not doing anything with it. Yes, we've had sex.*

You will ask your attorney *what does any of this have to do with my divorce whether our families are friends whether we followed due diligence around dating what does that apply to in my divorce proceedings it seems like they're using this as a chance to be nosy I don't get their point can't we object to some of this and do they really have to know details about my sex life?* Wyatt will not answer a single question about his sex life or about abuse or cheating or anything. Your attorney will say *we're not going to waste more money and time asking questions that won't help your case at all and I can't sit in this room all week* he'll take Wyatt's deposition in a couple hours you will be angry that yours took days *I'm stuck paying my attorney the whole time they question me these people have me trapped I'm a prisoner I'm a prisoner and they have the right to bleed me out because apparently I'm a criminal skank for leaving my husband even after everything he's done to me I'm the one who gets treated like a criminal and no one will even LET me talk about our history no one will let the truth inform the process what is wrong with this world it's like Wyatt's the king and I'm asking permission to leave his harem and so there will be punishment I have my dues to pay* you will rant to your mom and dad *he's attacking me and he's attacking everyone and I have to show up to defend myself to defend everyone and what about the kids and the farm can't we just stick to the basic facts and get this over with this is not a complicated case I don't want to show up anymore I can't afford to show up anymore I want to walk away I want out this process does nothing for humanity this whole thing is criminalizing and I have already been beaten down enough but no one even cares about that why did they even ask all those stupid questions who cares where I was on November 18th what does that matter and why do they get to ask whatever they want* you will learn that they can always ask what they want and

205

you won't be surprised when they use time at trial more than a year later to ask you again about that old, unused prescription for anti-depressants and after that round of questioning you will wonder *what are they doing now* and you will watch Wyatt's attorney scrambling through his trial notes with Wyatt over break he will be reading from them to someone over the phone in front of the courthouse you will be sitting in your car eating a banana and watching them huddling over their notes and phones and you will wonder. At the end of the day you'll listen to your messages on the drive home will have one from Miles *hey there, I have some bad news it seems that someone filed a complaint with the medical board I'm sure it's Wyatt trying to take my license it seems he filed a complaint with the board that says I gave you drugs and split up your marriage while you were my patient. No one else would file that. So there's going to be an investigation and I tell you that man is really an angry, bitter man so give me a call but don't worry about it too much because this whole thing is ridiculous and it doesn't have a leg to stand on but anyway, just give me a call.* You will hold your breath you will be too stunned to cry you will stare blankly through the windshield and somehow make it home *everyone I touch is going to go down there will be no peace for me there will be no peace for anyone who loves me.*

You will worry yourself sick over Miles' license. *I'm ruining his life.* The medical board will send out an investigator and Miles will sit with him at the table with the evidence and the investigator will look through things ask a few questions and abruptly stand up to leave he will say *it sounds like an angry ex is wasting everyone's time. There is obviously no basis for this complaint. I'm going to dismiss the investigation.* Miles will call right away to tell you and you will breathe a sigh of relief and Miles will breathe a sigh of relief but Wyatt will never, never stop shouting to the world that you left him for your gynecologist.

He will tell the world and he will tell your small children. Gabe and Levi will be six and eight at the time, and Abby will be three. You will try to ignore Wyatt you won't always know what to say to your kids you will hug them you will hold them you will listen to them you will buy them relaxation CDs to help them fall asleep at night to guided visualizations but they will suffer. They will ask questions. *Why did you leave Daddy for Miles what is a gynecologist why didn't you call us all last weekend why are you making Daddy sell the farm can't you just let him keep it I love the farm I don't want you to make Daddy sell it why did you have to ruin our family for Miles why is your house so small why did we move here why is your yard so small why aren't the parents nice to you I don't understand why the parents aren't nice to you, Mom, and can we talk about my hair I just want to wear a hat tomorrow can you call my teacher because I didn't want to shave my head but he made me shave it and I started crying I couldn't help it and I told him I don't want to shave my head and I know you said to call you but he won't ever let me call you and he told the barber that if I cried then he should shave it even shorter I hate him he's so mean I hate him and when we got home he started tickling me because I was still mad and he sat on my chest until I threw up I thought I was going to die he thinks it's funny I hate Dad but why can't we just keep the farm I don't want to sell the farm why are you making us all leave I don't want to leave and I can't sleep I hate my whole life why can't I just be like the other kids why can't I have brown hair and I don't want it shaved I have to wear a hat and I hate my whole life.*

You will moan inside your heart you will call the guardian you will call your attorney *my kids are suffering this process has to end* they will say *that's unfortunate* they will say *there's nothing you can do.* You will stiffen up you will walk around ready for a fight you will make a strong declaration that Wyatt's tricks aren't going to bring you all down. *He got my twenties and so far my thirties but he doesn't get my whole life and I'm a strong mama I'm a grizzly bear mama and he needs to stop messing with our kids I am not going to tolerate this I am not going to let him bring us down I am never going to stop I am going to keep calling the guardian I don't care if he hates me and I'm going to keep these kids in therapy I don't care if the court laughs at me I don't care if they think I'm ridiculous I don't care what they say because something's going to bust someday soon this is going to stop and I am never going to cower I am never going to break down I am sticking with our spring break plans and I don't care what he does to try and ruin it these kids need a break and Aunt Margaret already bought the tickets and if Wyatt wants to pretend that he didn't agree to it right in front of the guardian then he'll have to take me to court what an ass he is anyway I don't know why he has to try and throw a wrench in it now why he wouldn't want the kids to have this vacation with all their cousins we're not taking anything from him and he still gets his week he's such a whiny little bitch I'm so sick of him trying to take me to court over every single trip. That man is not going to bring me down that man is not going to wreck our children I am going to fight for their right to a stable childhood all this is bullshit and all this is going down. I'm breaking his sick cycle I am taking it down.*

You will move forward with your spring break plans. You will insist that Wyatt pick the children up for his week. He will not pick them up, he will not take his week, he will instead file a contempt motion stating that you took his week, and you will go to court. Wyatt's brother-in-law Trent will serve you with the papers in front of your children. They will stare at you with wide eyes.

And this will be your way.

You will wear out you will need special care and attention your children will be worn out they will need some special care and attention you will hang your head you will imagine that you're stomping on Wyatt's face when you go for a run you will work to give your children everything they need *we'll just buy some pants for you to keep at your dad's house now here's some Chapstick now keep this in your pocket and make sure you put some on today it'll help your top lip get better* you will sit up with them to talk before they fall asleep at night you will play their music as loud as they want when you drive you will all rap right along with it you will deliver everything everywhere you will meet with their teachers you will sometimes not know what to do.

You will need energy you will need to study you will want to stay loving and spontaneous with Miles you will feel a little broken and scared after the medical board thing you will feel a little hopeless about your chances every time your kids come back from their dad's and ask why you didn't call them all weekend and why you had to ruin everything for Miles you will not know what to do except to reassure them that you did call *did you see my messages on your phones?* They will say *Dad took our phones and put them away* you will want them to feel safe and happy and excited about their own lives *they shouldn't be worried so much about my life or Wyatt's life they should be safe enough to worry about their own* you will want to make things better for them you will want to make things better for Miles *he's already had enough suffering in his life he deserves more I want to give him more* and over time he will want more attention he will want to start sharing a little more time he will want you all to start eating together two times a week but your children will be in such a state of chaos that you'll have to say *no, I can't start meals together the kids are really struggling and I need to give them more time.* Miles will feel so lonely for you he will say *I just want us to think about moving forward I don't want your divorce to be the center of our lives* you will agree with him but your children's therapists will also tell you that your children need more time and space *I will give them more time and space* which means that you will eventually have to tell Miles that you just can't meet his needs. *This is all still in such a dark space and I need to do what's right for my children and I just can't meet your needs.* He will assert his right to his needs and you will agree with him *I understand why you want to move forward I understand why you want those things and I love your family and I want that, too, but it's not about what I want and I'm just not able to be there in that way* and you will very sadly go your own way.

You will go your own way you will continue with your classes and your most determined plans but you will walk a little emptier you will look a little emptier of hope you will rely on your old habits of pretending nothing's wrong you will write a blog to stay cheerful you will focus on the positive you will paint freely to music at home alone on a Saturday night you will write in your journals you will write lots of poetry you will write another book you spend weekend after weekend cleaning house and standing blankly in your children's empty bedrooms. *I hope they're ok, please, God, protect them.* You will rearrange your clothes you will designate some just for court *when this is over, I'm burning this pile* you will throw your wedding dress in a dumpster you will throw your wedding album on a fire you will go out to dinner with your sister you will go out to lunch with a friend you will date a wine-and-cheese guy for a few months he will not pressure you and he will send poetry through your phone every day he will tolerate your obsession with writing he will think your head-scratching over sentences is quaint he will bring you ice cold beer in a dripping, sweating bottle along with searing hot shrimp still bubbling he will tell you that you are *sushi grade* and you will laugh and relax a little you will appreciate everything about the man there will be absolutely nothing wrong with the man except in the end what will be wrong is that he exists in your life you will be entering a time when you just want to be alone when your kids really need you to be alone.

I'm so sorry. I just need to be alone.

You will want to feel more than the need to be alone.

15.
WOMEN'S WORK

Women in psychology have historically been called
'hysterics'
more often than not.
It is still widely believed that the female nature
unconsciously invites exposure to
molestation and assault.
This is not just a small chapter in psychology,
it is the foundation.
And a similar psychological paradigm
extends to our children.
It makes a woman like me wonder
how I am to survive
let alone heal
and stand up for my kids
when hostility toward us
infuses the doctrine
by definition and by reaction
at every point.

You will work.

Your work will wake you in the morning at 4 am you will write a book will write a journal will write a poem. Before you leave your marriage and the farm, you will huddle in a blanket before Wyatt's heavy desk you will drink strong coffee and try to peak through the clouds. You will fail. To see clearly you will be so trained in your job, in your capacity to lie that your writing will come out more like a made up story than the truth about your life. You will be so good at pretending you will have an inner drive to pretend you will write *should I finally get a riding horse but how would I find the time I'm just so busy in the garden all this leaves me with no time to fix my relationship. I'm just going to have to leave.* You will not be able to write the truth and only later will you realize that you lie and you will wonder when you fell into that role and when it might end. You will wonder about lots of things and understand only a few, you will understand why soft people cover their mouths while talking about difficult things or why nice people can't continue when sharing bad news or why optimistic people often can't say the truth when it's right in front of them. Why they're so full of disbelief. *How could he DO something like that? Surely that's a mistake.* You'll understand why so many people look at most everyone else and see a soft spot inside *we all start out completely pure and wonderful and even though the world hurts us, it's always in there somewhere and in the right moments anyone's heart can crack wide open* and yet you'll watch those same people become automatically terrified of a burly man with tattooed knuckles even as they embrace the charismatic yet humble blonde man offering a drink with a smile you'll come to understand that people only see the soft spot in certain kinds of people and that appearances mean more than maybe they should and you'll know that's why even Children's Protective Services would dismiss a case called in by a therapist and a physician on a white dad in flannel living on an idyllic farm but would on the same day show up at a mobile home in the middle of a junk graveyard and start a file on a father living in poverty right away, especially if that poor dad shows up at the door without a tooth and especially if he's any shade of brown. Perhaps the rich dad molested his daughter. Perhaps the poor dad hasn't had electricity for a month. You'll know that the poor dad will be the one most likely to get it—not the rich—because you'll see these things happen. You'll stop wondering why we can't say the truth about these things you'll start to understand why people hide pain and oppression as if that means it isn't really happening you'll start to see that some people actually use those human tendencies to their advantage. You'll wonder why they'd do that and at the same time you'll wonder why you'd sacrifice decades of your life waiting for Wyatt's soft spot to crack wide open even as he smashed you up against the wall over and over again.

And you will look for answers.

A minister will have answers for you a minister will describe your work in the world a minister will tell you that wives are supposed to live as a consistent model of Jesus so that their husbands can eventually change.

You have a duty, you have a role.

Your aunt will find a quote from the Buddha: *Weakness invites aggression.* Both statements will trouble you deep down *am I stronger if I take it or does it just bring on more am I supposed to stand still to be strong am I weak for wanting to get away what is my role did I bring this all on myself?* You'll wonder what Jesus would do *but I don't have any special powers like that am I supposed to ask Jesus for special powers* then you'll wonder why you're so weak and where that weakness comes from and how you can get rid of it and you'll wonder later what all this means for children *why can't weakness invite protection isn't the Buddha's view ignoring my mothering and my nurturing perspective and the whole world seems upside down maybe that's why smaller people get blamed for everything and why blamers and haters say we all get the same chances when it's clear that we don't and why people use equality as a weapon instead of ensuring it as a right and why the whole world tells itself lies about all these things and why they say things like 'God made it this way and that's why I'm doing this to you.'*

You will have a job. So ingrained in you that you won't even think to quit your job you will be fully trained in making it look like things aren't what they are and that no one's being hurt you will spend most of your adult life telling yourself and everyone else around you that what was happening wasn't really happening your job will keep you from stating the facts and your success in your job will be the main reason your marriage lasted as long as it did you'll be so good in your role that you'll hide your evil story even from yourself it's why you won't write the truth it's why you'll instead write a page or two about the exciting things you have planned with some extra emphasis on your positive mission statement and some words on how inspired you are by your grandmothers you will write about flowers and sunshine but you will feel on the inside like a budding rebel even your act of writing will represent very questionable behavior every word you compose will be an inner act of pushing back against your role every lie will be a little opening to a future truth. What will matter is the act. Of writing. And in the months before you leave your marriage, you will wake every morning for your secret hours of self your fingers will fly over the keys and it won't matter yet that you can't write the truth what will matter is that you can write at all. After, you will put on a floral skirt and host a baby shower with a smile *yes, I'll send you the recipe. Glad you like it.* You will put on a happy face. You will put on a show. You will tell yourself as you're getting dressed *it's time to rally* you will spend fifteen or twenty years protecting him and protecting yourself and then you will start to question why you play his game so nicely one day in October while watching him smack the coach on the back at your son's football game you will hear other parents praising him *he changed everything for my son really brought him into the game* you will think *no one knows him no one knows the truth no one knows me or my story or why I do anything* and you'll watch the parents cheerfully circling around him and you'll wonder what if they knew and why don't they know. Why don't they know.

Why do I protect him. Why do I pretend and what keeps me in this role.

And you will sort through it. *I play Wyatt's game because people don't want the truth. They don't like my truth they don't want my truth and the few times I've tried to share, it brought on a vengeful retribution.* You will remember. The time you mentioned to a friendly football parent that there had been some rough times but you were moving on and you were so thankful to be free from abuse. What you got in return for sharing was a grand slam of a smack down a whole community putting you in your place because whenever Wyatt found out you'd uttered a word, even professionals would join in for the burn *we can take your children away from you* other parents would decide *she's a lying bitch going after him like that* you won't make the mistake of sharing the truth publicly more than once or twice in your life but it will take you years to realize that the real reason you keep holding on and telling the lies isn't just because of your own stupid optimism or your tendency to stick your head in the sand like your therapist says. It won't be just because you can't bear to see the truth or because you mistakenly believed that every person has a soft spot. The most real and powerful reason you'll lie and close your eyes is because you'll feel like you have to. *Weakness invites aggression.* When you tell the truth, you look weak and people attack. It's either your fault *why would she put up with that? She must've asked for it she must have a victim mentality.* Or worse *that can't be true she must be telling lies about him to manipulate people I bet she's trying to keep his kids from him she's one of those and that man is wonderful and she should be ashamed and they should take those kids from her, instead.* And when they don't see you suffering and crying and scratching around in cut-off sweats they'll shame you for having anything to say at all *she looks fine to me* but you won't be the type to walk around crying every day for fifteen years moaning *guess what he did today* you'll know very well that doesn't work any better, anyway, after trying it once and openly missing your children because when you shared that emotion even some of your closer friends would start to drift away, some more quickly than others.

People don't like the pain.

And they don't want to believe it. If you share the hard truth about a beloved personality, it will become nearly impossible to build relationships with anyone else around. Even the soft truth will bring on some punches from another team mom when you ask that both parents be invited to team parties for the benefit of your children. This football mom will respond with *what are you saying are you telling me what to do? Seriously telling me what to do? Well, fuck YOU you ugly bitch I know all about you everyone knows who you are you slut so yeah look away you prissy bitch why are you such a fucking priss I know all about you so go ahead and walk away* she will be swinging punches at you as you go. The little league team will be sitting right there in the corner next to you, your son's face will be red hot he will be picking the bottom of his shoes.

You will have a job. To protect your children. To do this job well, you will have to accept that no on wants the truth. Not even professionals. What you will get is a clear shut up *you got emergency room records?! No? Then shut your mouth don't you ever walk into my office again and even say the word abuse because I know your type and some people are just too sensitive and if you try to use something like that as a wedge between him and the kids I can immediately recommend that the magistrate give full custody to their father I do have that power as the guardian and are we clear?*

Are we perfectly clear?

You will learn that when the truth isn't pretty, expected, or delivered with a fair dose of charm, people will almost always put their faith in a lie.

You will have a job. Your job will take a lot out of you it will move you from optimism to despair. But you won't even notice that journey—the deceitful nature of despair will creep into you slowly over the years it's another kind of smoke entirely and it will fill you up to the rim and once you're full of it your lies will change from *we're a really strong couple just getting over a few bumpy places* to *he didn't mean that* to *yeah, we're doing ok we both love family life and that helps* to *he wouldn't do that* to *we're independent people I'm so excited you should see the children's garden I put in I'm so in love with life I can't decide what to do first* to *I caught him lying again and he looked straight into my eyes but that was a small issue and I believe he's telling the truth about this one because it's big* to *I've been having some problems with foggy brain lately forgot an entire party felt so ridiculous and terrible I'm going to see a doctor to find out what's wrong with me there must be something wrong with me just need to figure it out* to *when we split, of course he'll acknowledge I'm a great mom I've been their primary caregiver he's always said moms are the most critical* to *he will find something else to focus on and then he'll leave me alone* to *the court will never tolerate this there's clear documentation of him lying on the stand multiple times they will not tolerate this I cannot wait for justice to be served it will be so satisfying* to *his sister won't help him keep them from me after this summer she's a teacher she knows that's wrong she would freak out if anyone did that to her* to *I know there's no justice for me but I believe it must exist in other courts* to *all I have to do is change my energy so that I attract more positive things in life* to *the court cares for children this will not last for long* to *good people always win in the end I'll just stick to the high road and everything will work itself out* to *people will see who I am if I just continue to engage them and continue to do what's right* to *this is all going to end no one can keep that much vengeful energy going year after year after year* to *a mother's bond with her child can never be broken.*

You will lie.

Every one of those statements will be a lie it will be your job and you will lie to yourself and you will lie to everyone else maybe survival can bring on a whole different way of saying

217

things out loud maybe survival can change the truth entirely maybe survival can change reality so that it's not only the oppressive tyrant telling all the manipulative evil lies and causing all the hurt maybe it's also you, his victim, telling all the positive-thinking-he-wouldn't-do-that survival lies that's causing the hurt, too. Maybe it's the lies we tell each other maybe it's the lies we tell ourselves maybe it's the blinders we put on when we see something we don't want to see maybe the whole world and nearly every life could be different if we as a people could strip away our need to separate ourselves from those who are suffering if we could see and feel their pain and still stay open to the truth. If we could still say *yes, this is happening. I see you. I hear you.* And instead of asking *what is your problem what is wrong with you,* if we could instead spend more time on *who's hurting you what's their problem let's protect you let's care about your hurt let's make sure this can't happen again and again and again.*

You will realize this over and over and then you will sit at your son's basketball game years later and you will still act like everything's ok.

You will act like everything's ok.

Because the whole world's a confusing topsy-turvy act of *I'm ok, you're ok* and you will have another job that says *I have to keep it together for my kids.* What is right? What is wrong? When do you make things look better than they are? When is it hurting or helping your children? How will you know? You will want nothing but the truth. You will want so badly to stand in public with the raw honesty of your situation and who you are and what you've done right and what you've done wrong and when it's been hard and how you feel when your children refuse your calls and why they are refusing them and what they've been told about you. You will want people to know that no professional knows how to help you or your children, even when they start shoving you around to earn their father's applause. You'll want people to know what it is to lose your job over nasty rumors and lies to be pushed out of every social circle that touches your children's lives to be suspected of every rotten thing to be told that you're insane over and over to have your children hear that you're insane nearly every single day to be viewed by so much of their world as a dark, disgusting force when you're just in fact a regular old human being who will have lost everything by then who will have lost everything she loved because she dared marry the wrong man and he would never, never let her go would never stop working to destroy her until she was gone you will wonder why you believed his lies you will wonder why everyone else believes them, too, you will wonder what truth is in this world you will wonder how other people find their answers but the closest you'll come to understanding is that people build their own truth in ways that work for them and then you'll say a short prayer *please help me know what's true* and you'll wonder about all the ways we construct our own vision of God for ourselves and you'll forever remember Wyatt's face leaning close to yours as he shared his own personal version:

God wants people like you to be wiped from the face of earth.

You will work hard to stay.

You will work hard to earn your keep.

16.
CAN'T
DIAGNOSE EVIL

We work hard
to create assessments
that lead to diagnoses
hoping to minimize the risk
to society, but
we often give more sympathy
to the victimhood of the
offender
than we do to his or her victims.
In part,
we do this to shield ourselves
from the idea that we could follow all the rules
and still be hurt
or that some people
devastate others
for reasons we don't know how to heal
and may not ever understand.

You will not know evil no one will know it. You will not see evil no one will see it. It will look you right in the eyes, and like most people, you will think it must be ok if it smiles and pats a dog on the head *every human being on earth comes with the capacity to care*. Like most anyone else, you'll think that evil must be somewhat easy to identify it might come right at you with a gun or it might have squinty or buggy eyes or it might be a man trying to trick you into his car or it might be a creepy uncle who pats little children on the bottom all the time. Like most anyone else, you'll think that real evil lives absolutely somewhere else you'll believe that evil's out there somewhere else trafficking people or drugs or that it's kicking a kitten to death for a child to see or that it's flying airplanes into buildings or shooting schoolchildren in the middle of music class you will believe that evil does unfathomable things you will believe that evil is *out there* and *unfathomable*.

Also like most people, you won't live long if you spend every day obsessing over what evil thing might happen next. So you will assume that most everyone is good. You will assume that the car next to you isn't going to suddenly have a little fun by pushing you off the road and watching you crash. You will assume that if evil comes at you, there's a pretty good chance you'll see it coming and that you'll have a chance to do something about it. You will know how to punch you will know how to use a gun you will know how to gut a deer you will have taken a self-defense course in high school you will remind yourself to take that course again after you barely get away from that skinny white guy who came skulking after you through the parking garage in the dark with that long face and those big, bulging eyes you will not know what he might have done but you'll certainly not stick around to find out. He will walk after your car as you drive away.

Also like most people, you will think you know evil without ever really asking yourself whether or how you do. You'll have watched enough movies to be mostly petrified of gangsters. Urban gangsters, mob gangsters, gangsters of things and places that you won't even know exist you'll be sure that these are the *out there* people who are capable of hurting you but even then you'll also believe that *some of those guys are surely softies underneath and I didn't grow up the way they did I'm sure they don't all hurt everybody they meet.* And you'll grow

222

weary of the mislabeling and the way society attacks those who suffer so you will come to the defense of addicts everywhere you won't need to link evil to addiction the way some people do you will go home and find yourself watching some parole show on TV there will be an addict in trouble for breaking parole once again you will argue with the show out loud *well if I had to live through all that, I might want to get high, too, why is everybody yelling and shaming that guy he doesn't have any violent crime on his record he's never hurt anybody he doesn't even steal why is everyone yelling look at him hanging his head like that I just want someone to give that man a pillow.*

You will think that the judging of sad souls is actually what's evil so you won't want to toss any labels around *who knows the truth who knows anything* you will wonder why depression can be clinically diagnosed in the DSM-IV and then treated but racism can't *who decided that racism is inherent but depression isn't maybe they left it out of the manual because they haven't figured out how to medicate it or make money on it but then why was homosexuality in there at one point were they trying to medicate for that?* You will come to know that the focus of diagnosis seems to be founded on which diagnoses can make the most money and you will know exactly who wrote the book and so you will use it with extreme caution and when it comes to addicts and other hurt people, you'll wish you didn't have to use it at all you will say *most people who get the right kind of support are a lot less likely to hurt themselves or each other at all.*

But sometimes you'll wonder if that's realistic or if you're a fool *people hurt each other all the time men are constantly stabbing each other in bars* you'll be confused about evil you'll work on a residential construction crew for your grandpa for a few years and one of the nicest guys on the crew will have stabbed someone once *but that was a long time ago* and by the time you work with him, he won't seem dangerous to you at all and so you'll wonder, later, *was that guy swept up in evil? Is evil inside the person or is it inside the moment? Is evil a force that travels around?*

That thought will creep you out because if evil is a traveling force then it could come to anyone and so it could come to you *do we have to keep our guard up all the time it doesn't feel like I'm guarding against anything I never feel like I'm fighting evil inside myself. Maybe when I have bad dreams it's a way of working through evil things or maybe those snake dreams I've always had are some kind of evil coming to visit me in the night.*

Does evil come to visit people in the night?

You won't know the answers to those questions you won't know evil. Like most people, you'll be left to wonder *where does evil come from* when ambassadors and doctors are killed in troubled places or when children die in school. *Where did that come from what made that happen.* You'll think about it when you feel afraid. You'll think about it when something has happened that's so terrible you won't be able to reconcile it with the workings of your brain. *How could that have happened.* You will wonder about evil and sexual assault you will wonder about one of your ex-lifelong best friends and whether he could be considered temporarily or permanently evil after he snuck into the bathroom and tried to rape you in the shower when you were 21. You won't have thought of evil at the time instead you would simply smash his fingers smash smash smash his fingers while screaming and you would scream at him until he left you alone then you would cry and tremble and cry all through the night behind a locked door *who is that person* you will wonder about that whenever you think of him over time but you won't take any chances *I will never see that man again.*

You will be surprised by people. You will not be born with an understanding. Like most everyone, your ideas about evil will come from your education and your family and your government and your religion. You will have grown up worrying about the Cold War and anything else on the news *there's always plenty of scary out there* and you will have watched

224

Red Dawn with wide eyes will have wondered what people would do to you if they took over your country you will have wondered why anyone would want to hurt you *why would people hurt kids?* You will not be able to understand.

Like most people, you will have little formal education on other ways of identifying evil you will have heard about the devil but never really understood. You will have wondered why the devil would be red you will have wondered why the devil would have a tail. You will have wondered *what if God's red how would anybody know* you will have wondered why God and the devil angel had to argue in the first place *why wouldn't God just zap him if he was so mean, God can do anything.* You will have wondered why the devil would cause a car accident when you hear people talking that way and you will never in your life understand what people mean when they say those things *why would God just sit there and let the devil cause a car accident?* Your own family won't have talked about the devil, not that you remember, the only thing you'll remember your dad saying about religion at all is that *it's more important to walk the walk* he'll be tying up his farm boots he will send you off to church on your own he will say *I'm not going to go sit beside someone who gets all dressed up on Sunday and sits in church asking for forgiveness and then walks out that door and spends the rest of the week screwing people over.* You will have read the Book of Revelation in high school and felt petrified with your friends over the predictions of Nostradamus you will have graduated high school and headed off to college with no real ability to identify evil at all.

You'll find out later that no one you've ever met in your life could identify evil, especially when it's under their nose. You won't figure all this out until you've been married and abused and divorced and through graduate school and working as a therapist and a writer. You will be suffering. You will be looking for answers. You will have spent the last thirty-five years believing wholeheartedly that when someone's being

225

battered and smashed, the experts would without a doubt be able to identify the person doing it the person who was capable the person with a destructive intent. And if those experts happened to miss it at first, you will have remained certain that they'd see it in time. You won't have known that they don't possess the skills to see these things and that they don't have a clear awareness of the fact that they're missing these critical skills and that the least aware will be the experts who will be the most confident in their clinical expertise. *I can see right through him.* So while they flail around with background checks and interactional interviews that they believe provide all the necessary answers, you will have been left to fend for yourself in a world that either won't want to or won't know how to identify a lack of conscience unless it has a bright orange tag on it that says *criminal.* But you won't believe that only criminals are evil *the evil ones are more likely to slip through the cracks* you will begin to understand that Wyatt will always slip through the cracks and what makes it even worse is that you'll have been left not only to fend for yourself but also fully obligated to follow the rules of the system even as most of those rules will have kept you from fending for yourself. *That cop called me a crybaby for calling her and told me not to bother her with these issues so I guess next time she thinks I should go ahead and chase him off my porch with a gun or a crowbar or something and I certainly know how to use a gun but oh no, wait, I'm not allowed to do that, either.* So you'll have fallen forward at points with your hands tied behind your back. You will have been put up against not only another human being who's out to get you but also up against the whole system that will have been so easily manipulated into a weapon serving evil intent. You will have lost your assets and your credit and many of your relationships including your relationship with your children. You will have lost the power to protect them you will have lost the power to parent them. Wyatt will always talk more and louder. *Don't listen to her she should listen to you for once and no, don't bother calling her back there's just no sense to that woman she doesn't make any sense.* You will even be on the verge of losing Matt he will regularly report feeling hopeless *I just can't see us ever having a normal life together anymore there's always something terrible happening and that's just really hard* you will be sitting on what will feel like the secure, solid bottom of a hole but each time you'll start getting comfortable you'll find your ground's being swept away and there you'll go plummeting again with nothing to hold on to that might stop you. You will wonder how could this (still) be happening you will be looking for answers you will try hard to think positive *this positive thinking is getting so old what the fuck* you will pick up exercise once again you will text the boys the stats you kept from their last game you will keep their stats at every game but neither of them will respond. You will have consulted with experts in alienation you will have participated in advanced training programs you will try to host groups of your own you will have special knowledge and experience in domestic violence and yet you will know nothing absolutely nothing at all about clearly identifying and dealing with a person with evil intent and a lack of conscience to stop them from going through with it. You will have stereotypes to work with, most from the DSM-IV. A lack of remorse. A short fuse. Violent outbursts. Apparent lack of respect for the lives and well-being of other people and/or animals. An inability to form lasting, healthy relationships. A tendency toward addiction. A history of abuse and/or neglect and/or trauma. You will be taught that these are the characteristics of a person who might hurt you or someone else. But no one will point out that these traits are even more often linked to Attachment Disorder no one will teach you to tell the difference, and you won't have even thought to talk about a lack of conscience in class none of your case studies will have covered a lack of conscience either and you will be thoroughly educated in child abuse and neglect but will somehow have missed the part about parents who absolutely lack a conscience and how to identify them as being different from any other troubled parents you might meet. Was the issue featured in the series of four volumes on Child Welfare that you purchased and pored over? Was a lack of conscience the focus of some class that you missed? No. Later, when you learn to recognize a "lack of empathy," you will find it attached to phrases like "disruptive" and "criminal record," and you won't know to apply it anywhere else. You won't remember what you might have missed you will think *maybe I should've picked up a class in criminology* you will wonder to yourself why a lack of conscience might have been separated out from every other area and pinned exclusively to criminals why a lack of conscience wasn't something that you were ever trained to detect. Was there a screen you could have learned about? Was it a special skill reserved for the FBI? Was it deemed completely irrelevant for those focused on school social work or veterans or family systems or individual adult therapy? What about screening for foster parents? You'll wonder if it's because you're in social work instead of psychology, but then you'll wonder again, later, why so many psychologists remain so vocal about having more and better training than anyone else in the field when every psychologist you've ever met but one will also have lacked these identification skills entirely when it seems nearly every psychologist you meet has no real ability to detect deception. You will wonder, later, why the assessment training appears to have been reserved for the CIA and the FBI *is it because we as a society don't want to imagine that any other professionals will need the skills? And what about attorneys? What about training programs for guardian ad litems or anyone involved in approving care for all the already traumatized and marginalized children?* You'll have met enough of those children after they grow up to know that when a small girl experiences repeated rapes in a series of households throughout her childhood, then that little girl is pretty likely to have some sort of "dysfunction" when she grows up. And you won't have any tolerance for the people who point their fingers at her and demand that she be as capable as they are *it is, after all, a free country. We all get the same opportunities.* You'll want to scream at all those equality people that *you can't ignore the rights of this nation's children* you can't ignore them and then get pissed when any raped and beaten little girls and boys grow up to be traumatized and perhaps hurtful or addicted adults. No more pointing fingers only a few random traumatized people stand up later as some miraculous example of perfectly acceptable societal success and if every judgmental person imagines that *I would be like that I would be the one to break through the barriers* then all those judgmental people need to go back in time and prove it, prove to everyone that *life is a choice and we all get equal chances.* You'll want anyone who talks about equal chances to go back and be born addicted to drugs in complete poverty and then to be dropped into a foster system that's designed for good but exploited by people who lack a conscience by people who rape and molest and whip and beat tiny little six year olds and then you will want all those people to come out of all that still talking about equal chances and their personal tremendous success. *Thank you, dear God, for writing my name on the palm of your hand.*

You will be angry and yet you still won't understand the concept of evil. You'll learn enough to know that it's not politically correct to call anyone *evil,* especially when many terrible acts might actually stem from a physiological deficit *I would never use the word evil, it's not professional* but you will certainly come to understand that many of the very worst crimes are committed by people who lack the capacity to feel remorse for what they've done on any level. But when you gain that understanding, you still will not have learned that these individuals are more likable than most people that they aren't cool and distant that they aren't just a select few creepy murderers or high-profile con artists you won't know how to look for a lack of conscience in noncriminal and quite normal looking populations no clinical professors will have warned you about people who exude charm and talk excessively about *protecting the family* or *protecting the community* or *protecting our way of life* and you won't know that these types would ever stick around to raise kids you will have falsely believed that *if*

229

they can't form real attachments, they won't bother with raising children and besides most of them will end up in prison you will not know that your assumptions are completely erroneous you won't understand that many who lack a conscience keep their kids close and tight for their own purposes. You won't know for years and years that all your struggles and attempts to deal with Wyatt were just a waste of time because he's always been more dangerous than anyone anticipated or identified. You won't have ever found one ounce of protection or justice. You won't have found the peace of knowing. All because no one not a single professional in your divorce not a single clinical professor in your university not a single victim's advocate or attorney or psychologist or therapist not one single person involved will know how to see him clearly and no one will be able to tell you how to deal with the man when you can't get away from him when you have to raise children with him. Not one textbook not one self-help book will be able to answer that question. And that won't have been a flaw of your particular graduate program, it will quite simply be the way of the system you'll only later come to notice the widespread lack of professional training and community interest in understanding and you'll learn to see the void only by falling right in.

So let's talk about that fall.

Let's start with beliefs. When you filed for divorce, you will have automatically believed that the court system would work to be honest and equitable and especially to protect your children. *We protect the nation's children.* But when you share the word *abuse* with your attorney, he will choke a little on his coffee *now we don't want to get into all of that, unless you have any emergency room records?* You will have said *no he didn't break bones* you won't have considered all the times you went in to the ER gasping for breath or needing an IV for dehydration. *But I did dig up some police records from when he choked his ex-girlfriend they're pretty telling does it help if he has a history?* You'll discover

230

that no, not really, the court won't care much about that if it was from before you were married. *But I have some recordings of him threatening me? My life? And some other stuff? Like when he said that if I leave him he'll make sure I miss my children.* You will have stockpiles of journals and calendars and photos and tapes. He will say *don't bother. I wouldn't even bring it up the court doesn't react well to women who bring up abuse.* You will interview ten or twelve other attorneys, and they will all agree. This will infuriate you. The fact that the court is not interested in hearing or understanding issues of abuse—especially when there are children involved and especially when the court when the court becomes incredibly interested later in your dating life—will infuriate you, and it will fire you up even more when the court later tells you that adultery might be the *grounds for divorce* and the adulteress will be *you.* You will curse the private investigator who advised you *don't bother gathering evidence or hiring me because none of this adultery stuff really matters the court just wants to divide stuff up and get on with it* you will sit on the stand and answer question after question about every reason why you're incredibly spoiled and completely insane and absolutely slutty and why you've always been a terrible mom pawning your children off on other people and why you never had a connection with them and why you never did one worthwhile thing or contributed financially you will answer all these questions in a monotone you will answer them in a near shout the magistrate will butt in over and over *counsel, will you tell your client to speak up* or *counsel, will you tell your client she can't ask questions* you will remember that private investigator's advice and think *FUCK YOU you fucking asshole the court ABSOLUTELY DOES CARE and they especially seem to love petty gossip and now no one knows the TRUTH!* You will sit on the stand you will be treated like a criminal for days the opposing counsel will look at you with complete and unbridled disgust your attorney will ask you later why the opposing counsel's so vicious he will ask whether you have any idea *does that man have a personal vendetta against your family* you will say *I've never met him my family doesn't know him* your attorney will ask you whether you're absolutely sure he will tell you *I've been doing this for 35 years, and this is the worst case I've seen in my life.*

And in those moments when you watch Wyatt captivate the court room you will think *injustice* and you will be flabbergasted over the fact that you've been silenced that your real story only makes people look down on you more or blame you more or see you as more of a liar while it does nothing to inspire a good look at the man who's the perpetrator. In fact, the court will seem to feel quite sorry for the guy he'll get up on the stand and cry for the first time in his life over some story he's made up about the kids *I've always been there for them kind of like their rock they've never gotten very close to their mom she's just so unstable so I guess you could say I've been like their number one parent* and he'll say that he's brokenhearted over the way you split the family that he's brokenhearted over the way you hurt them all so much and that he's devastated by the time when you were screaming at them that they couldn't have their Dad anymore and they were clinging to him crying and sobbing *Daddy, Daddy, please don't go please don't let Mommy make you leave* you'll be flabbergasted by these outrageous lies you will tell your parents later *he is flat out LYING on the stand! Who lies on the stand you can't lie on the stand he took and oath and he's still lying on the stand he's sitting up there and putting on a show! He even whipped up some tears and choked on them a little he is making things UP! His story about the kids crying over him is crazy what happened is he snuck into the house and picked them all up in his arms and started telling them that mommy was trying to make him go away forever and that mommy didn't want them to see their daddy ever again and that he might never get to see them again in all their lives and he started clutching them and they had no idea what was happening and they started sobbing they asked my why I would make daddy go away forever they didn't want daddy to go away forever and I told them that I'm not doing that and I told him to leave and I tried to hug them but he just clutched them tighter and started wailing and saying see, I told you that mommy's trying to get rid of me she wants me to leave and they were an absolute wreck I spent hours trying to help them recover after I finally got him to leave I think he only left because he got them to the point of near hysteria and who does that to their kids and when he was leaving he looked back at me and smiled an 'I win' kind of smile and now he's twisting it all around in court how can he lie like that how can he do these things?* Your mom and dad will listen to this story and tell you to make sure that your windows are locked *don't ever leave them open* your brother will go out and buy you a big giant dog. *That man is a professional phony. He's going to take down his own children to get to you and in my mind that makes him a very dangerous man. If he finds you alone with no witnesses, he will kill you.* You will not take this in completely you will still be stuck on the idea of a soft spot inside every person you will think *that man was my husband didn't he love me at some point isn't that why he's so mad right now wouldn't that soft spot stop him short of killing me but then I guess I should be smart about this what if his anger was too big or what if it was too late?* You'll buy window alarms and door alarms and you'll let the dog roam the house you will never have known to consider that he might not have a soft spot even after you complete your graduate degree and advanced clinical program you still won't know that some very normal and noncriminal human beings just don't come wired that way and like everyone else, you won't have known to worry that he might be cold-blooded he *looks too all-American to lack remorse he doesn't really have the capacity to take down children without regret he clearly loves his children he's just a mess right now* you won't even have known to worry about a lack of a guiding conscience but what you and most of the professionals involved *will* think is that *she must be doing something wrong.* Or at best they might think *this is a very angry man a very, very angry man and divorce brings out the worst in people but given time he'll get bored and go back to his normal ways.* They won't care about your history they won't care about his history they won't ask you any helpful questions they won't want you to volunteer any information. You won't know that evil when left unidentified often gathers force in groups that it often seeps into systems that are designed for good, molding up their interiors with a wet stench and fusing up

233

their joints. You won't know to put together the words *systemic evil* even after friends advise you that the magistrate will blame you for everything that the magistrate is a hard ass toward women that the magistrate won't *ever* let you go back to your farm *I know one woman who fled with her daughter after a beating from her husband with nothing not even with her glasses and when she asked to go back and get them later this magistrate said you're the one who left without them, so no, you can't go back.* You won't know to use the words *systemic evil* even after you complete months of research on domestic violence issues in the United States even after you start complaining that there are gaps in the system and most courts especially rural courts treat battered women very terribly, so terribly that most attorneys will advise those women not to bring it up at all because it will lead to a lot of angry and humiliating questioning and in most cases a far more negative outcome. You will be outraged by this *who's going to protect the kids involved when battered women can't even tell their truth* your attorney will tell you *listen, you don't understand something, the court doesn't protect children the court doesn't care about children the law treats children like property of their parents so when you divorce, you're basically dividing them up. And why would they give equal parts to a woman who lets herself get beat up.* This will piss you off even more you will rise out of your chair *how am I letting myself get beat up I LEFT and why is that my bad and not his and what about children's rights!?* He will turn to you coldly *you think children have rights? Children don't have rights. You have rights. Your ex has rights. Your children are your joint property. They don't have rights.* Even with the outrage and the disbelief and the rush of dizziness you'll feel over this news, you will still not know to utter the words *systemic evil.* You won't know how to consider that the system lacks empathy. That it lacks remorse or a conscience and that without careful external monitoring that it can and often will become completely corrupted by judges granting favors to hometown attorneys while ignoring perjury and lies with the result of ruining second chances and wrecking children's lives and taking honest people down by serving itself up as a weapon

234

of destruction and the court will not feel remorse for being used this way it will destroy every asset it will take the equity a woman could use to buy a house for her children and it will divide it all up between the attorneys the system will keep a conflict alive for years a clever attorney knows how to milk an angry man like a cash cow *we need to file we need to appeal we need to object and I have a lot of friends who are experts and the magistrate is friendly with them, too, so you should consider hiring them it will really boost your case* and when it's all said and done, the court and it's inherent systems will have no sense of responsibility for the destruction, the bomb doesn't feel bad when it rips open a city and the system can look its victim in the eye and say with great confidence *this is entirely your fault you're the one who married the guy and we're all just doing our jobs.* Meanwhile, you will have put two attorney's children through college with nothing left for your own you will owe more than thirty grand on a card you've been living on while any cash you had went to your counsel you'll have spent the entire four year process thinking *this will be over any minute and I'll have my equity and they'll lift the restraining orders and I'll move forward I need to move forward buying and selling property is the only way I've ever made any good money and my hands are tied and my resume is worthless and then there's school and I've got to get out of here this needs to end now* and yet it will not end when you think it will it will not end that year or the next year or the next year or the next you will lose your capacity to plan. *I can't make plans.* So when it finally does end, you will still owe your attorney even more than you have and by the time it's done, planning will be pointless he will own your blood he will own your everything he will even put an illegal lien on the one piece of sentimental property you might have left over he will take you out to his car during a morning break from maybe the fourth day of trial and spring a piece of paper on you *I drew something up now you know you owe me some money and we talked about needing to address that, right, so you can either sign this lien or I'm not going back in there today and you'll have to go back in by yourself* and by that time, you'll be so hopeless and scared and lost that you'll just sign the thing and then sit and stare at the trees and cry *that land was my grandpa's it's our family farm he gave us each ten acres he was born with nothing and worked his whole life to have it and did you know I grew up there* you will look over at your attorney and in his not-listening he will be busy putting the paper back into his leather bag you will climb out of his Mercedes and think quietly to yourself *I hate that man I hate everyone.* You will fantasize about throwing rocks at the courthouse pillars you will fantasize about smashing his perfectly clean car to pieces with nothing but a crow bar and your hands your heart will pound with the sensation of throwing things swinging things but he will pat you on the back and say *let's do this thing, now you need to speak up, remember, but don't say things that might make the magistrate mad do you need to use the restroom we have a long afternoon ahead of us.*

The most treacherous form of evil is often invisible. This form can shift to engage it can take on the appearance and expectation of justice and goodness. It will play on your sense of belonging it will make you think you're doing everything right it will make you think it's doing everything right it will make you believe that it cares for you it will raise its arms in exaltation it will use captivating language it will be fueled by power and money and control and when it sweeps in and fills a system of justice it will be nearly impossible to nail down because such a system is not inherently evil and therefore not every piece and part of its giant apparatus will necessarily be out for blood. Some parts will be good, some people will be good, and that goodness will keep us hopeful and when we're hopeful we're most easily blinded. We're most likely to ignore discrepancies or to blame individuals or groups for their own fate when the inherently good system points itself at them and devastates their lives. With hope, we can feel that we're legitimately teaching our children that it's all good and that it's all about justice and that it's all about making things right.

And then those children will grow up. Like you, many of them will have ingrained beliefs about *the way things are*. You will take justice for granted you will believe that any historic or current flaws in the system are or will be naturally self-correcting you will believe that people who work for justice are actually and honestly working for justice you will believe that the people who work for justice are deeply and unwaveringly working to protect children and human rights and equality.

You will be wrong.

You will learn about evil in court you will learn even more about evil through your social work program. You will learn for the first time about recent eugenics programs and mandatory hysterectomies for fourteen year old girls all over the southern U.S. you will learn about poverty you will learn about homelessness you will learn that no one really knows how little is spent on social services in the United States you will wonder what kinds of conversations about budget everyone's trying to avoid by constantly talking about people on welfare when those people are not even taking a recognizable piece of the federal budget. *When you look at a pie chart, it's almost not even a slice. If it's practically invisible, then why do we talk about it the most have you ever thought about that.* You will learn about legislation that works against children in the United States and your old belief that we're the most protective and safe country to grow up in *in the world* will be dashed against the rocks along with your hope and your dignity and your faith in justice. You will learn that bribery and corruption doesn't only happen in the small courts of other countries. You will learn that money wins the case every time that the person who either doesn't have any or runs out first is guaranteed to take a loss and then have their nose rubbed in it over and over and over again—for as long as the aggressor likes. You will learn *that's what we call justice.* You will learn that most courts absolutely despise stay-at-home moms you will read the research and then you will sit on the stand while they mock your choices and laugh at you and your worthlessness outright even the court recorder will join in for those jokes the only straight faces in the room will be you and your attorney and the court martial. You will not cry. You will learn what it means to despair.

You will want to talk about the gaps that no one else cares to talk about *did you know about these huge gaps in the system* you will call your professors you will set up meetings you will call all the local domestic violence shelters you will arrange visits to the victims' unit you will call local violence prevention programs you will call national violence prevention organizations you will tell them *we need a consistent definition did you know that no one has ever agreed on a clear definition of battering how can anyone work together when the victims' advocates will screen you according to one definition of battering and confirm that yes you have absolutely been battered you have been isolated and controlled and beaten down and coerced and used and threatened and damaged and you need some help and then you will go to the cops and they will look at their definition for the word and tell you that no, you haven't been battered at all and that the only way a person can be battered is if they're physically assaulted and we can see the marks. That's it. And this legal definition of battering or domestic violence is even more troubling because lots of non-abusive and non-battering people can make a one-time mistake of physical violence when overwhelmed by emotion and then this one-timer may end up with a record that labels this person as a 'batterer' which can wreck that person's life but then there are smarter batterers who know you can choke someone to death in just a couple minutes with no marks and you can isolate another human being and treat them like a prisoner of war and devastate them in every way and hurt them physically without breaking bones and then this smarter and much more consistent and insidious batterer will know that all of these things fall outside of the legal definition of 'battering' and so they will never get a record they will never get a label and they will be empowered to sliver through life ruining and devastating everyone around them, including children. This insidious batterer can meet every criteria for every part of*

238

the definition of battering as presented by every domestic violence organization and every shelter and every victims' advocate in the nation but it won't matter when the victim goes to court because there will be no legal definition that aligns with the screenings and definitions that these organizations use to help victims see the 'truth' and begin to find help and begin to find 'hope'. So when these victims then go to the system of justice it will be more like they're bumping up against it and their 'hope' for justice will only serve to re-traumatize them because it's not going to be served let me tell you I've been there and all it does is create horrible confusion when all these people tell you that you've been wronged and that your experience is real and that you should find protection and justice and then you go for protection and justice and those people say what the hell is your problem because this is very clearly your problem because we don't see any records of broken bones and so what exactly are you trying to do here are you trying to take those kids away from their dad with your false accusations because that's not going to get you anywhere and don't come into this court talking about abuse if you can't back it up with X-rays. You will tell everyone that there's a gap *a huge gaping hole* and that no task force will make a difference until all the institutions agree on the definition of battering until all the people who might possibly make a difference see the value of screening and know the working definition of what they're screening for and see the value of taking extra precautions to protect not the rights of the perpetrator but to protect the rights of any potential victims including and especially any children involved because people who batter rarely stop with other adults people who batter most generally abuse children, too.

You will learn that the system of justice has deviated from its essential and foundational purpose. You will learn that good people may spend their lives trying to make justice but you'll be lucky if you ever encounter one of those individuals in the court itself. You will learn that evil comes in through every weak point through every flawed human being and that evil not only corrupts the person but starts to shift the entire way the system moves forward, almost like an epigenetic effect.

The system may struggle to self-correct, but most any honest and non-aggressive human being's experience of the system will be devastating and debilitating on every level. You will learn that the people you hire to help you navigate through the mire will devour your assets and your faith in general goodness along the way. You will have no choice but to walk through the process *you married the government* and there will be no way to leave unless you leave your children and all hope behind. You will stay the course you will not leave your children behind and you will maintain hope that something will shift that there might be some way that the people or the process won't destroy you. They will mostly destroy you.

You will learn about evil.

17.
FULL CUSTODY

Relationships don't end.
Things you thought you'd
fully experienced
and even finished
are buried deep in your flesh and bones and
they come back to you
in ways you see
and in ways you don't
over and over

again and again.

You will know what it means to live as a ghost of yourself on the outskirts of society. You will watch yourself walking through the grocery store from the outside you will wash your dishes you will resent the dirty cobwebs in the window above your sink you will think about all the cleaning energy you had when you were young *I wouldn't live with windows like that* you will walk away and turn on the TV you will be tired. You will be so tired you will be ready to put on your pajamas every day at four *if I could just have a month to go lay down somewhere* you will wish you had enough energy for more school *I want to go back to school for more I want to be an activist I want to do work that makes a difference* you will wish you had more energy for reading and research you will wish you were conducting fascinating interviews and that you had more

241

energy for writing poetry and painting canvases and baking pies for your children you will need more energy than you have for work you will need more creativity than you have for everything you will take on a few big projects, anyway, you will try to build a private practice as a therapist but it will not take off as quickly as you'd hoped *it takes so much networking and now we live 45 minutes away from the city and my kids need me out here and I need to do brand writing it's where I'm already established and I need to be better at balancing all this and I do want this practice to go and I want to do research I want to write I need to pay all these bills how am I going to pay any of these bills* so you will work mostly as a brand writer you will even work a little at brand strategy and on good days you will point out where it all intersects with psychotherapy *doesn't everything* but you will never feel as wholly able to invest yourself in anything as your colleagues sitting around the table you will watch them racing to wrap up a project so they can get to their boat for the weekend you will wonder what it would be like to have a house or a boat or even your own car anymore *how do people get there why am I still struggling along I'd love to go rest my brain on a boat on a Friday night* you will watch your colleagues celebrate their children's acceptance into different clubs and programs you will long for your own children you will wish you could take a week off with them and sit on a boat together maybe eventually the sunshine and swimming would help them stop feeling so angry toward you and maybe they would begin to speak even just casually even just to tell you that they caught a fish *I think I got one* you will remind yourself that you need to concentrate more on the work right in front of you so you will focus all your might on climbing out of the fog you will concentrate on concentrating you will long to shine *I want to fully invest in these projects I want to start even one day with a full well with a full tank I want to get out of bed with excitement over normal human things I'm so tired of forcing I'm tired of forcing everything I want to get dressed in clothes that aren't already worn out I want to breeze in with confidence instead of scramble scramble scramble I don't want to rally up some fake kind of excitement over the work I want to be truly excited about the work I want to feel it for real I want to feel excitement* *over anything and I want it to be for real* you will attend client meetings you will sit with clients and try to stay focused you will work to stay focused on the importance of the work for the client *this is about the client* everyone around you will have stressed out for days over the work for the client it will have been like a life-and-death moment was just waiting waiting waiting right around the corner you will watch your colleagues sweating bullets you will watch your colleagues sprinting up and down hallways you will watch your colleagues working to please you will watch the director freaking out over small changes you will wonder how freaking out people still get to be in charge you will wish you freaked out a little more over those kinds of things you will long for freaking out over normal details you will long for a fully engaged moment when you could know you were doing your best you will watch your clients watching you they will be waiting for you to blow their minds with some *shit-hot-strategy-and-creative* you will want it to matter so much that you'll be sweating bullets in your heart you will want to dedicate yourself wholly to the work but when you're presenting as a writer you will have a harder time pulling through you will look at the clients around the table and think also through the fog of your oldest son and the way he dreaded dinner with you this week on his thirteenth birthday *why do I have to see you, Mom, it's not like I have to see you just* *because you're my mom* you won't have seen him for weeks you will have purchased hopeful tickets for four on a zip-line and he will not want to go *you're just trying to buy my love you're just a* *trickster maybe if you'd stop lying to Dad for five seconds then anyone* *would want to spend time with you* you will work to put this out of your mind you will pour a cup of coffee you will work to connect to shake hands all around you will pour yourself another cup of coffee you will think about better sleep *I've got* *to get some better sleep* you will shake a few more hands you will work to manage the process you will work to remain engaged you will work to laugh over the blog your colleague set up for her European tour she and her doting husband will want everyone to watch their every move they'll even come up with a trip jingle that they've recorded together *that's so adorable* you will work to remain fascinated with the names of new restaurants you will practice maintaining genuine interest you will practice suspending everything but the present moment but then you will go home to your tickets for the zip-line and you will watch a documentary on *social death* and you will sob into your popcorn bowl for hours in self-recognition *I am dead in so many ways I am dead and who was I before, anyway, who owns these hands who owns these hands.* You will stare out the window without thought and wonder what you were looking at and where the time went, later. You will *rally* you will do what it takes to stay connected to the normal you will tell your son that you're going to pick him up for the zip-line no matter what and you will take him out to dinner his dad will call him five times as you sit together over your hot wings his dad will call you four times as well his dad will eventually leave you a message that he's absolutely infuriated *I see how you are I'm just trying to have a conversation about our parenting plan but you're just never available now are you you're just never available so you can forget next weekend with Abby if you can't even have a grown-up conversation then I'm not going to cooperate with your ridiculous requests* you will finally respond by text *you know I'm having birthday dinner leave me alone* he will leave you one more message *I'm just trying to have an adult conversation but that's obviously impossible with you so think about that next weekend because Abby's not coming with you how's that for karma maybe you should try caring about your daughter more than your food* you will try not to get upset you will turn off your phone and concentrate on your time with your son he will receive six more texts from his dad plus a call and at the end of the night he will ask *can you just drop me off at Dad's* you will feel sad you will feel empathetic you will know that there's no other acceptable choice he can make his dad will have texted him fifteen or twenty times altogether that evening his dad will never let him live in peace with you, the enemy. No, at every event his dad will check on him thirty times to make sure he's doing ok in your apparently ominous presence *are you doing ok with her and I bet Matt's acting like a total loser that's hilarious* and he'll say *I bet her whole family is acting all obsessed with each other like always and it's crazy how your Papau can act like things are so normal when he's totally lying to you that's just crazy, isn't it, well I really miss you, son, so act like an angel and keep them guessing only we have to know the truth and I can't wait to see you so text me as soon as you can and I'll just swing out and pick you guys up I'll get you out of there* and as a boy what he'll come to know is that he only feels peace when you're not around. He will know that he only feels peace when he laughs with his dad when they read your emails out loud *your daughter will protest later Dad reads your emails and texts out loud and they all laugh at you but if I read them over his shoulder he's not telling us what they really say and if I tell him then he tells me to be quiet that I don't know what I'm talking about but he's lying, Mom, and they all laugh at you.* You will feel sad for her you will feel sad for your sons you will remind yourself *I've been caught in that trap, too* you will understand their position *they love their dad and I understand how engulfing he can be, he can be the best thing in the world and he's really fun and he makes this their only choice and if they act like they love me they get punished. And he's made me into the other, the evil force, and so any person who hangs at my house must be a crazy loser like me and those boys don't want to be crazy and you know what, in their world, it looks like this whole small town community is backing them up on it. The whole world outside of us, and so they block out my whole family and their dad has them believing that even my parents are deceitful liars and when any of us try to connect with them he convinces them that we're chasing them around like stalkers and that it's not normal and that we're trying every day to ruin their lives. It's so backwards but how would they know. It's so confusing. And Levi plays with his little cousins on my side but how long will that last. Gabe won't spend time with any of us since we've moved out here her he's stopped staying with me at all he'll hardly spend the night here and it was torture for him to come for Christmas.* You will not know how to comfort your children you will not know how to draw the line you will cry when you talk to your mom you will stare across your yard

245

why won't the boys throw the ball in this yard you will run your fingers down the clothes in their closet *why don't they miss their things* you will cry to Matt you will take ten photos every time you see them you will try to take a piece of them with you when they leave and you will stretch out every moment you will post photos of smiling children on Facebook you will act like nothing's wrong *no one on the outside can fathom what's happening here, anyway, and if I start talking about what's really happening, most people will just distance themselves from me they will start to wonder what's wrong with my whole family why the kids would push away from their mother which leads straight into blame and people saying that their kids would never do that or that you can never break a connection with a mother if she's any good but I don't know why we think that rock hard soldiers can be completely brainwashed as prisoners of war but not pre-adolescent boys who are looking for answers from their father about what it looks like to be a man and I have no idea why people think that alienation can't happen or that it's not as deep as it really is even my dean blew me off and said that relations with ex's are just difficult and my situation will smooth out soon but it's been six years since I left and Wyatt still fires up the boys every single day and no one but me seems to notice that it's poison for them and it's not fair for their lives but if no one can hear what I'm saying then what's the point in sharing when even the court system only make things worse for the kids and there's never any enforcement because parenting plans are apparently unenforceable* so you will scramble to project a normal life *people reject you when you're down* you will scramble to build a career *it's going well and we're so excited* you will motivate friends and colleagues to run races with a steady flow of weekly emails *this is the week for eight miles and it's time to start thinking about some mantras that can help you through* you will give money you don't have to charities *we all have more than anyone else so even if I'm in debt I want to teach my children how to give* you will blog about raising children and sticking to your values you will post photos of your daughter washing eggs and holding fluffy yellow chicks you will babysit your nieces and nephews *sure, I always have time for you* you will treat your friends to lunch even when you're buried in debt *I used to be the best with money and now I don't even feel like I care what's the point all my saving and investing amounted to nothing it's all been given to him and my attorney and it's all just an illusion in life and it's either going to miraculously fix itself or I'll die tomorrow, anyway* you will listen to your friends worry and fret and stress over their budgets you will think they actually have it pretty good *no kids and together they're making three times what I do* you will never tell them your opinion you will have long lost your interest and capacity to see anything you do as having any kind of impact on your future you won't even be able to visualize a future any more all it will be is gray blank space and so you'll say *don't worry about it, I'll treat* and you will tell yourself later *I can't stand worrying about money I can't stand listening to rich people obsessing over how much they don't have when everyone around me has plenty.*

You won't have plenty you won't have any money left at all you won't have credit to start over but what you will have is a deep hole of debt you will pay for $1.25 of gas with your last five quarters and vow *never again—never, ever again* only to find yourself pumping out $.75 more not two days later using some change you found on your parents' kitchen counter. You will remember the way you used to make your budgets and follow them with no doubt that you could make a difference that you could build your dreams and you will remember the way you used to make scrapbooks and party invitations and birthday calendars *I was a different human being I miss that innocence that idea that things matter.* You will long to feel things like that again you will remember what it felt to make dinner for a man and serve it with candles and crazy panties and a smile but you will not make romantic dinners you will not make scrapbooks you will not take joy in creating small mementos of love you will join with a fairly non-romantic man and you will live quietly together you will hold his bent arm as you walk you will teach him the names of the birds on the feeder and he will teach you the names of every mushroom in the yard and you will cherish his patience and you will cherish his voice and you will cling to him sometimes

247

at night and you will sometimes push him away and you will laugh with him and you will cry. He will wipe your tears he will run his fingers across your hair he will sometimes cry, too *I had no idea it was going to be this hard.* You will want to save him from the conflict you will be sure that he's eventually going to leave because no human being would stick around for so much loss willingly so you will try sometimes to package all the alienation up in a box *we don't need to talk about this every day I want it to go back to the way it was when we were first together I want to be more freely loving remember that snow day when I jumped on your chest with that bottle of champagne and popped the cork down the hall and we had mimosas all morning long? I want to be like that again.* You will be afraid of losing him especially because your ex will start to insert himself everywhere in your lives he will use the boys' phones to access your online cloud of photos and documents, your Netflix, and even your texts back and forth to each other until you and Matt don't feel like you can have a real conversation over the phone because Wyatt might be listening especially when Wyatt starts to make direct quotes to you from your private conversations. And then Wyatt will start to label Matt as a loser to anyone willing to listen and he won't feel any obligation to tell the truth he will say *I don't think that guy has ever worked in his life and he doesn't even own that house what a loser and he's such a weirdo you should see him working out in their garage with a sandbag like he's some kind of badass or something you should see it he's such a joke he takes breaks every five seconds and they don't even mow their own grass why in the world would you even have a yard if you can't mow your own grass what is wrong with them that's so weird I swear you guys do not want to grow up to be like him you should actually look at anything he does and try to grow up to be the opposite of that.* Your boys will learn that if they screw up that they're *pulling a Matt* or *doing it the Matt way.* You will wonder *who would listen to that shit? It's ridiculous and what do people care and why is any of that his business and what does anybody else know about us and why would they care* but people will care you and Matt will live on the outskirts of the parent population in your little small town everyone will hear all about you from your ex and you will never enter a room or a gymnasium without a tremendous sense of anxiety about who will or won't talk to you and who will turn their head away but you will fake it you will insist *this is not going to ruin my life I'm going to volunteer to be Team Mom* you will try you will invite new people to meet up for happy hour or cards six or eight times before you give up *the Fitzpatricks just cancelled, too, maybe we're not that much fun maybe we're kidding ourselves* you will still have your friends back in the city you will have your families you will know what you stand for *Matt is an amazing therapist and I am an amazing therapist and I can write pretty well and we both have to live with meaning we can't just plow along* you will feel like you're plowing along you will rally yourself you will chase the boys down after their games to connect even for thirty seconds and Matt will try to keep it positive, too, *Good Game, Gabe* even when Gabe won't look in his direction or acknowledge his voice you will reassure yourselves *some parts of this are completely normal* you will text and tweet positive little tidbits to them you will post more photos you will smile for the camera you will never complain in public or show up in cut off sweats and you will not flinch or yell when Wyatt suddenly drives away as you're talking to Levi through his rear window. Instead, you'll jump back a bit so your toes won't get run over and you'll smile and wave *Bye, Levi! Talk to you later!* Then you'll complain to yourself *I think he'd quit these antics and leave me alone maybe if I really was alone if I'd live in subsidized housing far away and if I'd show up in cut off sweats then he would calm down some I think the court expected that, too. It's like if you leave your man, be prepared to lose it and they never believed I brought anything of value to that relationship, anyway* but you will not give him the satisfaction of whining in public you will rally you will stand tall you will do what it takes to keep up the lie. That you have a steady life. That your boys haven't cut you out completely. *No one understands and it's so easy for him to convince every person on earth that every part of everything is my fault. That it's karma. That I'm the one doing the alienating—keeping him from his daughter. He leaves her with me, which I love. But I call him and ask him when he wants to arrange to pick her up for his time just because I feel required to. But he leaves her with me, anyway, he doesn't pick her up and he even just assumes I'll pick her up and take care of her after school regardless of what day it is. And then he yells at me that I have no rights to my time with the boys because I'm the one who keeps Abby from him all the time. I can't help it if he doesn't pick her up. But he says it so much and so often that everyone believes it. The boys chime right in and yell at me, too. Everything is my fault. Everything is my fault. I feel so frustrated but more than anything I feel so bad for those guys. I've been where they are. Lost in smoke. He doesn't care if he ruins their lives. If he trashes their relationships. All he cares is that they do what he wants and that they bring him glory. If they cross him, he will take them down.*

They have no right to be or become who they are.

They will be who he wants them to be, or they will suffer and die. To him. Like me.

And history will have been rewritten. Your boys will believe that every ounce of conflict and frustration they've ever experienced in their lives will have come as a direct result of something you did they will drop friends who have any positive relation to you they will drop girlfriends if they find out the girl's parents have always known you they will reject the kids who live in your neighborhood after their dad has a long talk with them about how he thinks that *townie kids are either goth or ghetto-gangsta and you guys seriously don't want to be associated with kids like that you don't want to hang with kids who live in town what a bunch of freaks* so they will distance them from whole groups of people they will become suspicious of anything unlike their father they will learn to hate their own talents if there's a hint that they came from you they will despise and eventually reject entire populations and phases of their lives.

And as an enemy, you will lose all power to impact them as a parent. If you tell them to call you right away, their dad will say *don't worry about it are you going to play Call of Duty with me or not it's now or never and I'm seriously not waiting around* if you tell them that you're going to turn off their phones if they don't answer any of your calls their dad will laugh *I bet you ten bucks she won't turn them off what a joke. Seriously, bet me ten bucks.* They will place bets and he will intercept or monitor every single call or text you make. They will never have a conversation with you that doesn't stir up some turmoil from their dad he will stand right beside them at every moment and tell them what to say and if one of them happens to sneak and call you from the school bus for a private conversation, he will get it when he gets home. So they'll stop calling you at all and they'll be so well-trained that their dad will be able to say *you should call your mom* when company's over and they'll know to say *no* and they'll mean it. Because it's all about appearances and Wyatt likes to tell people that he encourages them to spend time with you *but they just won't have anything to do with her* and they'll be well-trained enough after a few years to know exactly what to say and do every time. And so you'll hardly get to talk to them at all and if you tell them that you're not going to turn their phones back on until they commit to returning calls from you and their aunts and uncles and grandparents, their dad will tell them to ignore you *just ignore them they're so obsessive and I'll get you new phones I'm paying for those with all that child support, anyway, so what can she say she never sticks with anything so just blow her off.* If you tell them that you're picking them up for family dinner whether they want to come or not, their dad will tell them to *say no just ignore her just don't answer the door just stay in the basement you don't have to see her you're old enough to decide and if she complains to the court all you'll have to do is speak up and the court will let you stay with me full-time, anyway. You're old enough and you don't want to be with her. Period. End of story. So we can take this to court and you can just tell them that you never want to see her again. Tell them the truth. I'll stand up for you. You want to go hang out with those losers for some family dinner don't they get together every single week isn't that weird what are they obsessed with each other and do you even want to be part of that it's just not normal and no, I didn't think so. You don't have to do what she says we all know you want to stay with me full-time, anyway. When are you going to tell her that you guys need to tell her that.*

You will struggle to keep a connection. You will tell them each week that you want to have your normal schedule that you want your time with them and that you love them and you want to see them. You will keep showing up for your time but they will say *no* and hide in Wyatt's car or basement and he will always be there to get them, even when you're trying to pick them up at school on your time and only once in a while under his direction they might say *yes and can you take me shopping for school supplies and then drop me back off at Dad's* or *can you take me to Dick's I need some new basketball shoes and then drop me off at Dad's* you will always say *yes* because you want them to have school supplies you want them to have shoes that fit you will pick them up whenever they call you for a ride to practice when they're out at Wyatt's house alone *at least we'll have a little time together in the car* and every time it will be *can you just drop me back off at Dad's*. You will not argue with them after your first few tries you will have given that up you will hug them and you will try not to fight. *We only get moments together. I have to calm things down and be steady. I have to try. Or else every brief moment we have will be a fight, and there will never be a chance to repair. And I don't want that.*

And they will come to you stirred up for a fight. Ready to defend their dad's honor they will come to you on fire they will come to you with an agenda every time. *So, Mom, I need you to explain something to me. Can you tell my why you think it's ok to take child support from Dad?* Or something like *Mom, we're not going to your stupid church you don't even have a real church can you tell me why we should go with you when Dad's going to a real church and why do you even go to church, anyway. Maybe you should listen harder. Maybe you should let Abby go with Dad for once instead of always keeping her away and Abby, you need to go back to Dad's with us and mom, you never let her come to Dad's so stop keeping Abby from Dad* you will sometimes mistakenly argue *do you not know that she spent five days straight with your dad last week and when was the last time you spent even one day here what makes you think you can ride her like that all the time?* They will call you a liar *Mom, you're such a liar and all you do is lie to Dad she never spent five days there you are such a liar, Mom. Abby, you need to come stay at Dad's with us* if you forget to care for their experience and instead get lost in the facts and the words, it will go back and forth, back and forth, back and forth—and sometimes you will forget. It will sometimes go well and sometimes it will go terribly. You will most times keep it smooth but you will sometimes have had enough you will sometimes blow up or walk away you will get so tired of the constant, constant stream and you will feel yourself getting weaker you will feel yourself getting stronger you will feel yourself wanting a break but there will never be a break.

Just before Christmas, your oldest will cancel on a hike through the Grand Canyon with your parents—three days before they're supposed to leave. You'll be able to tell that Wyatt let it lie until the end so everyone could get their hopes up you'll also be able to tell that he then spent about four hours every evening of that last full week riding both boys about why they shouldn't go on the trip and why they should cancel at the last minute you'll be able to tell by the flow of texts they send you every evening that Wyatt will have Gabe all fired up about how your parents are trying to ruin his seventh grade sports and your parents will be devastated they'll have spent months planning the trip with the boys and everyone was so excited leading up to it and it was supposed to be your parents and their three oldest grandsons hiking into the canyon but in the end, Gabe and Levi will be so pressured to cancel that Gabe will nearly explode and Levi will hide at your house for the four days leading up to the trip he will get "sick" and ask out of nowhere to stay with you for the first time in six months he will call you and ask you to get him at school *I'm just too sick to go back to Dad's can you call him and tell him I just need to stay here my phone is dead so I can't call* and he won't have any symptoms other than an alleged stomachache but you'll rub his head and cover him with a blanket and let him stay you'll figure that he has his reasons and he will absolutely have his reasons and he will be the one to quietly head out on the airplane to Arizona and the anger will rain down on him when he gets back but at least he'll have figured out a way that he could go. But Gabe will be another story. He will stay that whole week before the trip alone with Wyatt and he will need an outlet all the four hour conversations will be more than he can contain and so when you stop out to pick up a few of Levi's things for the trip Gabe will come outside to rant through your car window about what a trickster what a liar you are he will describe all the ways he thinks you've tricked him and all the ways he thinks your parents have tricked him and his father will come out to watch he will sit behind him in a lawn chair with a delighted smile and it will continue for five minutes before Matt will have listened to enough of the disrespect and anger and hate and misinformation he will have been watching Wyatt's happy expressions in the rearview mirror the whole time Gabe was ranting and he will want to make a difference so he will calmly step out of the car and walk to Wyatt and ask a dangerous question a very dangerous question *is this how you want your son to talk to people do you really want him to have relationships like this?* That's when the full out attack will hit for the next ten minutes you will hear nothing but your ex's voice laughing and cursing, both you and Gabe will turn your heads to watch in shock Wyatt will stand right up to rant *you think you have it figured out, Matt? What a joke are you kidding me are you fucking kidding me? Who are you, you don't even own the house you're living in where do you even work do you even have a job? You don't even have a job, do you because no one knows what you do you sit around on my child support I own everything you have I own everything in that house and this is unbelievable I can't believe you would even talk to me*

254

about my sons you're an absolute and complete loser, Matt, you think you're a good example for anyone? Matt will stand in calm shock and contained rage you will hear him repeat *I'm a good man, Wyatt* over and over but Wyatt will only amp it up *you think you have some kind of prize here?* He will be pointing at you *I'll talk to you in ten years about that one you just wait you'll come talking to me about her that slut left me for her gynecologist, Matt, her gynecologist and you think you have some kind of a prize? You think you have some kind of prize? Well good luck with that one I'll talk to you in five years because nothing is good enough for that one absolutely nothing I was making $350,000 and what do you make? Nothing and that's because you're a mooch do you even have a job probably not no one knows what you do you live off your girlfriend and both of you live off of me but good luck with that one nothing's good enough for her she'll walk away from anything you know why because she's absolutely on the bubble that one she has mental issues she has serious mental issues you can talk to my mom and my sister, too, about that one so good luck with her she left me and she left the farm and even her doctor man didn't make enough for her she left him too she can't maintain a relationship with anyone men just walk right in and out her door so good luck with her and I'll talk to you in ten years and who are you, anyway, you're a total loser living off of other people the boys can't stand you for a reason because you're flat out weird and a mooch and you have obvious anger problems and so good luck with all that you call yourselves therapists and even your own kids hate you sounds like you need to study more how can she even give advice to anyone else when her own kids hate her I'm telling you these kids can't stand that woman and she still calls herself a therapist and who are you how do you like living on my money I'll talk to you in ten you are so unbelievable this is absolutely unbelievable you want to talk to me about how people turn out well why don't you look at yourself a total loser and good luck with her she doesn't stick with anything she'll just take what she can get and walk out the door this is so unbelievable absolutely unbelievable I cannot believe you would even talk to me like that I cannot believe you would even ask me such a ridiculous question you think my boys should turn out a loser like you that's absolutely ridiculous good luck with that this is so unbelievable I cannot believe you would even talk to me at all.*

You will not be able to take it at some point will jump out of the car and tell him to shut his mouth that he's a liar and you left him because he lies and he knows it he will rage on he will not hear a word you say Matt will repeat over and over *I'm a good man, Wyatt* or *she's a good person, Wyatt* sometimes Wyatt will pause to laugh in his face but mostly Wyatt will take giant pivoting steps toward him and away from him swinging his arms and pounding his fists in the air. Matt will stand still your children will be dumb-founded your daughter will start to sob in the back seat once you step out and speak up and then her brothers will try to pull her from your car to take her inside their dad's house she will grab the car handles screaming *NO! NO! NO!* you will walk around to take her from them and hold her she will cling to your neck they will tell you that they *hate you* you will tell them that you *love them* they will almost run away from you inside the house and you will get back in the car and shut the door and rock your daughter and turn on the radio and try to drown out the sound of Wyatt's ranting, raging voice you will see his body pivoting around the driveway in your rearview mirror. Eventually, Matt will simply walk away and will be back in the car, too, he will be pale-faced and stunned he will apologize right away *I'm so sorry, Abby. I'm so sorry I said anything I'm so sorry I said anything at all. I'm so sorry.* You will spend weeks and months sorting through that experience in your brains Matt will remain dumbfounded *I never thought it would go like that I'm so sorry. Here I specialize in character disorders and I didn't even see that one coming. I will never try that again.*

Later, you will hold him in your arms. *Don't worry, Matt. I've worked with hundreds of professionals by now. No one sees him. No one thinks he would do anything he does and he never shows that to anyone else so no one would ever see it coming no one even agrees with me that our kids need some therapy and I'm just glad he didn't hit you and I'm sorry I brought him into our lives I'm so sorry you have to deal with him at all.*

You will hold each other and cry. *The kids. The poor kids there has to be something in this world to help them how can we help them how can we make this better.* There will not be any apparent answers you will talk about attorneys you will talk about therapists you will know the court won't help you will talk to attorneys and therapists who agree *unless you have fifty grand ready to spend you'd be wasting your time* you will moan and tell your mom later *they love Wyatt up in that courthouse they'll crush me again and probably give him full custody no matter what I do* so you will talk about therapy and be advised that it won't work unless Wyatt agrees and Wyatt won't agree so you will talk about it some more you will talk about it for days you will talk about it for weeks you will talk about it for months you will talk about it for years.

How can anyone understand when no one else will ever see? When no one knows him. There's no way out.

You will despair. Despair will lead you to sometimes-phases of secret-self-destruction. You will stop exercising almost entirely you will forget to take your vitamins you will sit with a friend on a weekend alone and smoke his cigarettes while he plays the guitar. You will smoke one right after another until your lungs burn right along with your heart and your head will go numb you will feel good you will lay your head on his guitar and listen to him sing you will relax in the numbness you will follow the sound and then you will jolt back to the reality of what is. *Fuck the world that hurts my kids that hates me.* You will stay up too late ranting and raging in your journal. *Fuck the world. Fuck you. Fuck me.* You will drink wine you will drink more wine Matt will chop wood obsessively Matt will chop more wood. You will fire up your stove until the house is too hot for sitting you will crack a window and throw on five more logs *what are we going to do with ourselves. Somehow, we have to make a life. Somehow, we have to be able to ignore him if he knew he was at the center of so much turmoil if he knew how hard he was making it for us to envision a happy future there's no way to be happy when I know the kids are being hurt if he knew that his presence made a future seem almost unimaginable if he knew these things he would be enormously happy he would laugh and say it again he would say 'you need to stop being such a bitter person, Helen, you need to get on with your life' he would laugh all over again and say 'you familiar with karma, Helen?'* You will wish for his demise *I wish he would just disappear it's the only way the conflict will ever die* you will stare at the wood stove at the flames through the wine in your glass you will swirl it around and skip dinner you will not have any answers. You will have already asked all the questions. You will wonder what you're doing to keep the conflict alive *I want to stop the conflict I want to never talk to him again it seems like as long as I exist as a being, there will be conflict stirred up and pointed at me. I don't even have to respond to him for it to happen. I could move to China and it would follow me. I don't have to fight back. I only have to breathe.* You will go through times when you wish you didn't exist. *My children might know peace if I was gone. Eliminated from the earth. They might know a day of peace.* You will go through phases of disconnect. You will sit quietly and listen to your friends arguing and stressing and crying over a cat, absolutely overwrought by the way they'd suddenly acquired a cat from an ex *I can't believe he would just expect that I would take care of it I can't believe he would just make assumptions like that it's just like him and I just can't handle this again I can't stand how he expects me to be responsible he just assumes I'm there and we're right back to the same old fight it's so him. But you know, it feels good to talk about it thanks for spending some time listening I think if I take some personal time tomorrow to reflect on the whole thing I'll be ok but right now I just can't believe he'd just assume I want that cat* and you will work hard to connect with the emotion you will care enormously for your friend but you will also be plagued by secret jealousy of her worries you will wish they were your own you will wish you still lived at a high enough level to get worried about things like that you will wish you didn't feel so much like you were already dead.

Sometimes I feel like I'm already dead.

You won't tell your friends because you will only have a few close ones left it's just too hard for friends to linger when you're not available for afternoons of shopping it's just too hard for friends to understand your situation at all and they will have uniformly expressed that *we have to have standards and you're just not meeting our needs* you will explain that it's been a hard year or two you will explain that when it comes to your children you've had the hardest year of your life. They will not really know how to respond they will want to know whether your children are all that matter to you *we care for your ache but we want to matter, too, we don't feel like we matter anymore and it's hard to invest in someone who's not investing back* they will know more about how to respond to cat issues than to the loss of a child you will not know how to explain it all you will feel like an alien trying to explain another planet and the few friends you have left in the end will try to care for you and offer advice *maybe you could try saying something to your sons like it seems like you don't remember who I am and maybe that will help them realize and remember have you tried asking a question like that maybe I don't know what I'm saying but that's what's coming up for me.* You will love their effort you will lean over and lay your head on their shoulders and two of your friends will sit with you like that for as long as you need and you will warm in those moments and appreciate those two more than ever and you will want to feel on the inside of their lives but there will be an ache of aloneness-with-your-situation that will follow you wherever you go.

You will sit on a bus bench and watch homeless men and women on the sidewalk. You will watch their eyes you will watch their expressions you will think about God. These people are children of God. You will wonder where they came from who they called Mom when they were young. Who they called Dad. Where did they live? *Were people nice to this man? Did this woman worry over her eighth grade dance? Where did she get those shoes? Who bought her very first pair? Who taught her to walk? Does she have children? Does he? Where are they now?* You will wonder what keeps them on the outside. You will wonder if they fought in a war. You will wonder about longing and loneliness and the human spirit. *How far can it stretch? How far does it go? What keeps us all tied together? Are there times when we all fall apart?* You will wonder what it means to fall apart. Sitting on the bus bench, you will wonder. What it means.

You will go home. You will make dinners and clean up you will go to the movies you will send holiday cards and best wishes. You will schedule parents to work in the school concession stand you will plan the book fair you will long for stability and most of all for your absent children. You will walk through the halls of their schools you will meet with their teachers for updates when the boys refuse to share their homework and report cards. You will order more school photos online when your package never makes it to you from Gabe. You will look for connections you will want to know. How they're doing you will hang out around the edges and watch you will hang out around the edges and try to see. They will resent you they will tell you to stop trying. *Just leave me alone you're a stalker.* You will ask another set of parents over for dinner you will ask another set of parents out for drinks. They will cancel the week before they will cancel the day of. Wyatt will live happily at the center of the new parent groups and you will volunteer again to be Team Mom. You will miss your life in the city you will miss your children's neutral school from *before* you will miss the parents there who invited you into their homes you will miss the days when you sat in the evening light with those parents and watched their boys and your boys chasing each other around the yard with plastic swords you will mourn for your daughter's loss *she spent five years at that school and she's only eight years old that's a huge part of her life maybe I should've insisted that she stayed when her brothers left but it's 45 minutes away and I don't know how good it would be to have the boys so far away from her and I'm so broke but my heart just aches for her she misses her school* you will watch as she develops inexplicable stomach aches and you will take her to see a therapist when her pediatrician says that's what she needs and you will stand up for her right to make the same decisions her brothers make and you will hold her in your arms as she cries *I miss my old school I miss my old friends but don't tell anybody because Dad will totally freak out he hates that school but can we just go drive by it I really like that playground I just want to wave* and you will wonder whether you should move back you will feel like you are trapped. *If I try to move, the court will make Abby stay here with her brothers they will never listen to her no one's ever listened to her they will listen to her dad and her brothers they will listen to her dad they will only listen to her dad.* You will know the truth you will have experienced the reality of an oppressed perspective. You will not know what to do.

You will not know what to do.

You will start Abby back into therapy until Wyatt calls and cancels it. The therapist will feel bad but be more afraid of a lawsuit from him than compelled to help Abby along. You won't give Wyatt the satisfaction of an upset phone call you will instead ask the pediatrician for more referrals you will vow to find a therapist who will stick with it whether Wyatt scares her or not. You will make spaghetti and spinach salads for dinner. You will open an email from your sister *you really need to read this book I'm reading it with my staff it's about being happy no matter what. Happiness is a choice.* You will decide to be extra happy no matter what you will help your daughter with her spelling words you will help her gather supplies for her personal design of the-egg-won't-crack-in-this-if-dropped-from-ten-feet machine. You will lay in bed together and watch an episode or two of *Modern Family* you will crack up with each other you will stroke her hair you will daydream about what your life might look like if you were with a loving goofy husband complaining about the squeaky step and

261

fighting about the details of raising three kids you will text your sons *good night I love you* you will hug Matt when he comes in from his evening sessions *how were they* you will pause there for a moment to listen you will appreciate his scent *it's important to like the smell that comes out of your partner's skin* you will watch him eat warmed up dinner you will pet the cat you will feed the dog you will wash your face you will read a little you will wonder whether your boys have their homework done whether they'll be going to bed soon *do they shower at night or in the morning what did they eat for dinner I wonder if they need new shoes I wonder whether Gabe's feeling any better* you will not bother to call again today you will have heard them loud and clear *don't call me I don't want to talk to you and you're not going to make me feel guilty and you're not going to change how I feel about you so stop sending pictures* you will long for them and you'll wonder how they're going to grow up to know women how they're going to grow up to love women what man on this earth is going to break through to them now that they've cut out every other man now that they'll learn only from their Dad and from his Dad they'll be the only men left in their lives *and I've never known two men to mistreat and despise women more than they do. It's a family legacy. I really just wanted to break that up for the boys. I want to help raise them. I know I've made mistakes even big mistakes with them but I want a chance to make repairs and I want time to connect with them. Who will love them for who they are who will encourage them to make their own choices who will balance things out when their dad teaches them to point the Bible at women as a tool for justification who is going to tell them that rape is not the woman's fault who is going to talk to these boys more than their father when he says more words per day than anyone else on earth.* Your heart will rattle around your breathing will nearly stop you will find yourself staring at the wall you won't know how much time goes by you will look through and beyond Matt typing out his notes you will not see anything, really, you will find yourself frozen like a block of hot ice you will find yourself smashed by the weight of the atmospheric ocean you will eventually turn your eyes to your sleeping daughter leaned up against you and you will force yourself to wake up. *Some people find deep peace in life's painful moments some people can let all these things go some people have faith in the universe some people can be happy no matter what at least my kids are breathing at least my kids get a chance to be alive. That's more than a lot of people get I have to have some faith.*

I have to have some faith.

And then Wyatt will file for full custody of the boys.

Six years after you left but not even two years after you finally got out of court, he will file to go back again. The certified letter will be timed for delivery the day before you're supposed to have spring break with your kids.

And the letter will fall out of your hands

as you pause in the horror of all that it means.

Court.

The pause will linger.

Your heart will stop beating.

There will be nothing else to do. A heart can't just keep going on like that. But then somehow, it does. You will feel its beats start up again after a moment inside your aching ribcage. The universe will pound heavy on your skull and your head will fall forward under the weight. You will stare at the letter, lying there in the grass, and out of the blankness of no thoughts—nothing left to think—you will do what you do. You will rally. Pull out a standard phrase. Remind yourself to have some faith.

I have to have some faith.

You will remind yourself again and again and again about faith and you will work harder and harder each day to feel faith in your heart but then wonder and doubt will sometimes creep in, especially when you wonder about faith and the disempowered and how much different that can be than the kind of faith that empowered people have you will wonder about the faith of an eight-year-old Maltese in ˜Scottsdale when it finds itself without protection for a moment in its side yard and is run down by a pack of desert coyotes and torn to bits you will wonder about the faith of the brooding bird as her nesting tree is chopped out from underneath her you will wonder about the faith of the squirrels in your backyard when you let your dog out the door and he tears through a screen panel in a single bound, taking the most direct route to the kill. He will never catch them because they can run. Faster. Their faith is in their speed in their own ability to get away and no one's stopping them from using their greatest strengths so they will run up and around the tree and chatter at him and flick their tails in anger you will wonder what it would feel like to run. To have the power to escape. To grab your babies by the back of their soft necks and take off for a newer, safer nest. You will wonder what it might feel like to live a life unbound to have faith in your own freedom to have some natural power to protect yourself and your own and to live without the system to live without the system telling you to shut up and sit down and then you will think about Matt and his love for post-apocalyptic daydreams and you will remember him stroking your hair one night and talking softly, watching the ceiling *you know if the world went down, Helen, you'd be just fine. You're such a badass all we'd have to do is find your family.* And then he would pause. *But you know, it's more than being badass, when I watched you deliver those goats last Sunday it was different. I almost cried. You were so calm and you knew exactly what to do even with all those kids watching you. What a miraculous experience for your nieces and nephews. The way you turned that one around. That was beautiful. You're amazing.*

You'd be fine.

Matt would pause another moment in his daydream, and his hand would freeze still on your hair.

But you'd also have to be ready to fight. More than anyone I know. Because you know if the systems shut down he'd come for you first thing and you'd only have one choice.

Kill him or be killed.

He would come to kill you it would be more important to him than survival you know. If the world ever goes crazy, even for a day, you have to be ready.

If the world goes crazy, he will come to kill you quickly. If the world stays as it is, he will work to kill you slowly.

You will lay there quietly for a moment, thinking about your brand new attorney and all his square lines and angles. Square teeth, square face, square shoulders. Square building, square office—right next to the square courthouse. You hoped that the proximity would make a difference this time around. An attorney who belongs to this court. Someone who knows. Someone experienced in this county. Someone who maybe could bring this all to an end. So you'd pull your files together and march up his stairs to find him leaning back into his buttoned-down chair, reading over the latest paperwork Wyatt filed with the court. You'd take in his unsmiling look before the questions. *So tell me, why are we here? From what I understand, you haven't seen your kids much in a year and I just can't imagine how that would happen so tell me how did you get to a place where your kids don't even want to see you? I just can't see how that could ever happen to a connected parent so tell me what we're dealing with here? And I don't want to hear all about your ex. I want to hear about you. How you could let this happen.*

265

You will pause and look for a single sentence or maybe two that could explain and you will say

this is a very complex issue

he will interrupt you right there *well I'm more of a black and white person so let me just say that I need clear and simple answers and I also have to tell you right up front that I might be able to help you with this but I gotta say that if you want some kind of World War III then I'm not your man that's just not my style and I'm not going to spend the next three years in court with this* you will take a quiet breath *well I really don't want any kind of World War and I don't have a lot of faith in this process after my divorce* but he will interrupt you there again *yeah, I heard all about your case you're kind of infamous up here and you know I have to be honest with you I think it takes two assholes to make a divorce go on like that it really does.* You will think *this guy thinks I'm an asshole what the hell am I doing I cannot believe I'm in court again how is this my life* you will know better than to talk about battering personalities and abuse but you will venture to bring up alienation you will say *my children are being alienated from me* he will say *well I'm not the expert on that subject but I have to say that I really can't believe you two are still at it and so I need to know right up front whether you want to settle this or whether you're looking for a World War III because from what I've heard about you it seems clear that you must have some issues.*

And with that you will take a few breaths and try to argue and defend, bravely referring to your binders and texts as you try to explain abuse and alienation, but by the end of that first deflating interview, you will agree.

Yes, I do.

I do have issues.

I have issues.

266